MANAGING THE MANAGER'S GROWTH

Managing the Manager's Growth

VALERIE STEWART
ANDREW STEWART

A HALSTED PRESS BOOK

JOHN WILEY & SONS
New York

Published in the U.S.A.
by Halsted Press, a division of
John Wiley & Sons, Inc., New York.

Library of Congress Catalog Card No.: 78–70905
Stewart, Valerie and Andrew Stewart
  Managing the Manager's Growth.
New York, N.Y./Farnborough, Hants, England
Halsted Press/Gower Press, Teakfield Ltd.
268 p.
7810   780929

ISBN 0–470–26561–2

Printed in Great Britain

Contents

Figures

Preface

Managers must learn to do better, if we are to survive, let alone grow. This is not a blanket condemnation of the performance of industrial managers in the UK; we know some who must rank with the best in the world. But times change; the market and the social context make new and growing demands on managers, in industry and elsewhere, and helping them to master these challenges is itself a challenging job demanding professional skills.

This book is for anyone who has to help managers learn. We write 'help managers learn' rather than 'teach managers' because although formal instruction has an important place in management education it is by no means the whole of it; the creation of opportunities for self-development, outside the classroom, is just as important. We hope this book will be used not only by professional personnel and training people, but also by general managers and managers in small and medium sized firms where the responsibilities of training cannot be delegated to full time specialists.

The book is designed with management training in mind, but some of the techniques discussed will also be applicable to the training of specialists and professional staff—to the training of anyone who adds value by the use of brain rather than brawn.

The book begins by considering managerial effectiveness—what is it, and why is there so much debate about it? It then goes on to consider how adults learn, and some of the obstacles to learning; for it is a wonder, and a pity, that people who were born hungry for learning—as we all are—should have learned in their twenties and thirties to shield themselves from opportunities to change their minds. Most books on management training assume that the trainees come willingly; we think that a big part of the battle is actually getting them across the threshold of the classroom, which is why we devote some space to learning outside the classroom.

The following chapter examines some of the skills required to manage the manager's growth; the personal skills and discipline required of the trainer. There are suggestions for self-development exercises which the trainer may practise, and some recommended reading.

The next two chapters are about training needs analysis. There is precious little written about training needs analysis for managers, and the techniques used on operatives do not always transfer well; it's impossible to watch a manager from a distance and derive a statement of his training needs, especially if his job has a long time-span of discretion. You have to interview him, analyse his actions, interrogate his results. Thus there are detailed instructions on training needs analysis techniques for groups and for individuals.

After the training needs analysis, we review the options the trainer has available—what sort of procedures could he organise or suggest to improve performance? The remainder of the book analyses these options in detail.

Techniques for training in new knowledge come first; the most popular of these is the lecture, which it is fashionable to denigrate at the moment; however; a well planned lecture, supported by good notes, and given to an interested audience, is a very efficient way of putting knowledge over, and we devote quite a lot of space to methods of planning and organising lectures, as well as other techniques—case studies, programmed instruction, etc.—used to increase knowledge. The next chapter examines training in skills—the various types of exercise, and the equally important topic of getting rich accurate feedback to the trainees in time to help further learning.

These two chapters assume that the trainer is running a formal training course, so the next chapter is concerned with the house-keeping and administrative requirements of such a course. Then we go on to discuss the trainer's options if he decides to use an external course—the people who provide them and the questions he should ask.

Next we look at ways managers can be helped to learn without putting them on formal courses. There is a chapter on coaching techniques; coaching involves the line manager as trainer, with the training officer proper acting as support to the line; we have some suggestions for organising coaching programmes and for training the manager-coaches. Following this is a chapter on projects and assignments, where managers are given full or part time jobs ancillary to their proper jobs, inside the firm or outside, with the twin aims of getting some work done and learning something new. The overall strategy for such programmes is discussed, as well as specific examples of projects and assignments themselves.

We conclude with some speculations on what the future holds for management training, and the new challenges that trainers may face.

A word about terminology and layout. References and further reading are given at the end of each chapter, sometimes with comments about the references themselves. We hope that each chapter will stand alone; this means that some references, and some comments, are duplicated. For this we beg the reader's indulgence; it is less annoying than having to backtrack for a reference elsewhere in the book. Nearly all the chapters finish with some questions for discussion; the lone reader will find them useful to ponder over, or they could form the basis of discussion groups where a number of trainers meet. We refer to 'the trainer' as the person responsible for planning and organising the various activities; he need not have the formal label attached, as the term embraces anybody, including general managers, who has responsibilities in this area. We have tried to avoid jargon as much as possible, having sat through too many discussions where the differences between 'management development' and 'management training' and 'organisation development' were debated with enthusiasm directly proportional to the participants' lack of professional competence. For the sake of economy, though, we tend to refer to technical and non-technical training needs in a way that may need explaining; by a non-technical need we mean training needs that have to do with the management of people, primarily, and by technical needs we mean just about everything else—financial, administrative, marketing, report writing, engineering, etc.

We came to write this book because it wanted to be written. We have been on just about all sides of the management training problem: working as in-house trainers, as buyers of training, as attenders on training courses; giving seminars and training courses through research institutes, professional bodies, other consultants and our own consultancy; we have coached and been coached, and Andrew Stewart was sent from his home company on an assignment. We have seen the gamut of quality, from the courses that were downright dangerous through the pontificators to the people who actually got a kick out of helping others to do better. We've done hackwork, and made some horrible mistakes;

and once or twice we've had the thrill of teaching people a technique and seeing them do new things with it that we hadn't thought possible. We wanted to write about what we had learned.

Much has been learned from other people. We owe a long standing debt to Neil Rackham, and to Terry Morgan and his colleagues at the Air Transport and Travel Industry Training Board; not so much for specific ideas, though there have been plenty of those, as for the example of their approach—that the only way to tackle a problem is by researching it scientifically, rather than by forming opinions on the sidelines based on the last book you read. There is another large debt, to Nickie Fonda and Ken Knight, of the Brunel University Management Programme. Many of the ideas in this book were tested at Brunel seminars, added to and modified; how they do it we don't know, but they manage a consistently excellent and challenging programme from which we have learned much over the years. Others, as they say, too numerous to mention: including the people who taught us, by example, what *not* to do; the few horror stories within these pages are all true, and if anyone recognises himself and has the grace to blush, then well and good.

Thanks, too, to our editor at Gower Press, Malcolm Stern; editors must have a dreadful management job to do and we have always been conscious of skilful guidance.

Valerie Stewart
Andrew Stewart

1 Managerial effectiveness and contingency theory

A Why do we need to define managerial effectiveness?

'I don't need your ivory tower theories about management effectiveness. I can spot a good manager as soon as he comes in the door.'

Anybody who tries to improve managers' performance will encounter that argument, not once but many times. It is usually produced by people of little insight and limited talent who are scared of letting other people into such secrets as they have. If they survive, they do it by sticking firmly to what they already know. The rest of us, charged with the task of getting managers to perform better, think long and hard about precisely what that word 'better' means. That even the well motivated trainer gets lost from time to time is shown by the debate on evaluation of management training—management training existed long before there was evaluation of training, and opinions divide sharply on whether it is possible to evaluate training and whether it is worth while. We begin this book, therefore, with a short consideration of what managerial effectiveness is. While it is not an exhaustive treatment in itself, it is designed to provide a framework for analysis which the reader can then follow using the books cited at the end of this chapter. The technology and the administration of training are fascinating subjects, but we must know a little about what we're training for.

Most people can tell when their motor car is sick, their shoes don't fit, or there's too much salt in the stew. Why is it so difficult, then, to define what we mean by effective and ineffective management?

1 *Because a skilled performance always looks easy.* Sit alongside any craftsman doing his job well, and you think 'I could do that too'. He makes it look so easy that it's difficult for the amateur to spot the skills he is using. The mistakes of a bad craftsman are usually much more obvious, but even then it's difficult to make a mirror image of a good craftsman from looking at a bad one. It's the same with managers; the amateur

1

observing a good one finds it very difficult to point to the secret of his success. The swan gliding along the pond may be smooth and stately above, and flurries of activity beneath; quite a lot of good managers are like that, and it's not easy to see below the surface.

2 *Our management language is impoverished.* Probably as a result of the first factor, there is a shortage of language with which to describe management. Having a vocabulary helps one label phenomena and recognise them when they reappear; this is why the Eskimos have over sixty different words for snow. Without a good language, it is impossible to construct good theories and it is difficult to communicate with other people; so for many management trainers it's a lonely life with little sense of progress.

Language is better in some areas than others, of course. Technical management skills are better served than human relations skills. Management failure is better served than management success. There is more available to help us understand the top and bottom of the management ladder than there is the middle. And lately close analytical attention has been paid to the more neglected areas [1, 2] so the position is gradually improving.

3 *Every man his own expert.* There are three areas in which no one will admit to a poor performance: driving a car, making love, and selecting someone for a job. Nearly everyone has his own private theory of management effectiveness. And because the language difficulties make it hard to be a proper scientist in this area, just about any theory of management effectiveness has some face validity; until, perhaps, you see another theory. The science of management is not virgin territory; it's more like the girl at the bottom of the road, whom everyone claims to have personal knowledge of.

4 *People like different sorts of measures.* Having struggled to get a workable analytical framework, it is possible to produce a prescription for managerial effectiveness in a particular firm. 'The effective manager should always do the following things, sometimes do these things, and never do those things . . .' the trainer says. And someone in his audience retorts with 'That's not what I meant by managerial effectiveness! I want to know what kind of personality the chap's got. That's much more fundamental.'

There are several ways in which effective managers can be

described. *Personality* measures (his character, style, motives, etc.); *attitude* measures; *behaviour* measures; and *outcome* measures (what happens differently because of him): these are all valid ways of describing managers. Which method you choose depends on why you are doing the measuring; personality measures, for instance, are more useful in selection of effective managers than in training them, because most personality factors are difficult to train. Some people have experience of only one or two kinds of measure, so that the other sorts come as a shock; others think that one measure is more 'real' than another, when this is patent nonsense; the measure you choose depends on why you're doing the measuring.

5 *Social change is outdating the old prescriptions.* Organisations and the society in which they function have changed a lot in the last twenty years. Who you employ, how much you pay them, by how much you differentiate between shop-floor and directors, how you motivate them; what you make, how you make it, and who you sell it to: changes in these and other factors have been so large that a management style that was effective when a manager joined the firm could well be counter-indicated by the time he reaches middle management. Whole books could be written on the change in management style required by the provision of equal employment opportunities for women, for example.

The management trainer's task, to work through this jungle of difficulties and discover what he has to do for his own organisation, is not an easy one. Training managers to be better managers has got very little in common with training capstan lathe turners to be better at their jobs; for the trainer has not only to see the solution to the problem of poor performance, he has first of all to define the problem. It is small wonder, therefore, that people hanker after universal theories of management effectiveness that would take away some of the agony; but there ain't no such animal.

B Is there a universal effective manager?

In company with many writers on management, we say No, though aware that it is always difficult to prove a negative assertion. '"For instance" is not proof,' as the proverb has it; maybe a series of instances will approximate.

Until a few years ago there were very few studies in which

managerial effectiveness was compared across a wide variety of organisations. The gaps are now being filled—Rosemary Stewart's work is an outstanding example—and we wish that more of the Industry Training Boards, who are in a splendid position to compare between firms in the same industry, would publish their findings. The three examples given below are chosen because the first is an interesting comparison within the same industry; the second is a classic large scale study; and the third is an example, from within one firm, of unique clarity.

1 *Three plant managers.* We performed diagnoses of managerial effectiveness in three organisations where the problem in each case was at Plant Head level in the production division. Each organisation is large, multi-site, well established; two of them were in indirect competition for the same market. Call them X, Y, and Z. Comparing the diagnoses for the three firms, major differences in the characteristics of effectiveness began to emerge, of which Figure 1.1 is a brief extract.

The effective manager in Firm X . . .	The effective manager in Firm Y . . .	The effective manager in Firm Z . . .
states his position openly in internal negotiations	makes sure that in internal negotiations the other fellow backs down	plays his cards close to his chest in internal negotiations
will discuss his staff's personal problems with them under any circumstances	will discuss his staff's personal problems with them if their performance is affected	refuses to discuss his staff's personal problems with them
works better in a group than alone	is not affected by the presence of others	hardly ever has to work in groups
does not insist on his rank or seniority prevailing	will use his authority speedily	pays little attention to rank or seniority

Fig. 1.1   Comparison of some characteristics of effective plant heads in three firms

From this it is apparent that the qualities necessary to be effective in one firm could well be counter-productive in another firm, even in a similar job. An interesting light was thrown on this during the course of our investigations; by chance a manager in one firm was given the diagnosis for another firm, with the implication that this was his own firm's diagnosis. He returned the document to the personnel manager covered in red pencil, with rude comments about our imperceptiveness. Fortunately we were able to reassure him, and with the permission of everyone concerned we arranged for the three firms to swap diagnoses, to everyone's benefit.

2　*Rosemary Stewart's work.* In 1967 Rosemary Stewart [3] published an analysis of the diaries kept by a sample of managers in a wide variety of jobs in different industries. She demonstrated that they could be classified into five types:

> (a) the emissaries, people whose work brought them into close touch with the outside world, who might be out of the office for days at a time;
> (b) the writers, people who spend more time than average in reading, writing, doing figure work, giving dictation, etc., and who consequently are more solitary than most;
> (c) the discussers, managers who spent a lot of time in contact with others, especially with their peers in small groups or one-to-one relationships;
> (d) the trouble shooters, who spend a lot of time in fleeting contacts, in inspection work and in discussion with subordinates, and who rarely leave the premises or attend big committee meetings;
> (e) the committee men, who have fewer external contacts and more internal contacts, with whom they spend a marked amount of time in committee meetings.

Dr Stewart's analysis, which is taken much further in her later work, [1] makes clear that managers in different jobs have different demands made on them and therefore require different skills. The trouble shooter (typically a production manager or a floor manager in a retail store) needs to be able to get to a problem quickly, even when it is expressed in the language of someone junior to him and less well educated; and he is in positive need of a butterfly mind, as he will rarely finish one problem completely before the next comes up. The committee man, on the other hand, needs patience, forbearance, a sense of strategy, a feeling for group dynamics, and a willingness to negotiate. Chain-store managers seconded to head office for a while experience difficulty in adjusting to the increased time-span required in one's thinking.

Rosemary Stewart goes on to cite in detail the different requirements of different jobs; but even this brief extract has, we hope, made the point that managerial effectiveness varies from job to job.

   3   *Supervision—UK and US style.* Rackham and Morgan [4] describe the results of an analysis of supervisory effectiveness in the UK and the US operations of BOAC (as it then was). Their statistical procedures produced clusters of behaviours associated by the managers with effectiveness; in descending order of size, the clusters from the two countries are compared in Figure 1.2.

UK effective supervisor	*US effective supervisor*
Verbal skills—the ability to structure communications well and communicate clearly	*Getting things done/action*—the ability to put plans into action, meet deadlines, work under pressure
Task orientation—putting plans into practice effectively, meeting deadlines, cost conscious, setting precise objectives, etc.	*Sociable enthusiast*—cracking jokes, giving encouragement, seeking approval, easy to work with, etc.
People orientation—showing an interest in and concern for his people, standing up for them, etc.	*Non-defensive*—admitting mistakes, accepting responsibility for his people's mistakes, etc.
Rigid/change resistant—resisting changes, altering people's jobs without telling them, giving the impression of knowing the answers	*Laissez-faire*—not talking too much, not cutting people off, not putting pressure on people, not giving the impression of knowing the answers
Non-communicating—keeping people in the dark, working in isolation, covering up when things go wrong, reluctant to approach his boss, etc.	*Calvinist streak*—criticising his people's performance to his boss, checks up on people's work, punctual, keeps a constant watch on his people, etc.
	Knowledge using—putting his knowledge into practice, not over-concerned with unnecessary detail

Fig. 1.2   Comparison of effective supervisory behaviour in BOAC, UK and USA

The observant reader will be wondering about the last two clusters in the UK. We have the authors' assurance that they did not load their data into the computer the wrong way round, and that this really is the way effective supervision was seen by the UK managers surveyed.

   The authors' reasons for conducting the survey were connected with their concern for the transferability of a supervisory skills course, designed for a UK population, to a population from the US and Canada. It is obvious from their data that there are differences in what is perceived to be important in a supervisor, and in the emphasis given to the characteristics which the two countries have in common. Rackham and Morgan go on to discuss some of the changes made to their training course, and their training strategy, in the light of this research.

It seems that universal prescriptions lose force as soon as one comes down to the detail, or as soon as one starts to ask for the prescription in operational terms. Of the few general prescriptions that stand up to empirical analysis, perhaps the most promising ones are based on Elliott Jaques' [5] time-span of discretion theory. Jaques says that one fair way to compare jobs is first to distinguish between the *prescribed* component and the *discretionary* component, and then to see how long a mistake made in the discretionary part of one's job could go undetected (usually by one's supervisor). The longer the time-span of discretion, the more difficult the job. Jaques goes on to describe how the time-spans of different jobs should be structured within an organisation for maximum efficiency, and Gillian Stamp at Brunel University has investigated the possibilities of testing people's individual complexities so as to predict their time-span of discretion and hence their management potential. However, even this single measure is a summary of many complex statements, and in practice usually needs supporting with additional detail.

The trainer's job is to get managers to be more effective. We haven't helped him very much so far; we have reviewed all the difficulties that stand in the way of his even seeing the job he has to do. Now we turn to what *is* known about managerial effectiveness, and hope to make amends for the earlier gloom.

C   The contingency theory of managerial effectiveness

The universal effective manager does not exist. The requirements depend to some extent on your situation. This view is sometimes called the *contingency theory* of management, although it is not really a theory as it does not help one make unique testable predictions. However, in recent years data have been amassed which help to describe the contingent relationships assumed by the theory. When we collate the results of the studies of managerial effectiveness which we have carried out in a number of UK organisations (using the methods outlined in Chapter 4 and in *Tomorrow's Men Today* [6] we discover that there are five factors which all effective managers appear to have in common.

Characteristics of all effective managers surveyed

1   *Self-management*. Effective managers are good at monitoring their own performance; so they set themselves realistic objectives, they recognise their mistakes, and they learn from their mistakes. Should they get into a rut, they can pull themselves out. Under greater-than-normal pressure of work their performance improves. They can adapt easily to the unexpected, and if delays and frustrations occur then they get on with something else rather than persevere on a fruitless course. They get on with unpleasant tasks rather than postpone them. They can process information they don't like, accurately, and they stay calm if other people get angry with them. They are willing to work with enthusiasm on ideas that came from other people. If they don't know the answer to something, they admit it rather than resort to flannelling. Success does not make them over-confident, and failure does not cast them down utterly. They will accept help when it is offered if they need it. They have positive plans for their own careers.

In other words, they are 'proactive' rather than 'reactive', managing events rather than being managed by them, and with something in reserve for special demands. They are in control of their emotions, and they are not easily sidetracked.

2   *Management of subordinates*. Effective managers set clear objectives and standards of performance, and they check progress frequently and not just when things are going wrong. They try to train their people, by delegating to them the challenging tasks (if necessary reserving the donkey-work for themselves). If a subordinate gets into difficulties, the effective manager helps him find his own way out rather than taking on the job himself. If the subordinate does something wrong, his manager tells him so, but privately; the effective manager defends his subordinates from public criticism by other people, and will not defend himself by blaming his subordinate. Effective managers give their subordinates the credit for success rather than grabbing it for themselves. And when they have delegated something, it stays delegated—the manager is not constantly trying to steal parts of

it back. One of the bests tests of a manager's ability to delegate is the extent to which he can work off a brief which someone else has prepared for him; effective managers do this well. They also try to sell unpopular company decisions to their people with a good heart, rather than siding with them against 'those so-and-so's in head office'.

The effective manager's role in developing his subordinates is a very self-effacing one; taking on the donkey-work, giving them the credit, having the patience to help them find their own way out. Yet it is interesting that our research, based on empirical study, accords perfectly with what Robert Townsend [7] said: that leaders come in all shapes and sizes, but that the one good rule for spotting a leader is that his people always turn in a superior performance.

3 *Technical and financial control.* Insofar as their jobs require it, all effective managers exhibit technical and financial control; thus, they are good at estimating the resources—human and material—needed to do a particular job, and the time it will take to complete. They absorb technical and financial information quickly and retain it well, and they are on good terms with the jargon of other specialists with whom they have regular dealings. However, in nearly all cases we must distinguish between *control* and *competence.* A manager who wishes to be a practising technical whizz-kid will not do a good job of developing his subordinates; he will find delegation difficult, and standing by while they make their mistakes intolerable. Practising technical competence is not wanted in effective managers so much as the ability to recognise and develop competence in other people; the ability to buy ideas well; skills of project evaluation, planning, budgeting, and negotiation. Only in matrix organisations or other rarities does the effective manager need a high degree of practising technical ability.

4 *Company policy and public relations.* All effective managers are concerned to present a good picture of their organisation to the public, and they try to ensure that their firm is a good citizen. This shows itself in an awareness of the PR implications of their decisions, and in willingness to take up the 'figurehead' duties which are expected of a manager just because he bears that title. Effective managers are prepared to use their authority when this is necessary—if a decision needs to be taken quickly, for example. They keep themselves up-to-date on company policy, and on current events insofar as they affect the

organisation; given the opportunity they try to influence company decisions while at the formative stage, rather than try to get them changed after they have been announced; however, they will implement unpopular decisions with a good grace.

5 *Communications and clear thinking.* Effective managers have the usual range of communications skills—clarity, conciseness, and timeliness, and a good sense of direction. They do not lose impact on the telephone. They listen well—they can reproduce fairly the points of view of people who disagree with them. They pass information on to people who might find it useful, even though this may not be in their specific remit. They distinguish accurately between what they can and cannot control, and between fact and opinion. They can work productively in committee. Where appropriate, they can cope with the peculiar ways in which computers distort the information flow.

Wherever we have looked, we find these aspects, among others, characterising effective managers. For the sake of symmetry, we should now examine the ineffective manager in some detail; however, in empirical studies the ineffective manager comes out much less clearly, because (one hopes) they do not stay around long enough to give a strong impression. A short sketch of the ineffective manager, in his universal essentials, looks like this:

> The ineffective manager avoids doing unpleasant tasks, and cannot listen to unpleasant information without blocking his ears or distorting it. He refuses help, repeats his mistakes, won't admit his mistakes, and always appears to have too much work to do. He does not put priorities on what he has to do, nor does he plan far enough ahead to monitor the effect of his decisions. He passes more information upwards than downwards; he under-uses his people; he does not delegate as much as he could and he only delegates the donkey-work. Nor can he leave things alone once delegated, but is constantly taking things back; he cannot work to a brief that someone else has prepared for him. Under pressure his performance gets worse. He esteems technical excellence at the expense of commercial opportunities.

This central core of managerial effectiveness, the characteristics which are common to everyone, is supplemented by characteristics which vary according to the organisation involved. A simple account of the factors which cause effectiveness to vary, and the effects they have, must be added to the central core before we understand the whole of the manager's—and the trainer's—job.

Factors associated with variations in management effectiveness

This could be a very long list. Interested readers can pursue the subject in more detail in the books at the end of this chapter. Here we give some of the most common causes of variation, with examples; it is not an exhaustive treatment of contingency theory.

1   *The product.* What it is, how it is made, who uses it—all these affect the requirements for a good manager. In a high technology industry with many fail-safe devices, a good manager needs less technical competence and more human relations skills, because the opportunity to make technical errors has been designed away from him. In a seller's market a good manager may esteem volume of production over quality (up to a point); in a craft-based industry quality may take precedence. Managers in service industries and staff departments need more skill in objective-setting than do managers in sales or production departments, because success and failure are more difficult to measure here.

2   *The location.* We have already quoted a good example of the difference nationality makes to effective supervision in the same firm. The management style that's right for Croydon may be a wash-out in Cumberland; what motivates a Londoner may well be distasteful for a Glaswegian.

3   *Accountability.* A manager who is motivated by profit-making is unlikely to succeed in an organisation where (say) maintaining continuity of employment is the prime criterion. Skills are needed in the market-place which are not needed by the administrator; *fast* research may be needed in industry, but it is viewed with repugnance by some Government research establishments.

4   *Competitors.* In a competitive situation the effective manager may find that all he has to do is keep his people informed of the competition's activities. Where no competitors exist, the effective manager gets his people to compete against themselves, without at the same time competing destructively

against the rest of the organisation. The style of the competition may also mould the organisation's own requirements, by forcing it to imitate or to differentiate.

5   *Size.* In small organisations the technical requirements of the job are strong, for all managers. With bigger organisations comes the middle management layer—the managers who can manage *managers*, who can counsel managers about management problems, who have clear communicable insights into the business of managing. Big organisations also force consideration of issues like local autonomy, bureaucracy, the management of information, etc., which we shall come to at the end of this section.

6   *Age.* An old organisation makes different demands on its managers; it is usually more difficult to get changes accepted, political awareness plays a greater part, the plant is older and presents different technical requirements, the work-force may be older and need different methods of motivation and control. Organisations go through a clear ageing process, from creativity to consolidation to renewal or atrophy; they need different skills in their managers at these times.

7   *The manager's own seniority.* Junior managers need skill with tactics; directors ought to leave tactics alone most of the time and concentrate on strategy. Managing operatives or professional staff makes different demands from managing managers—trouble-shooting, objective-setting, delegation and control—these are all different. Special skills are needed by managers who are planning things that will happen after they themselves have retired.

8   *The organisation's success or failure.* Managing failure is easier than managing success. When things go wrong, people look for a stronger leader with lots of personal authority; they are prepared to make sacrifices for the common good, and they are largely self-motivated. The manager's job is to supply the figurehead, to make sure that people don't get over-motivated and therefore inefficient, and to stop useless scapegoating. This is easier than the manager of a successful group, who can't crack the whip, cannot point to an external threat, and must resist people's natural preferences not to analyse the reasons for success or to change while they are successful.

9   *The trade unions involved.* Non-union organisations usually demand a high standard of man-management skill from all managers; in heavily unionised firms this skill may be

delegated to personnel officers. Individual unions vary in their negotiating style, and in the pressures they put on managers.

10 *The legislative context.* Hire-and-fire trouble-shooting managers do not survive long in situations where employment is protected. Product liability legislation requires a certain technical skill from the quality control managers. Pay restraint requires managers to think of other ways of motivating and compensating their people. Some forms of equal opportunity legislation imply that some groups receive special treatment in selection, development, and promotion.

11 *The degree of uncertainty* in the situation. In an ambiguous situation the effective manager shields his people from excess ambiguity so that they continue performing well; he learns ways of structuring the environment so that it does not appear too ambiguous to himself, and develops ways of monitoring his own performance. When things are too black and white, he does the reverse, so that people learn to keep their options open.

It would be easy to go on listing factors and examples; but better if the reader starts to draw up his own list according to his own experience. As we stated earlier, contingency theory is not really a theory at all, not yet; for 'a first-rate theory predicts, a second-rate theory forbids, and a third-rate theory explains after the event,' and most of what is described as contingency theory falls into the last category at present. Trying to amalgamate the factors listed above, and others, into a working model of inputs and outcomes, would be a very difficult task indeed. However, a simple theory that allows one to make a number of predictions is presented by Handy [8] in a book that deserves to become a classic on organisation study. He gives four kinds of organisation culture: *power, role, task* and *person*. They are summarised in Figure 1.3.

Handy's model is unsophisticated enough to withstand the rough-and-tumble of everyday life in organisations, but subtle enough to allow it to predict differences between situations. If you understand what kind of culture you are operating in (and the culture may vary between different departments of the same firm, of course) then you can make some testable predictions about the requirements for managerial effectiveness in these firms.

This has obvious implications for the trainer. Consider, for example, how one would go about installing creativity training in

Power cultures are most often found in small entrepreneurial firms, the 'buccaneers'. The culture depends on a central power source (usually one person) with rays of power and influence radiating from the centre. The organisation works by anticipating the wishes of the centre, relying on precedent wherever possible—the centre may act on whim or impulse. There are few rules, and influence is important: 'politics' rather than procedure or logic dictate the shape of decisions. Power cultures are usually strong, self-aware, reacting quickly to change. But they depend so much on the quality of the person at the centre that he can literally make or break the organisation; and, of course, they are vulnerable when they grow too large for the man in the middle. Successful people in power cultures have low needs for individual security; they are politically aware, good at risk-taking, power-oriented, and esteem ends above means.

Role cultures are often described as bureaucratic; a high degree of departmental specialisation with a controlling group at the top. There are many rules and procedures; job descriptions, grievance procedures, authority definitions, etc. The job description may be more important than the person filling it; it is more important that everyone doing the same job perform to the same standard than that some people excel. Position power is important; personal power discounted. Role cultures work well in stable environments, so that today's rules and procedures can be carried over to tomorrow's. But they do not perceive change easily, nor react to it quickly. Successful people in role cultures esteem security highly, and like predictable environments. Specialists survive well, and so do people who prefer stolid goodness to occasional brilliance. Power-oriented risk-takers are likely to be successful only at the very top of such organisations.

Task cultures bring people together on the basis of a job to be done, irrespective of seniority or personal power. Matrix organisations are examples of task cultures. Teams, rather than individuals, do the work; teams that form and re-form as the job to be done changes. The advantages of task cultures are their flexibility and sensitivity to change; however, they do not often produce economies of scale or depth to expertise, and control—especially day-to-day control—is difficult. Senior managers can control by task allocation and resource allocation, but more detailed control presents problems. Task cultures are vulnerable in difficult times, because when people have to compete for resources they tend to revert to the use of personal or position power. Good managers in task cultures need to be self-motivating and self-managing, able to work in teams, with specialist as well as managerial skills and a liking for individual freedom and low status differentials.

Person cultures are not found in many organisations, though many people would like to think so. Here the individual is the central point, with all the other resources arranged to serve him and his personal objectives; sometimes groups of individuals with similar objectives come together to share these service resources. However, group objectives, superordinate to the individual objectives, do not exist in the person culture, for any one individual could veto at any time. From time to time person cultures exist inside other cultures, if there is one person who has a unique contribution to make on the basis of specialist skills or knowledge.

Fig. 1.3   Organisation cultures: Handy's model

each of these four types of organisation. In a role culture, much of the trainer's attention would be given to helping people sell their ideas, and to changing attitudes about innovation, because role cultures are suspicious of brilliance. In a power culture, where emphasis is already on speed of reactions to problems, the trainer would probably concentrate less on the production of new ideas, and more on methods for ensuring that fast evaluation of ideas does not lead to good ones getting lost. In a task culture, where organisation is based on mutual appreciation of talents, the trainer's task would be to encourage innovation in areas other than the main stream of each trainee's activity, because there is a danger that people might be used for what they are good at already and not given much chance to expand. And in person cultures the trainer's main task could be to get the person at the centre more used to listening to other people and working on their ideas, because this type of culture encourages the lone wolf. Sensitivity to slight variations in presentation and emphasis, based on a knowledge of the prevailing culture, makes the training more effective. The reader may care to ponder the different emphases required, for each culture, for training in (a) objective-setting, (b) budgeting, (c) participative management, and (d) report writing.

D Summary

Helping managers learn implies knowing about what makes managers effective. This is not easy, because skilled performances are difficult to analyse and people's implicit theories of management often stand in the way. Nonetheless, on examination it appears that there is no universal formula for effective management, and that requirements vary depending on the situation. All effective managers show skills in self-management, management of subordinates, technical and financial competence, company policy and public relations, and communication; but the product, age, history, market situation, and external environment make their own peculiar demands. The division of organisational cultures into power, role, task, and person cultures is a useful working theory.

E   Discussion questions

1   How does the relationship between a pop star and his manager differ from the relationship between a salesman and his manager?

2   What are the differences between a supervisor's job, a manager's job, and a director's job? What does this tell you about the different requirements for skills in each job?

3   A manager in a high technology industry said: 'We design and manufacture the equipment so well, and have such a good management information service, that the only mistakes our managers can make are people-mistakes'. Discuss with reference to your own situation.

4   Tolstoy said that all happy families are happy in the same way, and that all unhappy families are unhappy in their own way. Turning this statement on its head, and in the light of what you know about contingency theory, consider Norman Dixon's list of the factors associated with military incompetence [9] to see if there are any lessons there for avoiding managerial incompetence.

Military incompetence involves:

1   A serious wastage of human resources and failure to observe one of the first principles of war—economy of force. This failure derives in part from an inability to make war swiftly. It also derives from certain attitudes of mind.

2   A fundamental conservatism and clinging to outworn tradition, an inability to profit from past experience (owing partly to a refusal to admit past mistakes). It also involves a failure to use or tendency to misuse available technology.

3   A tendency to reject or ignore information which is unpalatable or which conflicts with preconceptions.

4   A tendency to underestimate the enemy and overestimate the capabilities of one's own side.

5   Indecisiveness and a tendency to abdicate from the role of decision maker.

6   An obstinate persistence in a given task despite strong contrary evidence.

7   A failure to exploit a situation gained and a tendency to pull punches rather than push home an attack.

8   A failure to make adequate reconnaissance.

9   A predilection for frontal assaults, often against the enemy's strongest point.

10   A belief in brute force rather than the clever ruse.

11   A failure to make use of surprise or deception.

12   An undue readiness to find scapegoats for military setbacks.

13   A suppression or distortion of news from the front, usually rationalised as necessary for morale or security.

14   A belief in mystical forces—fate, bad luck, etc.

F   References and further reading

[1] R. STEWART.   *Contrasts in Management*, McGraw-Hill, 1976.

[2] A. MANT.   *The Rise and Fall of the British Manager*, Macmillan, 1977
A thought-provoking book about the management job, going to its basic essentials, i.e. do we need managers at all?

[3] R. STEWART.   *Managers and Their Jobs*, Macmillan, 1967.
One of the earliest studies to examine the manager's job in detail, and amplified in her later work, e.g. *Contrasts in Management*.

[4] N. RACKHAM and T. MORGAN.   *Behaviour Analysis in Training*, McGraw-Hill, 1977.

[5] E. JAQUES.   *Time-Span Handbook*, Heinemann Educational Books, 1964.

[6] A. STEWART and V. STEWART.   *Tomorrow's Men Today: the identification and development of management potential*, Institute of Personnel Management, 1976.

[7] R. TOWNSEND.   *Up the Organisation*, Coronet, 1971.

[8] C. B. HANDY.   *Understanding Organisations*, Penguin Management Books, 1976

[9] N. F. DIXON.   *On the Psychology of Military Incompetence*, Jonathan Cape, 1976.
A superb book for anybody interested in the performance of organisations, not just military bodies; and an example of how to apply science to history, and to present the results clearly and without compromise.

2 How managers learn

A How does learning happen?

There are many definitions of learning, but they all agree that learning is a change in a person's *behaviour* as a result of an experience or experiences, and which is not due to chance, fatigue, or ageing. In case this simple definition seems a truism, consider the number of management trainers who take as their measure of learning the fact that their audience says that it has learned something, or that the audience stops fighting back. It is always better to look for real, observable changes in behaviour as a sign that learning has taken place. To help managers learn we need to know more about the conditions that facilitate learning. These can be summarised as follows.

1 *The learner must see a connection* between the antecedent and its consequences if he is to learn to manipulate it. If Mary Jones never realises that it is her weight on the pressure-sensitive pad that is operating the supermarket doors, she will continue to stretch out her arm fruitlessly; if the manager does not realise that every time his subordinates consult him about a problem he takes on the problem himself, then he will not learn how to encourage their openness and self-reliance.

People do not always see the right connections; the rat in the Skinner box saying to his companion: 'Boy, have I got this guy fixed! Every time I press this lever he has to give me a piece of spaghetti', has the same distorted view of the world as the sales manager who believes that it's his superb chatting-up of secretaries that gets the orders, when it's really the quality of his product. A chance occurrence or coincidence—aided by the lack of proper vocabulary which we discussed in the previous chapter—may be taken for cause-and-effect; this is how most superstitions begin.

Learning the connections is hindered if people lie about the true state of things. 'If we yield to your claim, we shall be bankrupt in six months', says the industrial relations manager, hoping that this will teach the union representatives to lower their sights; but if his forebears have been saying that for the past twenty years, then the negotiators will have learned either that there is no connection between claims of imminent bankruptcy and ability to pay, or that the connection is in their favour.

Some of the things that managers are asked to learn do not connect easily with what they already know, or they are not presented in a logically connected framework. Just as the first stages of learning a foreign language are difficult because the new grammar and vocabulary seem arbitrary, some management skills and techniques present people with a long list of unconnected terms and procedures to master before they get to the interesting part. Most courses on finance for non-financial managers, or computer appreciation, or other technical topics for non-specialists, present this hurdle. Children find it difficult enough learning French vocabulary, and they have a natural appetite for symbols at that age; even they find it easier when the teacher draws connections between the new learning and what they already know. Managers have much more difficulty, and the trainer presenting a lot of new information must be careful to avoid the appearance of arbitrariness.

2 *There must be feedback on performance* if the performance is to improve. Imagine you are standing in front of a blackboard, with a piece of chalk and a ruler in your hand, and you are blindfolded. You are told to draw a line twenty centimetres long. When you have finished your stroke, you are told to draw another, and another . . . and another . . . and another. Will your performance improve? Contrast this with the situation in which you are told, at the end of your first attempt, how much your line measured. Then you make a second try, and are told how you did. Most people learn to draw a creditable twenty centimetres by the second method; whereas by the first method performance is no better at the end than at the beginning.

This is what feedback on performance is all about—knowledge of how you did, in time to modify your later attempts. *Feedback* has become something of a jargon word lately, and has had its true meaning distorted. (Also, it's a term belonging to two sciences—psychology and cybernetics—and this causes confusion amongst even the purists.) Feedback can come directly from the learning situation, or it can come through other parties. If as the typist learns to type she sees the page for herself, misprints and triumphs and all, then this is intrinsically better than if she could not see the page but had to rely on an instructor telling her how many mistakes per page she had made, or giving her marks out of ten.

Some management situations provide direct feedback in unequivocal form; but for most managers feedback on performance is difficult to obtain, either because they lack the vocabulary with which to structure direct feedback for themselves or because the feedback is distorted by coming through another person or by coming late. The novice manager in a grievance-handling situation may be ill-equipped to extract direct feedback from the situation, whereas the skilled manager would be monitoring eye-contact, interruptions, admissions of difficulties, and (perhaps unconsciously) things like pupil dilation and the smell of the other's sweat. Because direct feedback on performance has been difficult for managers to obtain, there has grown a trend in training to have 'feedback time' during management training sessions, at which the trainees try to give each other information about their behaviour. When this is done well (and by well we mean: in structured, reliable form, using categories appropriate to the skills being developed and the cognitive and emotional strengths of the trainees) then it is a tremendous aid to training. Done badly, it degenerates into 'Now it's my turn to tell you how I feel about you' sessions, from which useful information is difficult to extract.

Trainers sometimes talk about 'positive feedback' and 'negative feedback', using those terms in a way that would make a cyberneticist or systems man's hair stand on end. The waters here are so muddied with jargon that we prefer to speak of 'knowledge of success' and 'knowledge of failure'. Both sorts are necessary for learning to take place, and the mixture of the two is a nice problem. Knowing that you have failed is useful; it helps avoid that path next time. Knowing that you have succeeded enables you to take the same path again next time, but may not make clear the *range* of behaviours which are successful. If a trainee is to learn the boundaries between successful and unsuccessful behaviours, then he must have knowledge of results from both sides of the boundary; hence, knowledge of success and of failure.

In practice people are better at spotting failures—especially other people's—than successes so that the skilled trainer devotes more effort to setting up success feedback systems. He will also be concerned with the *frequency* of giving knowledge of results in the stages of learning where the trainee has not yet developed ways of getting sound feedback from the situation himself.

Feedback serves two purposes: *information* and *reward*. To keep someone producing a particular kind of behaviour for a long time, the best way to reward him is on a *variable-frequency schedule* of reward; this means that on average he gets rewarded every nth time he produces the behaviour, but that the actual distance between rewards varies around the average of n. The effectiveness of the variable-frequency reward schedule may be observed by watching people play the one-armed bandit. Considering feedback as information, therefore, it seems that the trainee should receive it in generous quantities; viewed as reward, though, it should come on a variable-frequency schedule. The answer is that in the early stages of learning, the information function of feedback is predominant and feedback should be richly given; in the later stages, when the trainee has learned to set up something of his own feedback systems, the frequency can be dropped to a variable-frequency schedule.

3   *Opportunity to practise* is very important, especially when people are learning a new skill. You cannot learn driving by reading the *Highway Code*; you cannot learn to negotiate by reading a book about it or listening to a successful negotiator telling how he did it. The new behaviour must be performed over and over again, with feedback on performance, until it feels natural and looks easy.

Much management training breaches this rule, of course, unforgivably. There are many training courses (communication skills, interview skills, selling skills) where a group of trainees take it in turn to perform in front of the others who watch and give criticism. Often on such courses people get only one chance actually to perform; maybe two if they're lucky. The rest of the time is supposed to be spent learning, vicariously, by watching the other people. Needless to say very little planned change in behaviour results from these courses.

Skilled trainers learn to dissect the things to be learned into their component parts, and to arrange training so that the vital parts are gone over time and time again until they are over-learned. In later chapters we shall see examples of how training courses can be designed to enable lots of practice, and lots of feedback, in subject areas where trainees have usually been passive; indeed, some people go so far as to say that unless you can get a representative sample of the relevant behaviour on a training course *twice* during the course (once to diagnose it, and once to measure improvement) then it is not material for a training course and should be addressed some other way.

Practice is no good without feedback. We recall a conversation with a trainer explaining the design of his management course:

'We put them into small groups in the afternoon.'

'Why?'

'To teach them about working in groups.'

'Do you have anybody observing the groups, to give feedback, or anything like that for them to use?'

'Oh, no.'

'But they work in small groups back at the job, do they?'

'Yes, that's why they need to learn about working in groups.'

The logic of this seemed to satisfy him; he could not understand why we doubted that people who experienced difficulties in groups in their jobs would be helped by repeating those difficulties on a training course with no opportunity for them to analyse their problems and progress. Practice and feedback are the cornerstones of good training technique.

4 *Help with a poor vocabulary* can be useful in those areas where people's analytical capacities are impoverished—interpersonal skills, the language of unfamiliar specialities, etc. We have seen that lack of vocabulary hampers the search for usable definitions of managerial effectiveness; it also stands in the way of people constructing their own feedback systems and taking charge of their own learning. Some of the most successful innovations in management training have centred on giving managers a vocabulary; for example the work on behaviour analysis [1, 2] in which people are given simple categories into which they analyse their own and others' behaviour. If at a meeting you can count the number of times each person's suggestions are listened to, and each time they are ignored, and maybe even construct a simple ratio between the two, then you have a better understanding and potentially a better capacity for control.

Some of the techniques, like lectures and reading assignments, which are derided by the sophisticated, work because they give trainees a framework for understanding what they already know but have not put words around. We were once badly caught out by this; we were invited to view a training course designed for travel clerks with the intention of improving their sales skills. We thought that it was unlikely to meet its training objectives for a variety of reasons—design, teaching methods, opportunity for participation, etc. Yet when we followed up the course to see if changes in behaviour had resulted, there were measurable improvements in staff morale and in sales; as we later discovered, this was simply because nobody had ever even told them that they were salesmen before.

Good trainers learn to establish and improve their trainees' vocabulary if there is reason to suspect that it is deficient; thus, asking a class to take five minutes to note down the salient points after they have seen a training film improves their vocabulary, as does getting together discussion groups from different industries. Training *can* happen without a sophisticated vocabulary, and the acquisition of the vocabulary is not the same as training; but the two are mutually reinforcing.

Before leaving the topic of how learning actually happens, there is a fallacy which should be laid to rest. There was once a training course at which the trainees were given, each evening, a little problem to work on; cannibal and missionary and goat crossing the river in a boat built for two, or the man defined as a habitual liar who says that this time he's telling the truth, etc. Before breakfast the solutions to these problems were read out by the trainer. No further use was made of the material; when we asked what it was used for, we were told that 'doing logical exercises limbers up the brain'. This is, of course, the same reasoning that inflicted Latin and Greek upon generations of public schoolboys on the assumption that they would thus be better equipped to deal with the problems of Empire. It is nonsense; exercising one limited set of skills will not facilitate the development of skills in other areas, unless the organism is so torpid that the first set of exercises brings it from sleep to wakefulness.

B What do managers need to learn?

Being a good manager means that certain things have to be learned—*knowledge* about management, and *skill* in managing. Some people add a third factor, saying that *attitudes* must also be learned, although there is doubt about the extent to which one can influence some deeply held attitudes by training.

Knowledge is something you have; skill is something you do.

The two need not go hand in hand; there are skilful interviewers with no formal knowledge of interviewing, and there are experts with paper qualifications who cannot put their skills into practice. It helps to distinguish between knowledge about *things* and knowledge about *people*, and between skill with *things* and skills with *people*. Most managerial jobs need all four categories, but in different degrees; the distinction should be fundamental to the trainer because they imply different training techniques.

1   *Knowledge* can be got through books. It can be imparted in lectures and discussions. Films and cassette tapes can be used; correspondence courses and programmed instruction techniques likewise. Concepts are transmitted from one man's mind to another's, using the medium of words and pictures.

These are relatively simple training techniques, but they are often misused; they are vulnerable to overloading and to poor presentation. It is tempting to lecture to an audience for an hour, but the reality is that most of them will be unable to concentrate fully after twenty minutes no matter how well-motivated they are. Likewise, diagrams are drawn which are overloaded with information because the teacher couldn't bear to leave anything out, despite the fact that the audience doesn't know where to start looking and remembering. The principles for putting over large quantities of knowledge are well known (see Chapter 7, and Howe's book *Adult Learning* [3]) but they are also well abused.

2   *Skills* must be acquired through practice with feedback, the trainee actually performing the task to be learned rather than passively watching or absorbing information. This means that the trainees are busy; that they are repeating the tasks over and over again; that they are making mistakes and learning from them. Sometimes the process of skill acquisition is long and painful, and involves plateaus where no improvement is visible for a while; anyone who has learned to type remembers the early stages of rapid progress, learning where the letters were; then the period of no improvement, followed by a sudden rush of skill and the ability to type words; then another plateau followed by (for some of us!) the ability to type whole phrases. Knowledge-acquisition usually has a much steadier pace than skill-acquisition; learners of skills may find this disheartening.

The different techniques required to teach knowledge and skills are easily understood when *things* are the subject; learning how to calculate centripetal force is different from learning how to corner on a bicycle, and learning how to add probabilities is different from learning how to back the horses. For the latter of each pair there can be no substitute for experience. In theory, people recognise that knowledge about *people* and skills with *people* demand different training techniques too, but this requirement is not often met. Many trainers are happy to lecture about the skills of salesmanship, or persuasion, or grievance-handling, breaking the monotony only to show a film about salesmanship, persuasion, or grievance-handling. True, from time to time they may introduce a case study for discussion, so that people may rehearse their formal knowledge about how the problem should have been handled; actual skills practice is minimal. The excuse often is that skills practice is too difficult to organise, or that it would take up too much of the trainer's time; unconsciously the trainer may know that his lectures are doing some good by working on the vocabulary problem, and he also relies on the gullibility of his trainees in believing that they have learned something. Thus, poor training is perpetuated and opportunities for real performance improvement are missed; for it is not impossible to design skills training in a way that allows for lots of practice with feedback.

Trainers need to be clear, when designing or choosing a training course, about the balance between knowledge and skills that is necessary. An audience of personnel directors attending a seminar on performance appraisal systems needs a lot of knowledge, but very little skill-acquisition; an audience of first-line managers about to start appraisal interviewing probably needs the exact opposite.

C What hinders learning?

Every trainer meets at some time the manager who refuses point-blank to be sent on a training course; or the course member who sits with arms firmly folded across his chest daring the trainer to have the audacity to try to train him. It is part of most firms' mythology that managers don't like training and have to be persuaded to change, but why should this be so? Why should the eager child who runs home anxious to tell what he's learned today, proud because he's passed a test, turn into the surly manager asserting that anything that was good enough for his grandfather is good enough for him? What has happened on the way?

Among the many things that hinder adult learning, we can pick out these:

1   *Forgetting how to.* Learning is itself a skill that can be learned, and can be forgotten. There are simple mechanical skills that get rusty after a while—taking notes, using reference books, writing connected prose, sitting still for hours on end. There are analytical skills—taking the bones out of an argument, knowing how to test a theory, comparing the points of difference between two views. There are necessary skills of self-management—the ability to listen to a point of view you dislike, or that is presented in unpalatable form; the ability to force yourself to confront possibilities you'd rather ignore. In addition, many people never properly learned the scientific method of problem-solving, on which so many present day management techniques are based, and many of our managers are not really numerate above a very elementary level. Having forgotten, or never having acquired, these skills, the manager sent on a long residential course may spend a good part of it in shock, completely out of his depth.

2   *Fear of exposure.* For some managers, being sent on a course implies that what they were doing before was wrong and stands condemned. It is sometimes quite difficult to get accepted the point that what they were doing before was as good as could be expected, but that now they are going to learn to do something even better. The fear is strongest in areas where people have difficulty monitoring their own performance. Some courses, and some trainers, have not helped; they begin by making everyone feel inadequate—so as to make them feel that much better at the end of the course—and news of this filters back into the rest of the organisation.

3   *Self-protection.*Some people would rather be comfortable than efficient, and they go to extraordinary lengths to make sure that nothing interferes with their comfort; they make their own little models of the world, in which change and unpleasantness are kept at arm's length by a variety of devices and deceits. These people can be heard neutralising information which other managers might heed as warnings: phrases like 'She's only saying that because she's a woman', or 'That's the exception that proves the rule', or 'We haven't had any *official* complaints'. When such managers learn, it is by catastrophe; they have sealed themselves off from the small warnings, and it is only when the world collapses around them—they lose a major account, suffer

a damaging strike, get a coronary, etc.—that they change their behaviour. They reject training, as it is usually offered, because training might make them change their ways.

4 *Over-motivation.* We have all had the experience of being able to absorb and reproduce information easily, except on the day of the examination; making a perfect dummy-run presentation, but going to pieces when putting our case to the Board; or making silly mistakes in work which we are taking special care with because it is so important. It is possible to be too well motivated to perform well, and this applies in some learning situations. The trainee who comes to the negotiations course in a hurry because he is face to face with ASTMS next week may paradoxically not learn very much, because his need to know is so great that it interferes with steady performance.

5 *Uncertainty about the training's purposes.* People are recommended for training for all sorts of reasons besides a need to improve their performance; courses are used as rewards, punishments, staging posts, and places to put people while their future is being decided. Some courses have been designed with a hidden purpose; they tell the trainee that they are for training purposes, but they are really assessive. Training for the present job is sometimes sold as preparation for the next one. These and similar factors conspire to get in the way of trainees managing their own learning, even if they begin by being well motivated; additionally some managers have an odd view of what training involves, thinking that a prestigious speaker or a high course fee indicates the usefulness of the training to them.

6 *Unhelpful trainers' jargon.* The need for improvement in all aspects of management has led to a burgeoning of new management techniques, each with its own terms. Trainers, who have to be familiar with most management techniques, are extra-vulnerable to the trap of using jargon. In addition it is tempting to invent jargon to hide one's ignorance; the more ivory-tower the concept, the more people fight about definitions and territory. Most trainers have their horror stories of listening to interminable arguments about the difference between *aim, purpose, goal, objective,* and *target*; about the difference between *training* and *development*; about the transition point between *management development* and *organisation development.* To the outsider, such discussions look like a bunch of techniques in search of a problem—or like running away from the real world. No wonder that the average production manager,

to whom a concept isn't a concept unless it hurts when you drop it on your foot, looks at the jargon-ridden world of management training and decides he wants none of it.

7   *The Fat Aunt Ellen syndrome.* Having criticised trainers for using jargon, we now offer some of our own. The excuse is that we have not seen this obstacle to learning identified by any other name, yet there is little doubt that it exists and that it hinders learning.

The name comes from a maiden aunt of the first author—a formidable lady who bore a strong physical resemblance to Henry VIII—who determined to reform the author's (undoubtedly troublesome) character. She would do this by enticing her to commit acts of good behaviour ('Good girls help with the washing up . . . wash behind their knees . . . don't keep frogs in their blazer pockets', etc.) and adding comments after the good behaviour like: 'There, don't you feel better for trying to be helpful?' and 'You see, I was right after all, wasn't I?' Readers who suffered similarly will remember the waves of resentment that rose during these after-the-act comments; it's bad enough reforming your ways, without listening to a prayerful commentary from the sidelines.

Unfortunately many trainers behave like Aunt Ellen—trainers on courses and manager-coaches—when they are trying to educate someone out of bad practice. We have already seen that for some managers, admitting that they need training is admitting that they were wrong, and that this is too uncomfortable to bear. Given that they have moved, or been pushed, from their comfortable state into one where they have actually tried something new, they are in a vulnerable condition. They need to consolidate, to realise that it didn't hurt as much as it might, that there could after all be something in the new method. For a trainer to come along with a hearty slap on the back and say, 'Well, Joe, how does it feel to have joined the twentieth century?' or 'I knew you'd feel better once you did it my way', is likely to arouse the same resentment in the manager as the child felt *vis-à-vis* the aunt.

Sometimes it seems to us that this is the biggest single obstacle in the way of managers learning—the tactless way they are treated as they learn their new skills. Some of the training course techniques which have a lot to commend them in other respects place the trainer in a Fat Aunt Ellen role: the session at the end of the course where people are pressed to say what they will be doing differently next week, for example. Yes, people need to translate their learning back to their jobs, but an action plan demanded at a sensitive time may do damage. Trainers who think that their trainees are over-reacting to unimportant personal details like the trainer's apparent youth, or sex, or hairstyle, should realise that some trainees may feel very uncomfortable in the training situation and that anything indicating the trainer's inexperience will be magnified out of all proportion.

To the list of hindrances to learning given above, which are amplified for the interested reader in the books cited at the end of the chapter, we add a speculation. We wonder whether some middle-aged British managers are, quite simply, exhausted to the point of being the managerial equivalent of the dust bowl. It is interesting to follow the career of a manager in his late fifties, from the beginning; the Hitler war, which though frightening and dull and arbitrary nonetheless made many people realise their own capabilities *in extremis*. Then the let-down; instead of a reward for winning, with a bumper harvest and two bob off the income tax, we get bread rationing. Foreign aid is spent on free teeth instead of re-equipping factories; people continue to scrape along. Then comes the boom at the start of the fifties, and the optimism of never having had it so good, which obscures analysis of the structural problems underlying our economy; and thence into the stop-go-stop regulation of the business cycle by government, the constant changes of tax and credit structures, which gradually erode the credibility of *any* incentive or threat which managers are offered. If you sometimes reward your pet dog for staying, and sometimes beat him, and sometimes ignore him, eventually he will become a neurotic wreck who does nothing to draw attention to himself in the matter of staying; if carrots are waved in front of managers, only to be turned into sticks, then back into carrots again, sooner or later the managers lose interest in carrots and sticks.

We are not trying to make a political point here, except insofar as we believe in productive industry; what we are saying is that it is easy to forget that managers have memories, and that a manager whose plans have constantly been thwarted may have little left to learn with. If we are right in this speculation, then the need to 'sell' training becomes even greater, and the difficulty increases also.

D   How can managers be helped to learn?

Training is a product and needs to be sold, like any other
product. Products sell partly by quality, partly by publicity, and
partly by recommendation. How therefore can we sell the idea of
training?

1 *Actively push its benefits.* Never miss an opportunity to
remind people that training exists and people profit by it. Get
training events and their benefits mentioned in the company
newsletter; at sales conferences; at meetings with clients or
suppliers; in selection interviews and career counselling
interviews and in the material associated with the performance
appraisal programme. Get line managers involved in training:
talking on training courses, discussing course content, analysing
training needs, putting training plans into practice. Get senior
managers to attend courses alongside junior managers if it's
possible, so that the juniors realise that all the firm believes in
training. And make sure that the training department is itself
well trained and managed to a high standard.

2 *Make training courses easier than real life.* A training
couse is a place to learn new ways of doing things; new
knowledge, new skills. In order to practise the skills and rehearse
the knowledge the trainee is bound to make mistakes, if only to
test the borders of his new learning. A trainee who sails through
a course without making a mistake hasn't learned much. But the
course has to be risk free; the trainee can make mistakes in the
knowledge that it doesn't matter, no business disaster will result.

This is very important in the case of skills which people have
picked up as they have gone along, with no real insight into what
they are learning. The production manager who finds that he is
suddenly confronted with a work-force which has downed tools
manages to negotiate his way out; while he's doing it he may be
so wrapped up that he does not fully understand and remember
all he is doing. Maybe if he scraped through by the skin of his
teeth he does not want to look back and see how the negotiation
was conducted. Then the next time a problem happens, he
follows roughly the same pattern as before, because it served him
well . . . and so on. When he comes on a negotiation skills course,
he may be set in his ways and terrified to change because he
doesn't really know why he has been successful. The trainer
must persuade him to try one or two different negotiation styles,
and this can only happen if the manager sees that the situation is

risk free—a place to experiment, a place that is easier than real life.

Courses that deliberately put people under stress are therefore suspect unless there are very good reasons. Courses with secret report-back on participants are of dubious value; formal assessment events have a place, a valuable place, but not as training courses. After the new skills have been learned, then the trainees may test them on difficult tasks, but it should be clear that there is a difference between learning (in a risk-free, easy environment) and consolidation (where challenges are appropriate).

3 *Help trainees monitor their own performance.* Formal training courses are a tiny part of a manager's life. Coaching and on-the-job training sessions may take up more time, or occur more frequently; but most of the time the manager is working for and by himself. He is his own best trainer, given the tools and the motivation to use them. Good trainers therefore spend time helping people to diagnose their own training needs, set their own training tasks, and monitor their own performance. It is common practice, on courses like Problem-Solving and Decision-Making, for the trainer to give the class a problem to work on; then after they have flogged their way through he presents them all with the model solution. When enough people have chorused: 'Oh, I see,' he passes on to the next subject. Far better to arrange to work with each trainee identifying the trainee's own thought processes, reasons for making each decision, assumptions underlying each decision, etc., and thereby to lead the trainee to build his own version of the model solution.

4 *Recognise, but don't patronise, good performance.* Feedback on success is needed as well as feedback on failure; the trainer whose reviews or feedback sessions are biased towards the negative end of the spectrum is losing an opportunity to motivate his trainees. It may be more difficult to give feedback on good performance, and difficult to do it without falling victim to the Fat Aunt Ellen syndrome, but trainers should try. (Feedback on success sounds much less patronising if it comes from the other trainees.)

5 *Emphasise the link with real life.* All training is different from the 'real' situation to some extent, simply by being labelled training. Off-the-job training in particular may seem unrealistic, especially if the trainer needs to chop up the learning into small pieces or deliberately to make it simple. However, the trainees

must be reassured at all points that their training activities are relevant to real life; partly this is achieved by the trainers' remembering to tell them so, and partly it is achieved by good design—not choosing abstraction for abstraction's sake. Some training methods—for example role-play, or group performance of very simple tasks—are so remote from real life that trainees understandably find it difficult to make the connection, and this is borne out when the training is evaluated.

E Summary

Adult learning is different from children's learning because people are out of practice and because the motivation may not be there. Learning takes place under conditions of practice, with feedback on performance, and help in monitoring one's own performance if this is required. Knowledge can be learned by formal absorption—of which there are many variants—but skills need active practice. Learning new things may be difficult for managers because it is easier for them to stay in their comfortable rut, and the trainer therefore has to sell his training and make it non-threatening and effective.

F Discussion questions

1   A course in planning skills took as its material the present and future requirements of the trainees' customers. The trainees were however forbidden to bring to the course any written material relating to their customers. When they realised how much they needed this material, and asked the trainer why he had forbidden it, the trainer replied. 'To teach you that you should have this sort of thing in your heads.'
    What do you think that trainer meant by 'teach', and what inferences can you draw about the success of the course?
2   'I've never had an experience like it. They just sat there, not asking any questions or showing any response at all, however much I tried to get them involved. They didn't even laugh at my jokes. I had questions designed to provoke ever-so-slightly wrong answers, and some discussion, but they acted as if the questions were rhetorical. Then they put the questions to me at the end, through the chairman! I found out afterwards that their

managers, and their Central Personnel Department, got a report back on the performance of everyone who had been on the course. I can see the sense of this for typists, but this was a course for middle managers, on the management of specialist and professional staff!'

When do you think report-back on courses is justified? How should it be done? Who should do it, and to whom? What about the trainee's involvement?

3 'And so for your first year in an American company you are very much on trial, and your strengths and weaknesses carefully noted and assessed. There is no mollycoddling whatever. You are expected to ask questions, find things out for yourself, and be willing to accept the corporate culture. At the end of it all you are classified either as a man with potential or as one who is unlikely to make the grade. Either way you are left in no doubt where you stand.' (From Farnsworth, *On The Way Up*, [4]).

Under what circumstances is this method of on-the-job training likely to succeed, and under what conditions is it likely to fail? Can you think of examples in your own experience?

4 Airline pilots will commonly report mechanical faults in the aircraft with no hesitation. Human error, and errors at the man-machine interface, go unreported until someone has an accident; then people will freely admit that: 'Yes, that nearly happened to me once, but I was lucky,' or '. . . but we had enough height to get out in time.'

Why do people admit that some things need improvement, but not others? What could be done to encourage the better reporting of human and interface errors (to improve training and job design and equipment design)? Have you seen managers behaving as these airline pilots do, and under what circumstances?

G References and further reading

[1]N. RACKHAM, P. HONEY and M. COLBERT. *Developing Interactive Skills*, Wellens Publishing, 1970.

[2] N. RACKHAM and T. MORGAN. *Behaviour Analysis in Training*, McGraw-Hill, 1977.

[3] M. HOWE (ed.), *Adult Learning*, Wiley, 1977.
A useful summary of work in this field, outlining a number of

interesting approaches and giving learned but not too technical analyses of the main problems.

[4] T. FARNSWORTH.   *On the Way Up*, McGraw-Hill, 1976. Amusing and illuminating look at how to succeed in big organisations.

[5] J. ROGERS.   *Adult Learning*, Penguin Books, 1971. This is not specifically a book about learning in industry—the author has in mind evening classes, voluntary re-training courses, etc.—but it is so insightful about the problems people experience when trying to learn after forgetting how to that every industrial trainer should read it. Miss Rogers has written a later book (*The Right to Learn*, with Brian Groombridge) making clear her indignation about the facilities provided for people who wish to improve themselves.

3 You, the trainer

All sorts of people find themselves working as trainers: line managers and technical specialists, consultants and research workers, as well as people designated as training officers. Not all organisations can afford to keep a staff of professional trainers whose job it is to do nothing else; in some small firms the job will be done by the managing director in the minutes when he's not being chief accountant, company secretary, and head salesman. Whoever the trainer is, this chapter is addressed to him in an attempt to offer some hints and suggestions for improving his own abilities as a trainer.

A Types of trainer

Looking around the world of management training, three stereotypes of trainer can be discerned. There is the prestige performer: the man with the big name, the high reputation, who charges fees to match; usually he speaks to managing directors or very senior managers only, and his style is to lecture them from on high. Then there is the instructor: usually working towards increasing knowledge rather than improving skill, he can be found at any level and may be recruited from within the firm or engaged from outside. Finally there is a third type, the facilitator: he may not appear to be any kind of authority figure at all during the training process as he sees his job as helping people to help themselves rather than formally instructing them. These stereotypes are not the only ones possible; there are trainers who fall between them, and trainers who can switch styles according to the needs of the moment. Each type has its value, and its limitations.

1 *The prestige performer* is good for giving people a shot in the arm, a quick boost to morale; some of them can be funny and entertaining and they draw on a wealth of experience which gives the audience a feeling of sharing, of being party to a privileged conversation. They can help a manager to understand his own

35

experience, by putting it in a wider context, and the value of this to an isolated managing director of a small firm, for example, can be very great.

Prestige performers are also useful when the internal experts have decided on a change or reorganisation, and they want to have an outside expert commend it to their managers because this way the change will have more credibility. It is not uncommon for the training manager in Firm A to be asked to give a homily to the managers of Firm B, assembled to hear about their new performance appraisal system; and in a few months' time the training manager in Firm B delivers a speech to the managers of Firm A commending their new consultative machinery. Prophets are indeed without honour in their own country!

Expensive prestige performers can be used to give people a 'Hawthorne effect'. This can be a good or a bad thing, depending on whether the person who's paying the bill knows that that's what he's buying. A Hawthorne effect happens when performance improves when you pay attention to people *almost irrespective* of the kind of attention you pay; it derives from experiments where the working conditions of a selected group of workers were systematically altered to find the best conditions, only for the researchers to be confused by the fact that adverse changes in working conditions nonetheless gave rise to improved performance because the workers were influenced by the simple fact that attention was being paid to them. To a worn-out production manager the fact that the company is prepared to spend a three-figure sum, plus opportunity cost, to send him to London to sit at the feet of an American guru for an afternoon may actually improve his performance when he gets back. This is an advantage in some circumstances, but the disadvantages of using prestige performers solely for Hawthorne effects are numerous. First, one cannot predict exactly *how* performance will improve; second, some people are more vulnerable than others to Hawthorne effects, and the effects wear off after prolonged exposure; third, there is always the temptation for the trainer to claim that he was directly responsible for the improvements due to the Hawthorne effects. If he is humble enough to realise what he is doing when he sends people off for a visit to a prestige performer, then he is better equipped to use this stereotype trainer to its best advantage.

There are dangers in being a prestige performer, too. The roar of the crowd is exhilarating; it is easy to be drawn into telling managers what they want to hear, rather than what they ought to know. It is surprising how much insult an audience will take, and come back for more, if the insults are delivered in the right voice—preferably Harvard educated! This makes for simple answers to complex questions, for the speech that boils down to 'The important thing is to do it right', for the speech that looks for scapegoats elsewhere, for the rabble-rousing in preference to the rational. It may also be difficult for a prestige performer to change his mind; if you make a big splash exhorting people to decentralise in 1975, it is difficult to go on the boards again in 1980 advocating more control at the centre. Some good innovations in management and management training were never fully developed because people put their prestige on the line with the first generation and did not dare move forward.

Most trainers need to act like prestige performers some of the time, although not everyone can lay claim to a great name. Much of the advice helping people to become good public speakers will help the trainer wishing to develop his skills in this direction: finding out about the audience first, preparing well, putting key concepts in order on cue cards, preparing in advance the things you will say to introduce yourself and to conclude with; standing square, not jingling the change in one's pocket, not leaning on furniture for support, engaging eye-contact with members of the audience; cutting out the 'ums' and 'ers' and speaking slowly. More important is not to get carried away with the glamour of it all; addressing a sales conference in Ibiza may feel like the management trainer's equivalent of Judy Garland at the London Palladium, but it's a mistake to be dazzled by it.

Many trainers also find themselves engaging a prestige performer to come and speak to them. Reputation is some guide; the fee is no guide at all. Some charge massive fees; others—speaking for instance to evening meetings of BIM branches and similar—ask only for their travel expenses. The size of fee is no guide to quality. Judge by the number of questions they ask about your organisation, the amount they want to brief themselves, whether they submit a draft of their speech to you for comment or expect you to take what is given. Listening managers can be helped to make the transition from Hawthorne effect to managed performance improvements if they are encouraged to make notes on what they have learned, or propose to do differently, after the speaker has finished.

2   *The instructor* operates more like a formal teacher than
the prestige performer does. It is his job to organise and present
a body of knowledge in such a way that some of this knowledge is
transferred from him to the trainees. The instructor is at his best
when there is an identifiable body of knowledge which the
trainees realise they need to know—for example, discounted cash
flow, company taxation, microfilm data storage—and when the
trainees recognise and respect the instructor's competence.

A good instructor is master of his material well beyond the
point he is likely to reach in any one instruction session; some say
that they feel as if they need a backlog of eight times the
imparted information to feel safe and confident. Good
instructors know the span of attention of their audience—
surprisingly limited even when goodwill and interest are there,
and practically non-existent after a good lunch—and they adapt
their plans accordingly, varying lectures with films, tape and
slide presentation, case studies, programmed texts, syndicate
tasks, etc. In addition the good instructor arranges the flow of his
material so that people have opportunities to test their learning
at frequent intervals—he asks them qustions, gets them to ask
him questions, gives them examples and exercises of the right
degree of difficulty. One of the best tests of a good instructor is
the way he deals with questions; the bad one repeats the right
answer, parrot-fashion, whereas the good one tries to get inside
the questioner's head, to imagine what he must have
misunderstood or what assumptions he must have made in order
to ask that question; then he slants his answer so as to remove
the fundamental misunderstanding if this is at all possible.

Formal instruction has gone out of fashion a little lately, which
is a pity; properly done it can be one of the quickest and most
efficient ways of transmitting knowledge. Instruction often fails
because the material to be taught is not suitable; skills cannot be
taught by instruction, though the vocabulary to understand one's
own skills sometimes can. Instructors also get into difficulties
sometimes about the extent to which they should sell the idea of
training; should they assume that because the managers are
foregathered to hear about the Employment Protection Act, for
example, then it is sufficient to start lecturing from cold, or
should they spend a little while rehearsing the reasons why the
managers need to know about it? The answer is that in nearly
every case the instructor has also to be a salesman for his ideas,
and a salesman for learning; the managers may even have asked

to come on the course themselves, but one must still try to attract their attention at the start of instruction.

Instructors and instruction are probably more vulnerable than the other stereotypes to administrative constraints; because instruction usually happens to large groups of people, taken off their jobs for the purpose, the impression grows that the minimum period of time that can be spent in instruction is a half-day or even a day. It may actually be better to have half-an-hour a week for a year, but the administrator may try for a week's course all in one lump.

Formal instruction can encourage a passive attitude in the trainees, especially if the instructor does not try to vary the pace and engage people's continuous attention. This may give people the illusion of having been trained even when no training has taken place. This is especially so when an attempt is made to teach skills by formal instruction; interpersonal skills are very vulnerable here. At worst, there is an instructor telling people what a skilled performance—or more likely an unskilled performance—looks like, which his audience absorbs with easy self-deception to come away with the illusion that they are now skilled managers.

The development of instructional skills is treated towards the end of this chapter, and more fully in Chapter 7, on the design of knowledge-based training courses.

3 *The facilitator* sees it as his job to create the conditions under which people learn for themselves. The trainees may or may not realise that he is there, or that he has a 'contract' to improve their performance; they feel that they have discovered things for themselves, and do not usually discern the skill which the facilitator has used to create the necessary learning conditions. Indeed, they may even reject the facilitator, if he has made them confront aspects of themselves they would rather keep concealed; a good facilitator will not mind this, as long as improved performance results.

Facilitators work best when skills are to be learned, rather than formal knowledge imparted; they are especially useful when the skills are ones which managers don't believe they actually need. In some areas of management it would not be possible to send in a formal instructor from the training department; there are senior managers who will only accept instruction from people they believe to be more skilled than they are, a constraint which excludes most trainers who are not also senior line managers.

Nevertheless a good facilitator can work with these managers to create the conditions in which they learn something for themselves. Facilitatory training styles are also useful when there are many people to be taught but they learn at different paces or start from different base-lines; when there are very few people to be taught, so that formal instruction would seem nonsensical; or when there is a strong need to change deep-seated attitudes as well as convey new skills.

The facilitator's task is perhaps the hardest of all management training tasks, and the one about which there is the most mystery; in the late 1960s the approach calling itself Organisation Development became fashionable, with an implicit style that involved the trainer sitting on the sidelines for most of the time, letting the team get on with their job, but from time to time making an 'intervention'—a comment, question, piece of feedback—which the group were supposed to take up. A number of books, simple and arcane, were written about intervention methods. Strange forms of training evolved—Coverdale, T-groups, sensitivity training, etc.—in which there seemed to be a deliberate turning upside-down of the traditions of management education. Some people tried their hands as facilitators, only to realise that this is a more difficult job than its apparent inactivity would suggest.

The good facilitator needs a wide variety of skills. He needs to know about group dynamics, and how to manipulate them. He needs to know about exercise design, in order to plan a programme of self-discovered learning for people to take in the right order and at the right pace. He needs to know how to motivate people to learn—what the balance should be between enjoyment, frustration, patience, challenge, and speed. He needs a good deal of personal strength and self-control, because the trainees will turn on him from time to time; it is a lonely job, and not one that is easy to describe to others; nor is it very rewarding, in the sense that the prestige performer understands the rewards of training, because the trainees are likely to forget that you're there if you are doing well. There is no round of applause at the end of a facilitator's involvement with the learning group.

Because of its apparent lack of controlled activity the facilitator's role is one in which abuses are possible. There is, for example, a natural order of group processes which will happen in any group of trainees thrown together with a series of tasks to do.

First they look for a leader—to the person designated as leader, by which they mean the trainer, first of all, and when that is unsuccessful they struggle amongst themselves to find a leader. When the leader emerges the group does well for a while, under the structure of firm leadership, but sooner or later they revolt against their first leader and another crisis emerges. At this point they turn again to the trainer for help, and if he is taking the facilitator role he will refuse to be drawn into active leadership of the group; at this point the group can become very hostile indeed, and the trainer's life is quite an uncomfortable one. Usually, though, the group settles down to a more fluid pattern of operations, with some insight into its own behaviour and some self-control. This makes them happy; they do well; they can see the end of the course in sight and they become positively euphoric with self-congratulation.

This will happen in just about every group of trainees given a series of tasks and left to get on with it. If the trainer does not exert himself at all he can guarantee that they will feel low on Tuesday evening and exalted on Friday morning, ready to go home convinced they have learned a great deal. They may not actually do anything different when they get to the office, but they will nonetheless say the course taught them a lot. A poor or unscrupulous trainer need do little to take advantage of this natural human tendency; he may actually manipulate the group's feelings by setting them specially difficult tasks just after the beginning of the course, making them feel failures. The bounce-back euphoria will be correspondingly greater, and he can get himself a reputation as a great trainer.

There is even more reason why this unscrupulous manipulation results in good course-reports in the teeth of evidence that the courses do not change behaviour; this is the phenomenon known as cognitive dissonance reduction. Briefly explained, it is this: people do not enjoy holding conflicting thoughts in their minds, and they will go to some trouble to make sure that conflict is not perceived. They can do this by building walls between different parts of their minds, for example the biologist who believes Archbishop Ussher's theory that the world was created in 4004 BC. Or they can adjust one of the thoughts to make it compatible with the other; and if a manager just come from a long and trying training course with an unhelpful trainer finds himself holding the thoughts: 'That was an upsetting, disturbing, unsystematic experience,' and 'I stayed there a week, and it cost the firm £500 plus the cost of having me away for a week' then he may reconcile the conflict by adding a third thought: 'It must have done me some good.'

This kind of tactic, practised by people emulating some of the more successful facilitators, has got management training a bad name in some quarters. This is a pity because the good facilitator knows what he is about, does not try to manipulate people for his own glory, and has a unique contribution to make in getting managers to learn.

Our three stereotypes—prestige performer, instructor, and facilitator— all have their uses. A good trainer may need to be bits of all three. Yet it is a sad fact that many people in training positions find themselves there without ever having had any teaching in the art of being a trainer. There is no diploma course turning out management trainers as such, and it might be a mistake if one were to be introduced; need it be the case however that the new trainer picks it up as he goes along? In our experience the untrained trainer thrust upon a group of expectant managers with no idea what he's going to do or how he's going to do it is just as likely to be found in big organisations as small ones, and in professional training organisations and consultancy firms. The Industry Training Boards are gradually helping here, and research is going on to further our understanding of instructional situations and instructional techniques; but for the average trainer it's a lonely life, and a bit of a scramble at times. We suggest therefore that the reader might like to try some of the following exercises, which are designed to help the trainer improve his own skills at a personal level. Some come from us; some have been borrowed from other people; all of them work.

Exercise One. Practise, as a conscious discipline, keeping silent while a trainee tells you something that he has learned. Resist the temptation to phrase it for him, or to finish his sentence, or to re-phrase it after he has finished; for it is much more important that he tell you in his own language, however faltering, what he has learned, than that you tell him in trainer's language what you think he's learned. Remember that when people dined with Gladstone, they came away thinking that he was the wittiest person in the world, but when they dined with Disraeli they came away thinking that they were the wittiest persons in the world. In the early days of this exercise it helps to keep a count of the number of times you successfully suppress the urge to intervene.

Exercise Two. Practise sitting so still that people forget you are there. Concentrate on suppressing every movement you make—fidgeting, scratching, smoking, writing, adjusting position on the chair. Then concentrate on keeping your breathing rate steady and slow, and on making slow comprehensive sweeps of the room rather than taking short glances. Then learn to concentrate on taking in what you see; watch how people talk to each other, watch the pattern of action and reaction, watch their faces and their body positions and listen to their words. Don't plan your next lecture, or plan what you will say to the group next; just concentrate on taking everything in and giving nothing out. Your test should be when you ask a group of trainees discussing a problem with you in the corner, to tell you when you left the room and how long you were gone; if they believe you had gone when you were really there all the time you have won.

Exercise Three. When you have mastered the previous exercise, add to it the ability to build up a mental map of the group processes. How you do this depends to some extent on your own imagery; you may like to imagine a running total of behaviours adding up over the heads of each group member, or imagine the members joined by different coloured lines—colour indicating the quality of transaction, thickness of line indicating degree of interaction. The map should be robust enough for you to be able to recall it later, away from the group.

Exercise Four. Look back at your last training course, or to the people you have given on-the-job instructions to lately. Name the person you found most satisfying to teach, and the person you found least. Now make a list of the differences between them—all the differences you can think of, including the obvious ones and the frivolous ones. Does this list itself teach you anything? Can you generalise from your list based on these two people to your experience of training in general? Now get another trainer to do the same, and compare your list with his. Has he detected characteristics which you missed? Does he find things satisfying which you find otherwise? Why? What does he do about them?

Exercise Five. In a group of trainers, each person writes on a small card a brief account of the worst mistake he ever made as a trainer—of course, it has to be a mistake that he *knew* he'd made. The same is done for the best success he feels he had. All the 'failure' cards are pooled, and all the 'success' cards;

someone then starts a discussion of the failure cards, looking at trends, differences, and courses of action. Could anything have been done to prevent the failures? Who could have done this? What more could the trainer himself have done? Is the problem likely to recur, and could it have been prevented? The process is repeated for the successes. At the end of the discussion each trainer writes down two or three things which he will try to do differently next time, and some notes about how he will tell whether his efforts are successful.

Exercise Six. Do you have any lecture notes? Pick a place at random, and list as many questions as possible that naïve enthusiasts in your audience might ask. Do you have replies (not necessarily *answers*) to each of these questions? Now make another list, this time of the questions that might come from a hostile trouble-maker and your proposed replies. Have a close look at your answers—are they likely to increase or decrease hostility? It is easy to produce a reply which squashes somebody, or makes him look a fool in front of fellow trainees, but this is a dangerous tactic for the trainer to follow. If you can get a fellow trainer to do the same, and compare his notes with yours, so much the better.

Exercise Seven. Pick a technical book off the shelves at random, preferably one which you will not understand easily. Write a thousand-word review of it for a journal of your own choosing. While you are reading it, make a note of the points you don't understand, and go to a technical expert for clarification; don't show him the passages you don't understand, but try to re-phrase the points in your own language. What has this taught you about presenting technical information to an intelligent layman, and what will you do differently as a result?

Exercise Eight. Try working from someone else's lecture notes. Has this taught you anything about your order of presentation? your way of organising material? your visual aids? the way you apportion your time? the way you treat questions? the shorthand notes you make for yourself? What corners do you cut when you make your own notes, and why?

Exercise Nine. Find a trainer doing a similar job in a different firm, and ask if you can sit in on one of his courses—returning the hospitality later, of course. Try to see the actual course, experiencing it as an ordinary trainee would experience it; don't have privileged discussions first in which the content and purpose of the course is explained to you. Write a report for yourself, describing the similarities and differences between you, and the things he does that you could usefully borrow. Your Industry Training Board may be able to negotiate a swap for you if you feel shy.

Exercise Ten. Take one of your existing training courses, or training plans, and turns it upside down. For example, instead of offering managers training in doing appraisal interviews, why not offer training in how to be appraised? Instead of offering courses for sales managers telling them how to sell, design a course in effective buying. Substitute listening skills for public speaking skills. Offer a course on accidents, instead of on safety, It will give valuable insights even if you decide to keep on training the normal way; but from time to time it improves performance actually to turn the training upside down.

Exercise Eleven. Talk to some managers about the training they have had; what do they remember best, what did they find the most valuable? How much of what they say they learned was planned by the trainer, and how much is the looking-back 'Ah, that taught me something' response? Think about the differences between trainer-planned and learner-retrospective kinds of learning. What can the trainer hope for and try to keep under his own control?

Exercise Twelve. Go to a prestige performance, or to a second-rate seminar given by someone using instructional methods to teach skills. Derive for yourself a checklist of things to notice in his statements: how many times, for example, does he say things which amount to 'Be skilful,' or 'Do it right,' or 'There's a lot of it about,' or 'That's an interesting problem you've got'. How many times does he use words like data, media, criteria, with a singular verb, thus indicating that he doesn't care much for precision of thought? How does he cope with questions? How does he cope with objections? How wide a range of industries is he drawing on for his anecdotes? How does he react when people in the audience start discussing the problem with each other instead of with him?

Exercise Thirteen. Spend a little of your training budget taking out to lunch one of the people who plan programmes of public seminars and training courses. Ask them how they do their marketing, how they discover what managers want. How do they deal with the problem of giving managers what they *need*, in the teeth (sometimes) of what they say they want? How do they evaluate their training? How do they publicise sensitive topics?

How do they choose their speakers? Ask what motivates them—how do they tell if they've done a good job at the end of the day?

Exercise Fourteen. Suppose you have to cut the costs of your training activities by 10 per cent. Where would the cuts do the least harm in the short term? Is this different from the long term view? Where would the cuts be most visible to senior management? to the trainees themselves? Where would they be least visible?

Exercise Fifteen. Make a note, somewhere, of your own personal objectives for the next eighteen months. What skills do you wish to improve? How do you want to be judged? What do you want to have contributed to your organisation? What challenges are you most looking forward to? What innovations do you want to put forward, and how do you plan to get them accepted? What new developments do you wish to consolidate? If the answers are mostly negative, and you find yourself constantly wishing it were Friday, then start to tackle the problem of your own enthusiasm and motivation first. You've no right to bully managers into doing their jobs better if you don't enjoy yours; besides, it'll show, and you'll find they won't listen to you.

B   Reading list

The choice of a reading list for a management trainer could be very long. We list here the books we wouldn't be without, either for their solid worth or for their provision of sudden, blinding insights. We have not listed those—like Rackham and Morgan's book, for instance—which are frequently referred to elsewhere in this book; they would nonetheless find a place on our desert island.

[1] C. B. HANDY. *Understanding Organisations*, Penguin, 1976.

A book that takes on the messy reality of organisational life—politics, incompetents, peculiar products and personal fancies—and makes analytical sense out of it without retreating into the ivory tower. Consistently illuminating, either for reference or for dipping into.

[2] M. DUNNETTE. *Handbook of Industrial and Organisational Psychology*, Rand-McNally, 1976.

A large and expensive volume of articles covering a very wide range of industrial problems, commissioned from experts in the field, and with each article having a very comprehensive bibliography. There are articles on subjects that don't even figure in other books' indexes; it is where we always start looking if we have a new problem.

[3] M. ARGENTI. *Corporate Collapse*, McGraw-Hill, 1976.
A slim volume, nominally about how and why organisations fail, but also about the people who make them fail—what they do, that information they have, how they use it, etc. For background to the training needs of middle managers, this is an informative book.

[4] R. TOWNSEND. *Up the Organisation*, Coronet, 1971.
Full of anecdotes, insights, and nasty questions; worth reading at any time, but especially when you've forgotten what you're doing and why, or you have to train managers who have fallen victim to the same disease.

[5] *The Arrow Trade Union Studies*, published by Arrow Books and by a variety of authors, are useful for two reasons. The first is that these are books written to train trade unionists in the basic skills they need, some of which are directly opposed to 'management' needs by definition. Managers need to know what the unions are thinking. The second reason is that the books are themselves a model of how to put across complex information—about statistics, or the law, or behaviour in groups—in simple, understandable form, with useful exercises, without being patronising. They do in four sides of paper what some management trainers maintain takes several days to achieve.

[6] G. S. ODIORNE. *Training By Objectives*, Macmillan, 1970.
Splendidly trenchant book about how to design training. In his continual emphasis on the need to have an end-point always in sight, and on the need not to spend people's time and money wastefully, the author is clear and firm. His anecdotes are plentiful and interesting, and he is not afraid to be rude about some management training fads.

[7] C. ALBERTS. *The Good Provider: H. J. Heinz and his 57 Varieties*, Arthur Barker, 1973.
This is good entertainment—a well-written biography which stands up in its own right as well as providing insights for the management trainer. Extracts from Heinz diaries show his novel approach to marketing, to welfare, to quality control, etc., as well

as his struggles when he had the chance to bribe his way out of bankruptcy. We wish there were more biographies of successful businessmen; this one is a delight.

4 Diagnosis of training needs: group methods

A Beginning training needs analysis

Top of the management trainer's agenda is the diagnosis of training needs—what, exactly, should he be offering his managers, what do they need to do better? Training needs analysis is the bedrock on which good training is built; if the analysis is done properly, then many of the problems of evaluating training become amenable, as we shall demonstrate in the chapter on evaluation. However, training needs analysis is not a simple matter, because of the difficulties associated with analysing managerial performance; it is not always possible to do it by just asking managers what they would like to do better, or by standing over them counting their deficiencies. The trainer has to dig a little deeper, looking for clues.

Training needs analysis techniques can be separated by two distinct dividers. On the one hand, there is a distinction between *group* techniques and *individual* techniques; the first useful at a macro-level, for strategic planning, for deciding training priorities, and the second useful whenever particular individuals' training needs come under scrutiny. The second distinction is more subtle. Some techniques are aimed at discovering *deficiencies* in people's present performance; others are aimed at discovering what *ideal* performace should look like. Obviously the trainer needs to know both the ideal and the reality, but the technique he uses determines which one he learns about first.

In this chapter we present a range of techniques to be used when analysing the training needs of a *group* of people. In each case examples of the kind of output generated by the technique are provided for the reader to work on. Some of the group techniques can be adapted for individual use, and vice versa, and they reappear, wearing a lens of different focal length, in the chapter on individual techniques.

B Critical incident technique

The principle of this technique is that the trainer interviews a

49

group of managers representative of his target population and asks them to tell him about the most difficult problem they have had to deal with in the last period of time. The interviews are usually done with one manager at a time; the period of time chosen is related to the manager's reporting cycle, on the basis of 'one-and-a-half times his reporting cycle'. Thus for an office manager for whom one week is very much like another, the interviewer asks about the most difficult problem in the last ten days; for a director of research and development the period might stretch to six months. (Longer is not advisable as memories fade.) The trainer might begin the interview—after the usual assurances of confidentiality, lack of interest in individual weaknesses, etc.—with a question: 'Can you tell me about the incident in the last six weeks which has caused you the most difficulty?' and goes on to interpolate questions, should they be needed, such as:

when?	one-off problem or regular?
why?	your problem or someone else's?
who with?	what caused it?
at what cost?	will it happen again?
how was it solved?	any long term effects?

and so on.

It is usual for people to talk freely in such interviews—after all, it is not often that they have the chance to unburden themselves about their problems—and the trainer should take full notes, only interpolating if the interviewee seems to be running dry.

When a number of interviews have been conducted the trainer sets about the task of classifying the records, looking for trends in the problems. It is best to seek a few simple dimensions, of two or three categories, and classify each problem along a number of those dimensions, such as:

alone/other people involved
technical/financial/managerial
type of product involved
if other people involved, insiders/customers/suppliers/other
if other people involved, senior/peer/junior/other
producing new ideas/servicing old ideas
new problem/old problem

etc., etc.

The actual dimensions used will suggest themselves as the

trainer goes through the records. It is useful to make notes of the costs of different types of problem, also. Ten to twenty dimensions is a manageable number; below that one is probably losing detail, and above that it may be difficult to isolate trends.

As a result of this rough analysis the trainer will have an idea of where the shoe is pinching tightest. In one organisation that was putting a great deal of effort into training managers to be creative and produce new ideas, a Critical Incident study showed that about 75 per cent of the serious problems centred on servicing their old ideas. (It was an R & D laboratory, communicating its research results to the outside world; senior managers had no idea how much time and effort the junior people were putting into maintenance work.) In another organisation a drastic switch in training priorities from technical to human relations training resulted from a Critical Incident study which demonstrated that all the incidents leading to lost business had their roots in lack of human relations skills, not technical skills. The technique will not give detailed coverage of all the training needs; it is unlikely to pick out the niggling, sub-critical training needs that rarely surface in a full-blown 'incident'. But it does yield a great deal of information for relatively little effort; it gives the information in a way that helps set training priorities; and it helps to indicate organisational areas where people had not thought of looking for training needs.

A Critical Incident interview can take as little as half an hour, or as much as an hour. For the sake of balance you may choose to ask about the incident that has gone most successfully, but people usually have more difficulty thinking of successful incidents, and the data are fuzzier as a result. From time to time a critical incident interview can turn into a counselling session unless the interviewer is very careful; the interviewee may say: 'You're the expert, tell me what I should have done.' Or the interview uncovers an incident so shocking that the interviewer has difficulty repressing his tendency to take immediate action. Accidental counselling should be avoided at all costs, although critical incident information can be gleaned as a by-product of an organised counselling programme.

Occasionally the interviewer meets with the type of mind that cannot cope with an open question, and wants to be offered a range of alternative answers from which he can choose. This usually happens with third-rate computer people, who have

Problem incidents for junior managers

delays caused by computer failure (3)
delays caused by instrument failures (3)
self writing an over-ambitious computer program (1)
taking over someone else's computer program (1)
undertaking a social survey without the relevant skills/experience (1)
coping with staff changes on the project (2)
being put on a committee where one is the oldest but the lowest status (1)
meeting an unrealistic deadline (4)
having one's terms of reference changed many times (2)
suddenly being told that one is not meeting the required standards (1)
getting technical facts accepted in the teeth of political opposition (1)
doing technical work while being pestered by external anti-technologists (1)
getting co-operation from an outside source of help (1)
doing full scale trials for the first time and forgetting about security (1)

Problem incidents for middle managers

having to chair an unruly committee (2)
having to write a report in a hurry because of previous silly delays (2)
having to write a shorter report than the facts justify (1)
failing to motivate a lethargic, but competent, subordinate (1)
managing a subordinate who flatly didn't want to do the work (1)
having relations with an outside contractor ruined by arbitrary company
    policy (1)
coping with staff shortages (3)
having as a subordinate someone who is brighter than oneself (1)
being removed from one's life work to suit someone else's political aims (1)
taking over a project from someone who did not want to let it go (1)
having to do unskilled work oneself because no-one else is available (2)
having no hand in policy-making (1)
having difficulty debugging a computer program (1)

Problem incidents for senior managers

having no secretarial support, which makes all other problems worse (1)
being delayed by procedural difficulties in producing a report (2)
having to correct silly mistakes on reports passed for clearance (2)
conducting technical disputes with outside experts (1)
not being able to fire incompetent subordinates (1)
having an ageing work-force who have run out of steam (1)
having to take on a new appointment with no job description at day's notice (1)
deciding the lines of future work and getting them accepted (1)

Fig. 4.1   Critical incidents of managers at three levels

taken on the colour of their surroundings to the point where they
cannot respond unless someone programs them. There is no
alternative but to go on rephrasing the question until the human
spark re-awakens; fortunately they are few and far between.

The major political consideration that has to be taken into

account before embarking on Critical Incident is the implied commitment it carries to the people who are interviewed. They have seen someone from the training department come and spend time interviewing managers; if nothing tangible results they may feel let down. Analysis takes time, and people have short memories, so it helps to let them see something resulting from the survey after a reasonably short period of time.

Example. In a Critical Incident survey of managers in a scientific organisation, the incidents shown in Figure 4.1 were discovered. Obviously in the full analysis they were treated in more depth; however, what training needs can you deduce from examining the raw list of incidents?

N.B. It is possible for Critical Incident studies to reveal training needs in people other than the ones being interviewed, of course.

C Self-report questionnaires

In a self-report questionnaire the manager is asked fairly bluntly what training he thinks he needs. The way the question is put varies; sometimes the managers are given a list of courses to tick, sometimes they are given a list of skills to tick, sometimes they are given a blank sheet of paper. Obviously this technique is vulnerable to distortion from a number of sources; the manager may not have insight into his own training needs, he may not know enough about the training courses on offer, and if the questionnaire is just another piece of paper in his in-tray then it is likely to be filled in in a hurry.

Self-report questionnaires are much more useful on the technical and financial sides than on interpersonal relationships. A good questionnaire takes a little time to set the scene, by asking the manager to refer to his year's objectives or to think of his most recent critical incident; only then does it go on to ask him to tick the courses he would like to attend (or the ones he would like more information about) or the skills and knowledge he thinks he needs. The middle managers in the previous example, *after* the Critical Incident survey, were asked what training they would like; these are the answers they gave:

management training (4)	statistics (3)
management of people (4)	survey methodology (1)
encouraging creativity (1)	finance (1)
joint problem solving (1)	negotiating skills (1)

problem definition (2)   interviewing (1)
management by objectives (1)   technical updating (2)
experimental design (2)   influencing company policy
                                (1)

These answers are not condensed, except for the men who asked for technical updating; they are a good example of the lack of detail inherent in most self-report questionnaires. The technique is commonly cited as a means of doing training needs analysis—which is why it is mentioned here—but it rarely produces the wealth of detail, and the 'human interest', that some other questionnaire techniques do. The next three techniques involve the trainer in making inferences about training needs from what people say, but they have a better yield.

D   Structured interview

In a structured interview the trainer visits a number of managers with a list of prepared questions that, he hopes, will throw light on their training needs. Obviously the questions vary from firm to firm, and from situation to situation; the best way to design the interview format is to do some free ranging interviews—critical incident perhaps?—and then to write out the questions in a way that makes them as open as possible. Even for an interview with people one knows well, it is better to have the questions prepared; otherwise some of the questions will lead, or be ambiguous.

This is an excerpt from a structured interview format which we used in a general search for training needs among managers of a diverse variety of functions and levels:

1   What sorts of things in your job give you the most satisfaction?
2   What changes would be necessary to make your job more effective? Who could make these changes?
3   What sorts of activities take up a lot of your time? Does this please you?
4   How far are you responsible for planning the way you spend your time?
5   What proportion of your activities do you have no choice about?
6   What aspects of your work interest you the most? the least?

7 Whereabouts in the firm is the work you do initiated?

8 Do you often come under pressure for quick results? Where does the pressure come from? How do you react?

9 How are your standards of performance set, and by whom?

10 How do you get feedback on the results of your work?

11 How, and by whom, does the work you are engaged on get stopped?

12 How much public presentation of your work and your department's work do you have to do?

13 Do you find yourself working very much in committees?

14 How much do you have to do with the data-processing department?

15 Do you have much to do with unions or staff associations?

16 Do you find the job different from what you were expecting?

17 Has anything you have ever been involved with come unstuck because of sheer lack of technical know-how on someone's part?

18 Have you any skills you feel are being inadequately used?

19 Where do you see your career going, over the next year? five years?

20 What training have you had? Do you remember any particular training activities as useful, or useless? Why?

21 What training do you think you need, either that you know is already available, or that you would like to see introduced?

22 Suppose you won the pools and decided to retire, so that you have to be replaced. What sort of person would you advise them to recruit to replace you? What technical knowledge should he bring with him? What training and experience would you want to give him in the first three months? What advice would you give him? What sort of mistakes do you think he would make at first?

The answers given should allow one to deduce training needs. Some of the questions will be more fruitful than others; for example, when we asked questions 9 and 10 of some technical managers we were met with blank stares, because the idea of setting standards of performance and organising feedback systems had not occurred to them. They thought that the technical job set its own, unique, non-negotiable standard of performance. Question 22 is generally useful, even when the manager has not been very forthcoming for the first part of the interview; so is question 18. The reader should try to design his own interview format, roughly following the lines shown above. Then with a little practice he will find that he can run through the interview as if it were a conversation, allowing the interviewee to bring up topics himself, ranging over the field of questions, getting coverage without making the procedure too wooden.

Interpretation is best done in stages. First, compile a rough list of all the reactions to each question (including blank silences). Then go through asking: 'What needs to be done better?' and 'What skills are being exercised here?' bearing in mind that while the major concern is with the training needs of the people being interviewed (unless you have a very weird sampling system) it is permissible to deduce other people's training needs and desirable changes in the system. It is wise to get another person to go through the material independently and to discuss any places where disagreements occur. Only when this stage has been completed is it permissible to interpret the results in terms of global training needs, or training courses; too many training needs analyses are spoiled by overgeneralising too early in the game, as when a need to make points more concisely becomes labelled a 'Communications Need' and sets everyone looking for a Communications Course.

Structured interviews are usually better than self-report analyses for anything other than the most straightforward training needs, but they do take time; they are usually hit-and-miss affairs, with only some of the questions paying off; it is difficult to get standardised administration between two interviewers, or from the same interviewer on different days; and where we have had the opportunity to compare the two, Critical Incident technique yields more information. The implied commitment of Critical Incident may tip the balance in favour of structured interviews from time to time.

E Diary method

This method of training needs analysis goes into much more detail than the previous techniques; it can even be used as an individual diagnostic tool if the manager co-operates and if this use is planned in advance. The principle is simple; managers keep diaries which record their activities under a range of heads, and the trainer then analyses them to deduce the demands being made on the manager and the skills necessary to do the job. Thus this form of training needs analysis moves away from the identification of deficiencies toward the description of actual performance and the deduction of ideal performance—an important characteristic to note when getting managers' commitment to taking part.

In describing the diary method we draw heavily on the work of Rosemary Stewart, who was one of the pioneers in the use of this technique in analysing the manager's job.

Diaries can either be general—sweeping over the whole range of training needs—or highly specific, when one or two training needs are to be examined in detail. The introduction of new procedures, for instance those demanded by the Health and Safety at Work Act, may be the cause for narrow field diaries to be sought; a supervisor in a garment factory is asked to place a tick in the appropriate place each time she deals with one of the following:

Workshop tidiness
materials obstructing free passage
made-up goods obstructing free passage
dangerous goods stacked at unsafe heights
personal belongings lying around

Machine maintenance
machines being serviced with power on
untrained people attempting to service machines
unsafe parts not being properly disposed of
machines left uncleaned
operatives transferring machines without permission
machines not being switched off during breaks

Personal
long hair in danger of being caught
smoking in prohibited areas
liquid refreshment being passed around work stations

shoes making foot controls difficult to operate
pregnant operatives lifting heavy weights

The example above is taken from the first draft of a diary which was to be issued to supervisors controlling women working sewing machines. The supervisors ticked each item, and used a code to indicate whether they had taken action themselves or told someone else to take action or had taken no action. They were not expected to say how long each incident had lasted, or who else was involved. Readers with experience of the situation may like to add to, or improve, the first draft diary given here.

Much fuller diaries have been used by Rosemary Stewart and by others attempting to get a broad picture of managers' activities. In one diary [1], Rosemary Stewart asked managers to record the length of time spent in each activity below, and information about who else was involved and the degree to which the activity was planned, thus:

Activity
Talking: on the telephone
        with one other face to face
        with more than one other face to face
        was the contact scheduled?
Touring (inspecting the work-place)
Mail
Other paperwork
Other activity (lecturing, travelling, operational work, etc.)
Contact
Alone
With boss
With secretary
With subordinates
With colleagues (i.e. peers reporting to the same boss)
With peers (i.e. people of similar level not reporting to same
   boss)
Other senior
Other junior
External: please specify
New contacts
Interruptions
Place: own office
      other: please specify
Nature of activity
Crisis (drop everything to sort out)

Choice (need not have done that day or any other time)
Deadline (done for a definite time deadline)
New work (different from anything done before)
Recurrent tasks
Urgent work
Unexpected work

In addition to this diary Rosemary Stewart gathered an analysis of mail in and mail out, and supported the diary with a detailed questionnaire. It is obvious even from the abridged transcription above that computer analysis is necessary to detect trends in the information gathered, and Dr Stewart gives a lively description of different types of job analysed into *choices, constraints, demands,* and *skills required,* which is essential reading for anyone wishing to emulate her detailed use of the diary method.

In designing a diary the trainer should go through the following steps:

1 A pilot investigation to see what the approximate training needs are, and whether they are general or specific to one or two areas of skill.

2 As the diary's purpose is to exhibit the demands being made on the manager, the trainer should decide the specific demands he wishes the diary to record; whether duration of activity is important; whether information about other people is important; whether he needs information about the manager's discretion in choosing the activities; and whether he needs information about results from the activities.

3 Each of the desired categories is broken into appropriate codes—one for type of activity, one for contacts, and so on. If the length of time spent in each activity is important, then an appropriate breakdown is given. It is important to make the manager's task as easy as possible—he should make ticks rather than write substantive information.

4 A questionnaire containing the diary is assembled, with a statement of its purpose and instructions on how to fill it in. This is sent to a sample of managers *after* first having been piloted on one or two willing managers. At the pilot stage two things should be clear: there should be no questions included whose answers would not provide useful information on training needs, and the method whereby the questionnaires will be analysed should have been decided on.

5 The returned questionnaires are analysed and a report

prepared on the demands made on managers—broken down into different managerial groups if this seems appropriate. Full discussion of these demands is then followed by decisions about training needs and the provision of training.

Diary method fails if the purposes are not made clear to the people taking part: are they being individually examined, or taken as part of a group? It also fails when people include questions because they look nice, rather than because they have something, potentially, to say about training needs; and when people have not thought about the statistical analysis they will need after the diaries have come back, so that they finish up losing information and credibility. Properly done, though, diary method gives a full coverage of the ground—fuller than Critical Incident by far. It can bring out the dull, day-to-day training needs that nobody bothers to look for normally. It checks the reality of the manager's job against his job description, often with thought-provoking results. It takes time, and needs skill and a greater degree of familiarity with the organisation than some other techniques require, but it produces more information.

F   Performance questionnaire

This is a good technique to use at the interface between training needs analysis for managers, and organisation development. We have described it in detail elsewhere; [2] in broad outline it works thus.

Having identified the level of manager whose training needs are to be investigated, the trainer designs a questionnaire which contains a series of bipolar statements describing managerial behaviour. (An excerpt from such a questionnaire is given in Figure 4.2.) The questionnaire is distributed to managers of the position under consideration, and perhaps occupants of that position and those of their colleagues who have close relationships with them. Each is asked to think of the most effective holder of the given job they know, or have working directly for them, and to describe him on the questionnaire—anonymously, but warts and all. When the completed questionnaires have been returned to the trainer a second round of duplicate questionnaires is issued, with the request that this time they describe the least effective job holder they know; again, anonymously, but warts and all. A simple statistical analysis then reveals which items discriminate between effective and

21	He would not take security precautions that could offend his customers	....	He would risk offending his customers by his security precautions
22	When he is outside the depot he is easy to track down	....	When he is outside the depot he is difficult to track down
23	He would rather deal with a new customer	....	He would rather deal with an established customer
25	He would rather buy high quality goods and risk the higher price	....	He would rather buy at a lower price and risk the low quality
25	If his people are in difficulties he takes on the job himself	....	If his people are in difficulties he helps them find their own way out
26	He pays little attention to the activities of the competition	....	He watches the competition's activities closely
27	He learns from his mistakes	....	He repeats his mistakes
28	He makes many speculative purchases	....	He makes very few speculative purchases
29	He absorbs financial information quickly	....	He absorbs financial information slowly
30	His handwriting is clear	....	His handwriting is untidy
31	He is ambitious to go further in the near future	....	He is content to stay at his present level for the time being
32	He lets his staff find out about new lines for themselves	....	He briefs his staff on new lines himself
33	He laughs and jokes a lot	....	He is serious
34	He is easily excited by success	....	He doesn't react much to success
35	He is slow at figure work	....	He is quick at figure work
36	He under-estimates the success of planned ventures	....	He does not under-estimate the success of planned ventures
37	He tells you his troubles	....	He keeps quiet about his troubles
38	He takes a long time to get to know customers	....	He gets to know customers quickly
39	He has a tidy desk	....	He has an untidy desk
40	He stays calm when people get angry with him	....	When other people get angry with him, he gets angry too
41	He prefers dealing with the ordinary routine, rather than special promotions	....	He prefers dealing with special promotions, rather than the ordinary routine
42	He treats reps as equals	....	He treats reps as inferiors

Fig. 4.2 Extract from performance questionnaire (retail sales managers)

ineffective performers; other analyses yield a list of items associated with effectiveness and a list of items associated with ineffectiveness, which can then be turned into pen pictures such as those given in Figure 4.3.

There are a number of advantages to this technique. Firstly, in getting perceptions of real people rather than ideal types one

The effective manager: a pen picture

1 *Self-management.* He takes the unexpected in his stride, and he keeps calm in emergencies. When he has made a mistake he admits it, and he learns from his mistakes; if he doesn't know the answer, he says so, but if he asks for help about a problem he tries to have a solution to suggest. He is willing to ask for help if he needs it. He plans several steps ahead, and he thinks before he speaks. He can understand something even when he doesn't like it, and if other people get angry with him he stays calm. He gets on with unpleasant tasks; instructions need be given him once only. He has a tidy desk and clear handwriting; when he is out of the depot he is easy to track down. He tolerates other people's eccentricities, and he is ambitious to go further in the near future.

2 *Management of resources.* He stocks to meet peak demands; he would rather be overstocked than understocked. He staffs to meet average demands, and he estimates accurately his staff's capacity for work. He puts priorities on what needs to be done, and he distinguishes correctly between urgent and non-urgent tasks. He is on time implementing price increases.

3 *Management of risk.* He neither over-estimates nor under-estimates the success of planned ventures. He makes decisions quickly, but without jumping to conclusions. He would rather buy high quality goods and risk paying a higher price. He prefers dealing with special promotions rather than the ordinary routine. When a line is losing money he puts more effort into it.

4 *Trade awareness.* He sees his job mainly as that of a seller, not a buyer. He keeps up-to-date on changes in the trade. He keeps up-to-date on local market changes, and he watches the competition's activities closely.

5 *Financial competence.* He absorbs financial information quickly, and retains it well. He is quick at figure work, and his operating balance is as even as seasonal factors allow.

6 *Security and hygiene.* Cleanliness and tidiness are high on his list of priorities. He won't tolerate any fiddling by members of staff, and he spots crooked customers and van salesmen quickly. He takes staff into his confidence on security matters, and he would risk taking security precautions that might offend his customers.

7 *Relations with subordinates.* He communicates downwards when necessary. He gives clear instructions when delegating, and short, clear instructions at all times. When he puts someone in a new job, he checks progress often. He gives his staff the credit for good work; if they are in difficulties he helps them find their own way out. He is willing to discuss his staff's personal problems with them. His staff seem happy.

8 *Relations with boss and head office.* He communicates upwards when necessary. He accepts changes imposed by head office, and reports any discrepancies himself. He asks for advice on personnel problems.

9 *Customer relations.* He puts the needs of the customer over those of the staff, and he will never turn away customers no matter how inconvenient the

Fig. 4.3 Outlines of effective and ineffective managers, derived from performance questionnaire results

time. He would rather deal with a new customer than an established one, and he gets to know customers quickly.

10 *Relations with other outsiders.* He treats reps as equals, and his relations with the unions are good.

11 *Personal involvement.* He gets personally involved in all aspects of the business, and goes down to the floor at all times. He checks progress frequently and briefs staff on new lines himself. He works long hours and is willing to get his hands dirty. He expands his own role and responsibilities as much as he possibly can.

The ineffective manager: a pen picture

1 *Low profile.* He plans one step at a time, and checks progress rarely. He needs chasing after having been given instructions, and he is late implementing price increases. His discrepancies have to be discovered by other people. He refuses assistance. He leaves some aspects of the business to others, and he avoids doing unpleasant tasks. He doesn't take in information he doesn't like. If he doesn't know the answer, he flannels. He feels that some jobs are too low in status for him. His relations with the unions are poor; he keeps business out of his social life; and he is content to let his manager dictate the scope of his role and responsibilities.

2 *Labile reactions.* He is easily thrown off course by the unexpected. He repeats his mistakes, and says the first thing that comes into his head. When other people get angry with him, he gets angry too. His desk is untidy.

3 *Management of resources.* He deals with each matter as it arises, and he cannot distinguish between urgent and non-urgent tasks. He over-estimates his staff's capacity for work, and he will turn away deliveries that come at the wrong time.

4 *Management of risk.* He jumps to conclusions quickly, but takes time to make a decision. He prefers to play it safe, and when a line is losing money he stops putting effort into it.

5 *Financial competence.* He absorbs financial information slowly and retains it poorly. He is slow at figure work, and his operating balance is more uneven than seasonal factors would warrant.

6 *Security and hygiene.* Cleanliness and tidiness give way to other considerations as far as he's concerned. He doesn't spot a crooked van salesman easily, though he won't tolerate any fiddling by members of staff and he will risk offending his customers by his security precautions.

7 *Trade awareness.* He pays little attention to the activities of the competition.

8 *Customer relations.* He gets involved with his customers only when they come to the depot, and he would rather deal with an established customer. For him, the customer is sometimes wrong, and he will turn away customers who arrive at the wrong time.

9 *Relations with subordinates.* He delegates the donkey-work. He gives long, detailed instructions, but when delegating his instructions are unclear. When he puts someone in a new job, he leaves them to get on; he checks progress rarely, and when his people get into difficulties he takes on the job himself. He tolerates a certain amount of absenteeism.

moves away from the standard 'good guy' picture towards a diagnosis much more representative of the organisation's own culture. Performance questionnaires, especially when derived from Repertory Grid technique (about which more later) are very sensitive measures of organisational culture. Secondly, because the questionnaire asks managers for their own perceptions of effective and ineffective behaviour, the trainer is in a strong position to undertake some organisation development work based on his diagnosis. He can present his picture to senior management with the words: 'This is how your line managers view effective and ineffective job performance in X job. Do you wish this picture to be perpetuated, or do you wish it to be changed?'. In our experience the detail of the diagnosis is so fascinating that senior managers get easily absorbed in it and respond well to interrogation about whether it should be perpetuated or changed, but in the case of the manager who says: 'I don't want ivory-tower training people telling me how to run my business' the trainer has a cast-iron excuse. He is not presenting a view of training needs as perceived by some outside expert; he is presenting the organised perceptions of the people actually doing the job, and if the manager chooses to reject the trainer the line managers will carry on thinking as the questionnaire results show. It is a good card to be able to play, especially with managers who are cynical about the value of outside opinion.

The results from the diagnosis should be interrogated with the question: 'Perpetuate or change?'. Then, information can be used all over the organisation, for performance questionnaire results are useful in selection, appraisal, promotion, and counselling, as well as in training. Ideally one selects those items on the questionnaire which are amenable to training, and then uses them as the basis for diagnosing the deficiencies of people whose training needs are under scrutiny; the questionnaire results give an ideal against which individual trainees can be measured.

The best way to construct a performance questionnaire is to base it on the constructs derived from Repertory Grid interviews. This interview technique is described in the next chapter, where it appears as an individual method; if interviews are stopped at construct elicitation, with a preference question asked about each construct, then information can be gathered from a few grid interviews which will enable a good questionnaire—about 100 items—to be designed. If it is not possible to do grid interviews, then the questionnaire should be based on other interviews with managers or on observing managers in action; but the more the questionnaire uses managers' own language, the better it will be.

A well designed performance questionnaire contains statements which are objectively observable, like 'In internal negotiations he plays close to his chest/In internal negotiations he lays his cards on the table'; it is easy to take these results and turn them into good, measurable training.

The drawbacks to performance questionnaire are, firstly, its requirement that at least thirty people complete the questionnaires for the statistics to be reliable (fifty is preferable); thus it is not possible in small organisations or at the very top. Secondly, if the questionnaire is *not* designed in managers' language, and/or if the managers are not asked to think about real people, warts and all, then the result will be a poor response rate and regurgitated 'ideal types'. The strengths of performance questionnaire are the detail it goes into; its sensitivity to organisational culture; and the opportunity it gives to negotiate about whether the perceived picture of effectiveness should be carried on into the future. For these reasons it is our own preferred method whenever major organisational issues are being debated.

G Content analysis

Here is a rarity for the personnel researcher: a training needs analysis that does not impinge on the people being investigated. Non-reactive research, as it is called, is difficult but challenging; the trainer who uses content analysis technique can find himself entering new areas with new challenges to his ingenuity.

To use content analysis technique the trainer obtains access to written records and combs through them systematically looking for training needs. He can look for skills being exhibited, of for deficiencies shown, or for demands being made, or all three. He can do it on a group basis, or occasionally for an individual. Because he is going back over historical data he is not disturbing anyone in the field; they need not know that the training needs analysis is going on. Neither can data be faked, as sometimes happens in real-time training needs analysis. The big problem is, of course, getting access to the right kind of written records when not everything that happens in an organisation is committed to paper; thus although content analysis is applicable outside a wider range of needs than might at first be thought, there will be some areas that it does not reach.

Most trainers have performed content analyses at some time; the training and development needs mentioned at the bottom of most appraisal forms are collated and systematised, the reaction sheets to in-house courses are read and noted. If the trainer can get access to line managers' working files in some form, though, the scope is greatly widened.

For example, in one organisation we gained access to the project files kept in the Research and Development Department, and went through a sample of files classifying each item on each of the questions shown in Figure 4.4. This categorisation was developed after an initial search of the files; we were looking to see what sort of demands were made on managers' skills so that the broad priorities of the training department could be fixed, and as a result of the content analysis some re-thinking began. The numbers against each item in the categorisation represent the items in the files which fell into each category; each file item (a memo, a letter, etc.) was classified on each question but for the sake of clarity we have omitted the 'other' category which fell at the end of each question.

Though the reader may be able to make some judgements about the training needs of these managers from Figure 4.4 alone, it is interesting to note how the results of the content analysis departed from expectation—as indicated in earlier discussions. It was not obvious to people, until the analysis revealed it, that managers spent so much of their time working in areas where no laid-down standards applied. Much of their training had hitherto been directed at getting them to understand and apply the appropriate technical standards, without the realisation that most of the time they had no standards to guide them. Nor was it realised how much time managers spent in selling their work, particularly inside the firm; nor how much time they spent on servicing old ideas rather than on innovating and developing new ones. It is one of the strengths of Content Analysis, when applied like this, that it highlights the balance of different activities and allows this to be compared with existing beliefs and provisions for training.

Content Analysis can also be applied to look for deficiencies in performance where these will be revealed by the written record.

1	*Technical*						
	Engineering	144	Science	20	Psychology	12	Economics 53
	Non-technical						
	Public Relations	81	Legal	37	Personnel	7	

2	*Inside the R & D Department*		*Outside the R & D Department*	
	with seniors	38	with head office	62
	with peers	21	with other labs	46
	with subordinates	30	with suppliers	54
			with customers	24
			with individuals	36
			with media	12

3	*Problem definition*		*Problem solving*		*Service/Maintenance*
	easy	23	easy	37	160
	difficult	24	difficult	10	

4	*Working against standards*		*Working without standards*	
	testing against standards	67	laying down standards	30
	advising about standards	60	advising, without standards	120

5	*Doing the work*		*Selling the work*	
	147		inside the R & D Dept	10
			inside the firm	54
			outside the firm	42

6	*Excess resources*		*Shortage of resources*	
	people 12 money 1		people 13 money 24	
			other 18	

7	*With technical peers*		*With laymen*	
	201		serious 80 cranks 19	

8	*Urgent*	80
	Non-urgent	204

9	*Long term issue*	117
	Short term issue	164

10	*Old project*	160
	New project	119

11	*R & D initiated*	106
	Initiated elsewhere	180

Fig. 4.4 Content analysis of project files in an R & D department

Looking at draft reports, in an attempt to analyse report writing skills, we found the following:

Strategic errors
Facts not distinguished from opinion	7
Benefits not clearly stated	5
Context missing (and needed)	4
Purpose of report unclear	4
Political implications of work missed	4

Unawareness of audience's special needs	4
Making statements that could easily be taken out of context	3
Claiming too much in the title	1

Grammar and syntax

'Data', 'criteria', 'media', used with singular verb	21
Subject not agreeing with verb	17
Spelling mistakes	15
Inappropriate use of bracket commas	14
Misplaced apostrophe in possessive cases	14
Misplaced qualifying clause	7
Confusion between *its* and *it's*	5
Use of jargon abbreviations without definitions	4
Use of quotation marks to indicate emphasis only	2

Presentation errors

Unreadable handwriting	5
Tables too dense	5
Terms not defined clearly	4
Results given without mentioning sample size	3
Paper, to be read verbatim, obviously too long for time allowed	2
Different type-styles used on final document	2

Editing and management errors

Paper too late for publication deadline	5
Editor offers clarification, author responds 'I know what I meant'	5
Editor puts check mark instead of specifying what he does not understand	4
Editor, having asked for report, forgets why he wanted it	3

Again, the results were interesting compared with the popular wisdom—and with the report writing course that was then being offered. We found very few errors of layout or house style—matters on which the course concentrated heavily. We found a large number of errors in the management of reports: the way they were asked for, the way a middle manager got his junior to re-draft something they would both present to senior management. And we found a very large number of grammar and syntactical errors. These topics were not treated at all in the training course, either because people assumed that grown men would know the difference between *its* and *it's*, or because it had not occurred to them to see the training needs. The content analysis results were presented; everyone knew how they had been derived, that there had been no faking or hiding information; and the course in report writing was re-examined in the light of the new information.

These two examples of content analysis show something of the range of the technique. It always needs a feasibility study first, unless it is obvious where one looks for the data; and imagination is needed to think of places where traces of training needs will be visible. Because it is non-reactive, and can be checked, and can be carried out at leisure, it is a useful technique for any trainer to know; new trainers can be inducted into their training jobs safely by giving them some content analysis to do and letting them find their way round at their own pace. Care needs to be taken about breaching confidentiality, so that personal records should be used with the utmost discretion if at all; the day-to-day paperwork of the business should generate enough to satisfy most needs.

H Behaviour analysis

Behaviour analysis is a special case of content analysis, in which people's actions and statements are categorised in a running analysis performed by themselves or (more usually) the trainer. The whole topic of behaviour analysis and the contribution it can make to training design and evaluation has been thoroughly treated elsewhere [3, 4] and we recommend the dedicated reader to peruse one or both of these references.

In behaviour analysis the trainer watches what goes on in a group and categorises each person's behaviour under a series of simple headings. He may use a form like the one in Figure 4.5, making a check mark every time each person exhibits behaviour in the categories analysed. After a while spent thus observing, the trainer summarises his information in a way that allows him to deduce the training needs of the participants and also something of the way the rest of the training course should be organised in order to meet those needs. Behaviour analysis usually precedes the relevant training by only a small amount; trainers do it at the beginning of training courses, or during management meetings which they are attending as consultants. It is possible to perform

Observer: VS	Exercise: Planning to interview						
Names / Behaviour categories	Fred	Joe	Jill	Daisy	Allan	Bob	Σ
Proposing	ЖII	I	III	ЖI III	ЖII	ЖII	
Supporting	ЖII III	II	ЖII I	ЖII ЖII I	ЖII	ЖII I	
Building	II	I	I	ЖII I	I	ЖII	
Disagree/ criticising	ЖII ЖII III	III	ЖII	ЖII ЖII ЖII II	II	I	
Seeking information	ЖII I	II	ЖII I	ЖII ЖII III	ЖII I	ЖII I	
Giving information	ЖII ЖII ЖII II	III	ЖII III	ЖII ЖII ЖII III	III	ЖII I	
Other		I	I		II	I	
Σ							

Fig. 4.5   Behaviour analysis form

a behaviour analysis and then wait a while before training—when sales people have their customer behaviour analysed by an observer, for example—but to get maximum benefit there should be on-course analysis as well. Thus behaviour analysis falls on the boundary between group methods and individual methods—it is performed in groups, analysing group behaviour, but it gives information about individual training needs as well.

The categories of analysis need careful selection, with due regard to the type of training undertaken. For a course in general interactive skills the following categories might be appropriate:

proposing
supporting

building
disagreeing/criticising
seeking information
giving information
other

The trainer looks for a number of things: the overall level of contribution of each person (too high? too low?) and the relative importance of different kinds of behaviour. *Building* behaviour is usually important in a cohesive team; people consistently low on this behaviour may need help and practice in increasing it. People with a high level of *proposing* and *giving information* may need help in learning to listen. Later on the trainer might discard these categories and look at some more, for example:

caught proposals	bringing in
escaped proposals	shutting out

defending/attacking	backtracking
admitting difficulty	jumping the gun

Here, the trainer differentiates between *caught proposals* and *escaped proposals*, i.e. between the ones that get some attention— even a refusal—and the ones that get none; this is useful when helping someone get his ideas accepted. The ratio of *bringing in* to *shutting out*, i.e. how many times the person invites contributions from elsewhere, and how many times he rides roughshod over other people by interrupting and talking over them, is useful whenever one is examining teamwork and participation. The ratio of *defending/attacking* behaviour to *admitting difficulty* tells the trainer a lot about the trainee's way of coping with challenge; does he respond antagonistically, or is he prepared to admit that he might not be completely right? In committees and groups operating to an acknowledged formal structure, the ratio of *backtracking* (going over old ground or old procedures) to *jumping the gun* (leaping ahead to matters that should not yet be treated) is a useful quantity to feed back.

Each of those pairs of behaviour tells one something about the training needs of the people concerned, especially when expressed in ratio form. These simple ratios can be fed back to the people as part of their training, and they can be helped to analyse themselves.

If the training were in counselling and grievance handling, the trainer might analyse into categories such as:

supporting
testing understanding
using personal names
reflecting questions back
giving direct guidance/ advice

and the trainees would be encouraged to develop more of the desired behaviours while the trainer relied upon behaviour analysis to check progress.

Only the briefest outline of behaviour analysis as a training needs tool can be given here; its uses are very wide indeed, because of the immediate impact it has on the training process itself. The trainees may learn to use it; trainers can use it to modify the courses so that no two courses are the same; behaviour change during and after training can be measured and thus some evaluation of the training is possible immediately. Although we recommend a study of the references before putting behaviour analysis into practice, some guidance is possible here.

1   Start with simple category systems—ratios even—and as few preconceptions as possible about what is *right* and *wrong* behaviour. In the end your aims will probably be *flexibility* of style, and *accuracy* of self-analysis; so avoid value judgements.

2   Have more than one trainer observing, in the early stages of learning the skill, and check your level of agreement frequently.

3   Don't do behaviour analysis if you like running clockwork training courses that are the same year after year. Behaviour analysis gives an opportunity to modify the training as it happens.

4   Do give feedback on behaviour once you are certain of your reliability and have enough information, say after a day on a week-long course, midday on a two-day course. Feedback comes easier if you are non-evaluative and try to present the results in simple form, using ratios where possible, for instance.

I   Discussion questions

1   What sort of training needs—and whose—could you discover by looking at: performance appraisal forms? customers' letters? the company newsletter?

2   One problem interfering with good training needs analysis is

that people overgeneralise and reach conclusions too early—translating 'He needs to write in the company style' into 'He needs a report-writing course', for instance. How many examples of this can you think of from your own experience?

3   Are the training needs of a group of people different from the sum of their individual training needs?

4   'I was setting up a training programme for sales managers and thought I had better know something about the future product mix. So I went down to Corporate Planning and asked to look at the seven-year plan. I was told in no uncertain terms that I could not have access to this or other planning documents, and was asked what on earth I wanted them for—I was Personnel, wasn't I?'

Has this happened to you? Have you done it to anybody else?

J   References and further reading

[1] R. STEWART. *Contrasts in Management*, McGraw-Hill, 1976.

[2] A. STEWART and V. STEWART. *Tomorrow's Men Today*, Institute of Personnel Management, 1976.

[3] N. RACKHAM, P. HONEY and M. COLBERT. *Developing Interactive Skills*, Wellens Publishing, 1970.

[4] N. RACKHAM and T. MORGAN. *Behaviour Analysis in Training*, McGraw-Hill, 1977.

5 Diagnosis of training needs: individual methods

A Introduction

There is no clear borderline between group methods and individual methods of training needs analysis. Some methods are applicable irrespective of number, and the convenience of the trainer and the total numbers concerned decide how the method is to be applied. However, when we look at individual methods it is clear that they vary according to *when* they can be administered; some, like the diary method, are best dealt with as part of the daily routine, whereas others, like behaviour analysis, are most often applied at the beginning of a training course. Thus a new set of options opens up for the trainer; if he carries out a training needs analysis at the beginning of a training course, he can adapt his course to take account of the needs revealed. Maybe he can perform a mini-analysis halfway through and make further adaptations, and a check at the end to see what the course has accomplished. Using the information dynamically like this is possible when the individual's surface (by which we do not mean superficial) features are under analysis— technical knowledge, sales behaviour, negotiating skills, etc. More fundamental problems of attitude, motivation, or career direction require attention over a longer period than the average training course.

These tactical considerations influence the choice of method; so does the politics of training. It is vitally important that in discovering someone's training needs the trainer does not put him off the idea of training; sometimes one has to sacrifice a little accuracy or speed for the sake of getting someone to discover and report his own training needs instead of suffering the trainer to do it for him. There is not the anonymity of the group to shelter behind, and the trainer must be extra-careful not to expose people to condemnation or ridicule.

The first three methods of training needs analysis have all been examined in the previous chapter; here they are adapted for individual use.

B Diary method

The principle here is the same as for the group method; the manager keeps a diary, and the trainer analyses for training needs. The difference is in the way the diary is treated once complete. Two forms of diary are possible; the 'how many times does each of the following incidents happen?' type, and the 'classify everything you do under the following heads' type. The first type is most useful when looking at technical skills, as in the example given of the supervisor in the sewing room; this kind of diary could be sent through the post to the trainer without much loss of information. But the second kind of diary, where the whole of a manager's day is recorded, maybe for days on end, is most profitably used as the basis for a discussion with the manager about his training needs and personal development as he sees them.

To do this, the trainer designs the diary, maybe allowing a little more latitude in the way activities are categorised. He sends or takes it to the manager, with instructions, and when it comes back he analyses it, looking for unusual degrees of emphasis, repeating patterns of activity, and so on. At this stage he should not think about 'training needs', but concentrate on getting to know this manager and the demands made on him. He prepares a memorandum of the outstanding features of the diary, trying to confine himself to six or eight points. An example, taken from analysing the diary of a manager in a large management consultancy, reads:

(a)   a large proportion of familiar (i.e. not new) problems
(b)   customers come to him, rarely the opposite
(c)   equal amounts of internal and external trouble-shooting
(d)   large amount of time spent in meetings
(e)   no time recorded reading business journals
(f)   no time recorded preparing for appraisal of a subordinate.

Here the trainer is using what he already knows of patterns of activity in the rest of the firm, and making implicit comparisons. Armed with these notes and one or two other questions, he visits the manager to discuss his 'development needs'. (For some reason this is a much more acceptable phrase than 'training needs', but it needs using with care.) In the interview he feeds back information from his analysis of the diary in a neutral fashion, thus:

'You seem to spend a lot of time dealing with familiar problems—problems of a kind you have had to deal with before. How do you feel about that?' and 'You've put down a certain amount of time spent in trouble-shooting, and it seems just as likely to be spent sorting out one of your own people as sorting out a client. Would you like to tell me a bit more about that?'

These questions are supported by more general ones: what are his job objectives, where does he see his career going in the next two years or so, what training and development activities would he like? If the trainer can maintain a neutral tone in feeding back the information, avoiding any suggestion of judgement or condemnation, then there is the basis for a good probing interview.

As this method is best suited to a long look at training needs, rather than a beginning-of-course snapshot, it is likely to lead to long term as well as short term training plans, with a fair amount of on-the-job training or self-development activity. If the trainer can find a way of interesting the manager sufficiently for the manager to see the value to himself of keeping a diary, then the manager can be enlisted to continue the diary for his own purposes to monitor his own progress.

C   Content analysis

The written traces an individual leaves behind can be analysed to discover his training needs, in exactly the same way as the traces of a group. Here the main problems are getting hold of a reliable sample of data from just one person, and getting his permission to conduct the analysis; he may be offended if he discovers that someone from the training department has spent the past week going through his personal records. If these problems can be overcome, then content analysis is possible and some of its advantages—off-line, no disruption, checkability, etc.—come into play.

One obvious source of data for content analysis is the performance appraisal records. An individual can be followed through several appraisals, seeing what training needs are recorded for him, what faults he persists in, what kind of jobs give him difficulty, and so on. More subtle, but often more informative, is to study all the appraisals done by one appraiser over a period of time, looking for his blind spots, the skills he has difficulty developing, the appraisees' comments (if the system collects them), and so on. The same principle can be applied to the interview records of particular selection interviewers, the visit reports made by managers with customer contact, and similar data.

Reports in various stages of drafting give information about training needs, in report writing and in the technical field with which the report is concerned. A file of customer complaint letters, and the replies of the manager who has to handle them, is also good hunting ground. In a large organisation, with managers spread around the country, the trainer can haunt the telex room studying how people use this singular medium of communication.

As well as delving into the past for written material on which to base a training needs analysis, the trainer may ask people to generate material specially for the occasion. He could ask, at the beginning of a training course, for the trainees to spend a couple of hours writing an essay on: 'My job,' after which the essays are analysed in time for the rest of the course to be adapted to accommodate the needs revealed. In the analysis, the trainer might look for the balance between technical and interpersonal tasks; the range of people with whom contact is made; any consciousness of whereabouts the writer's operation fits into the strategy of the whole organisation; the balance between backward and forward looking, between optimism and pessimism, between enjoyment and misery. This is a useful tactic with which to open a general management training course, though the trainer must take care to be seen to be using the material; there is nothing more disheartening than to produce material which the trainer says he will use, only to find oneself on the receiving end of a standard package.

We repeat the cautions given in the previous chapter when considering content analysis: look for patterns of activities first, only going on to infer training needs later; and get someone to cross-check the analysis so that idiosyncratic judgements do not creep in.

D   Behaviour analysis

Behaviour analysis is about individuals in groups, and the focus of attention can be on the individual or the group or the interaction between the two. However, at the individual level behaviour analysis can happen outside the context of a training course: for example, the trainer may accompany a salesman as he visits clients, performing a simple behaviour analysis on the interaction; he may accompany a manager through a performance appraisal interview, or a negotiation, or a grievance-handling, categorising the behaviour that he sees. The results can then be used as the beginnings of a counselling interview, or for the design of a training course, or both.

The trainer who wishes to use individual behaviour analysis as part of a training course must realise that this decision will influence the whole conduct of the course. The basic strategy is to collect enough information about individuals to be able to feed back a coherent and reliable picture, and then to get the individuals themselves to make plans for improving those aspects of their behaviour which they feel dissatisfied with. In making these plans they enlist the help of the trainer in producing exercises or allocating roles appropriately. The standard training course departs, in favour of the dynamically programmed course with the trainer drawing on his task library for exercises suitable to the needs of the moment.

Let us follow the progress of one manager taking part in a simple interactive skills training course where behaviour analysis is used. The course lasts a week, and for the first day the members are split into small groups with a variety of tasks to perform—discussing a case study, analysing data about a current organisational problem, making plans to interview their Divisional Director when he visits them mid-week, etc. These tasks are chosen to allow a wide variety of behaviours to be exhibited; some require planning, some negotiating, some information analysis, some creative thinking; some are done to strict deadlines, others not. By the morning of the second day the trainer has a series of ratios for each of the people on the course. Our manager, Dick, shows the following characteristics:

$$\frac{\text{Caught Proposals}}{\text{Escaped Proposals}} = \frac{16}{62} \qquad \frac{\text{Supporting} + \text{Building}}{\text{Disagreeing}} = \frac{8+2}{55}$$

$$\frac{\text{Asking for Information}}{\text{Giving Information}} = \frac{63}{128} \qquad \frac{\text{Bringing In}}{\text{Shutting Out}} = \frac{12}{47}$$

Clearly Dick has a few problems. He makes a lot of

suggestions, but very few of them get any attention (remember, a proposal is classified as 'caught' even if it is rejected; the key is that someone has noticed its presence). He gives out a lot of information, but doesn't ask for much; he doesn't seem to be paying attention to other people's ideas—look at his low score for Supporting and Building—and he is prepared to interrupt other people and carve across their contributions.

An experienced trainer will have no difficulty in identifying the skills that Dick needs to acquire if he is to work with others as part of a team. The art, however, lies in getting Dick to discover this for himself. So the bulk of the morning of the second day is spent in giving each trainee a summary of his own behaviour, as in the summary above, and the equivalent ratios for the group as a whole. Dick is able to compare his ratio on proposing with that of a total group, which is Caught: Escaped: 125:311. He sees that he is out of line, and discusses it with the trainer: 'I come up with a lot of good ideas, so why won't these chaps listen?' The trainer points out to him the ratio of Supporting and Building to Disagreeing, asking him what this tells him about the way he is treating other people's ideas. How much listening is he doing? How much is he asking for other people's contributions? How much is he pushing them aside?

The great merit of behaviour analysis is that with its information, these questions are not rhetorical. In most other training situations Dick could turn away, saying: 'That's what you think, but I know better.' With the B/A information in front of him the trainer can show precisely how much Dick is ignoring other people, and how he compares with the rest of the group; he may even ask Dick to take his analysis form and analyse the group himself—a good tactic if video equipment is available. Provided therefore that Dick is not confronted with too strong a condemnation of his behaviour, he can be encouraged to concentrate on one or two ratios which he would like to improve using the next series of exercises as a vehicle. The trainer suggests to him that in order to improve his Supporting and Building/Disagreeing ratio, he should follow the rule that he may not criticise any idea without first of all stating three things about it that are good. If there are enough people on the course with problems in Building behaviour (and there usually are) the trainer introduces a Building game: an idea or object is introduced into the group for discussion, but *every* contribution must build on the previous one.

After a few exercises like this there is more B/A information to be fed back; a new picture of training needs has emerged. After a second discussion with everyone, and individual learning objectives for everyone, the course continues adaptively. On a long interactive skills course it is common to find people are looking at their behaviour analysis after each exercise and making plans accordingly. The level of sophistication of training need rises; the course that starts with listening difficulties may finish up with people split into very small groups practising self-categorisation, learning flexibility of response, etc.

Behaviour analysis is a seductive tool; because it examines people in groups, and because it gives rapid feedback on performance in groups, it is tempting to use nothing else. It is important to stress that the trainer must know beforehand what assumptions he is making about performance in groups and the kind of behaviour he wants to train people towards; for example, is it legitimate always to seek increase Building behaviour and decrease Disagreeing? If the objective of the training has to do with teamwork, then it is legitimate; if the training is to increase managers' ability to spot security risks, then building behaviour has nothing to do with it. Like the Repertory Grid technique, discussed later in this chapter, behaviour analysis is a powerful, widely applicable procedure; one must have a clear sight of one's objectives if the technique is to work well.

E   Tests and quizzes

One simple way of assessing training needs is to ask people questions and see how many right answers they give. In technical (i.e. non-interactive) areas the paper and pencil quiz, and its variants, are useful neglected devices for analysing training needs.

For example, as part of a diagnosis of the training needs of personnel managers, a quiz could be administered containing questions like the following:

1   How many warnings must an unsatisfactory performer be given before dismissal? ....

2   How long must a woman have worked for an employer before being entitled to maternity leave? ....

3   Give two examples of conditions of employment that might be construed as indirect discrimination against women..........

4   Joe has been on the hourly-paid staff for five years and four months. How much notice is he entitled to should we wish to dismiss him? ....

5   Consider the following list of our suppliers. Tick those that operate a closed shop. Name the main unions recognised by each of them:

Bloggs Ltd   Cocklecarrot & Sons
Jam & Crumpet Inc.   Lunar Exploration Ltd
Mackenzie's Patent Unicycles   Bacon Renovations

6   On average, how long must a newly-recruited salesman stay with the firm before the cost of recruiting and training him is recovered? ....

7   What is the payment to the widow of an executive aged 55 who dies while in our employment, if his salary was £7,500 plus £450 profit-sharing last year? ....

It is easy to see how this can serve as a diagnosis of training needs, and how it could be used at the beginning of the training course to start a lively discussion amongst the trainees. One of the earliest books on evaluation of management training [1] showed how a simple quiz like this one also serves to put people in a better frame of mind to take advantage of the training; for if they get feedback on their results—by being allowed to mark their own papers—they become aware of their areas of ignorance and are motivated to do something about it. A repeat quiz at the end of the course—perhaps parallel in form with the first quiz, with different questions but covering the same ground—serves to evaluate the training and to reward the trainees with the sight of their own increased knowledge.

Quizzes need designing with some care, if they are to be fair. First the trainer needs a clear statement of the ground the training needs analysis is to cover; if the quiz is to precede a ready-designed training course, then the course objectives must be clear. If this does not happen then trainees will wonder whether all the ground has been covered fairly and with no irrelevancies. Then the questions need framing; the trainer must decide on the degree of openness in answers that he can cope with. At one extreme is Question 3 in our example, asking the manager to produce two instances of conditions of employment that discriminate against women; at the other extreme is the kind of question where a range of answers is provided and the victim ticks the one he believes is right. The second kind are easier to score, but more difficult to design, and there is the possibility of introducing bias by suggesting some answers and leaving out others. Open questions where the trainer feels confident that there is only a small range of possible answers are the best compromise.

Care must also be taken to avoid the 'What would you do?' type of question, for example:

> A subordinate newly transferred to your department appears to have a drink problem (breath smells, hand tremor, long lunch breaks, etc.). Would you:
> leave it a while to see if it got better?
> follow him to the pub and confront him when it was time to return?
> ring his wife to see if she could offer advice?
> suggest he join Alcoholics Anonymous?

It is easy for people to kid themselves—and the trainer—when they answer this type of question. Most people know what the right answer should be; they can all be skilful at a safe distance. Much better to use questions that test actual knowledge.

Either tests and quizzes used at the beginning of a training course should be changed for each new course, or the test papers gathered up and people placed on their honour not to reveal the content of the test.

An interesting variation on this theme is to play a game of Just-a-Minute with people already on a course, killing two training objectives with one stone: the game is good training in communication, and it helps the trainer do some training needs diagnosis. It works like the radio game of the same name: there are two teams of participants, or one panel competing as individuals, with a chairman who has a list of topics. One person is chosen to begin and is given a topic on which he has to talk without hesitation, repetition, deviation or inaccuracy for one minute; the other players can challenge him, and if correct they get a point and take up the subject themselves. Subjects are chosen for their relevance to the training course: new products, very old products, organisational acronyms, names of customers, suppliers, pieces of legislation, names of forms, etc. It's a game, not to be taken too seriously, good for an after-dinner session on a long training course when people feel they should be working but don't feel up to much.

F Psychological tests

Long books could be written about the use and abuse of
psychological tests in industry. Their use in training needs
analysis is limited but positive; above all else, trainers need to
know the limitations of psychological tests before embarking on
ambitious projects using them.

Tests measure a number of things: abilities, attitudes,
personality, interests, motivation. They come in a number of
forms and with differing degrees of restriction placed on them by
the bodies who distribute tests. Some are good, some of unknown
reliability; it is a jungle, and the trainer who wishes to investigate
psychological tests thoroughly is recommended to one or both of
the books given at the end of the chapter [2, 3] and should also
consult a psychologist before going ahead.

We begin with warnings about psychological tests for one
simple reason, ofter overlooked: there is no point in testing
someone in areas that cannot be influenced by training. Testing
a group of school-leavers for manual dexterity because you want
to select some for training as typists is a legitimate use of testing;
manual dexterity can be trained to a considerable extent in the
young. Testing a fifty-year-old manager to see how he rates on an
extraversion—introversion scale will not help at all in deciding
his training needs; you may need an extravert in that job, but if
he's introverted he's going to stay that way no matter how hard
you try to train him to be otherwise. The test might profitably be
used in *selection*, but that's another story.

Psychological tests can be used, with care, in diagnosing
training needs in the area of ability and aptitude; the short quiz
quoted in the previous section was an example of a psychological
test. Basic intelligence, factual knowledge, critical thinking,
verbal abilities, mechanical aptitude, numerical aptitude, ability
to think logically, computer aptitude . . . the list is long. With
managers, though, we ofter take these abilities for granted or
assume that they cannot be changed. It is on moving into areas of
personality and motivation that we strike trouble, for a number
of reasons:

1 Most tests of personality were designed for administering to
clinically sick people, and they ask questions about areas that
should not be of interest or importance in the industrial context.
2 Many features of someone's personality or motivation are so
deep-seated that they might not change with training, and any

training that did change them would change the whole person, not just the person at work.

3 There is nothing to stop anyone from producing a 'personality test' or 'counselling instrument' and selling it for profit. He does not have to prove its reliability and validity before putting it on the market. Some popular psychological instruments used in industry fall into this category.

It is easy to buy a test for the wrong reasons, to do an impossible job, and to damage people in the process. Care is needed therefore.

Tests of personality/attitude/motivation are best employed when one is taking a long term look at the development of an individual; they are less likely to help with an urgent training problem. Tests should also be used as the basis for a counselling interview, rather as happened with the diary method. It is not possible to recommend one test that will do the trainer's job, but a combination used successfully by a number of people is the 16-PF (Form C or D) with the Self-Description Questionnaire, Work Preference Questionnaire, and Job Climate Questionnaire produced by Fineman. [4, 5, 6] The 16-PF is' a personality test (16-PF stands for Sixteen Personality Factors) which has been adapted to give a shortened version, suitable for use in industry, which does not ask many clinical questions. For any individual only a part of the picture revealed by 16-PF will be vulnerable to training, and that over the longer rather than the shorter term, so care is needed in handling the information generated. The three Fineman questionnaires are a major contribution to testing in industry; they are short, well researched, and give coherent and useful information. The first measures the need to achieve, the second measures the kind of organisational culture he would like to work in, and the third measures the satisfactions and dissatisfactions that he experiences in his present work-place. Taken one at a time, or all three together, they form the basis for a very fruitful discussion of training needs and development in the medium to long term.

Though we advise that the trainer should consult a professional before embarking on the use of psychological tests, there are two words of warning that should be uttered in case the reader is approached by a test salesman trying to sell him a particular test. The warnings are:

1 Make sure that the population on whom the test was standardised is roughly compatible with your own. American

tests may not work well in the UK. Tests of sales ability standardised on toothpaste salesmen will not work when used on computer salesmen. Tests of executive ability standardised in an entrepreneurial organisation may not have much to tell when applied in local government.

2   Make sure that the test salesman can quote figures showing the test's reliability and validity. These should have been published in one or more of the psychologists' learned journals, and available for any psychologist to study. If the salesman responds: 'We know it works,' or 'Our customers are still using it,' or 'People say it's very thought provoking,' show him the door; he's marketing a test which has been designed for profit and which the designer is reluctant to put to the scrutiny of his professional peers.

To summarise the use of psychological tests in analysing training needs: they need using with professional guidance; they can help in difficult decisions, but should not be relied on for most day-to-day purposes; and they should be considered as an aid to long term developmental planning rather than short term diagnosis of immediate training needs.

G   Repertory Grid

Like testing, this is a subject meriting a book in its own right. Grid is a method of interviewing someone in a detailed and structured way, and of recording the results in such a way that changes can be measured and detailed maps drawn. This necessarily brief account covers only a few ways Grid can be used.

A grid interview begins with the selection of a number of *elements*. These are concepts representative of the area of interest of the interview. We shall take for an example a novice safety manager being interviewed to discover his training needs; the elements selected are eight named accidents which have happened in his plant or that he knows about. (For the sake of intelligibility, we substitute eight 'public' accidents, but the principle is the same.) The eight elements are written down on eight 3×5 inch cards. They are:

Aberfan	Flixborough
Staines Trident Papa India	North Sea oil blow-out

Titanic   Harrow & Wealdstone rail
Seveso   crash
                                  Battersea fun fair tragedy

The interviewer checks that the interviewee is reasonably familiar with the eight items on the cards. Then he takes the cards three at a time, according to a pre-arranged schedule, and placing the triad in front of the interviewee asks the question: 'Can you put two of them together so that they resemble each other and differ from the third?'

Eavesdropping on the beginning of the conversation with the safety manager, it goes like this:

Interviewer: Aberfan, the Staines Trident, and the Titanic— can you put those together so that any two are like each other and different from the third?

Interviewee: Well, the last two are methods of transport, Aberfan's not . . . Aberfan had a slow build-up, and the other two were quick . . . or you could arrange them differently, say that Aberfan and the Titanic were both designer error, in a way, but the Staines business was other people putting stress on the driver.

Interviewer: Thank you. Now try these three.

Interviewee: Flixborough and the Battersea Fun Fair both resulted in deaths, but no-one was killed in the North Sea oil blow-out . . . Flixborough and the blow-out were both things that happened pretty quickly after someone made a mistake, but the Battersea fun-fair problem was that no-one had done maintenance for years.

Interviewer: Thank you. Now try these three.

Interviewee: Seveso, Flixborough, and the Harrow rail crash. Well, the first two are chemical plants, or course, as opposed to rail travel . . . the first two had long term effects, the rail crash didn't . . . Flixborough and Harrow are both British accidents, of course . . . Seveso and Flixborough are both fairly recent, the Harrow one was over twenty years ago . . .

The interview procedure, cumbersome though it appears at first glance, is a very good way of getting at the distinctions the interviewee makes when he is thinking about accidents. The interviewer records each of the bipolar distinctions produced— called *contructs*—against the triad which gave rise to them. If the reader cares to continue the process, drawing more triads for himself, he will discover how compelling and searching a procedure it is; and how the interviewer has actually suggested none of the content produced in the interview. Grid procedure is almost completely free from the bias inevitably introduced into other techniques by the need for the observer to formulate questions and make interpretations.

If our novice safety manager had continued in that vein, by inspecting his constructs we could make strong inferences about his training needs. For example, Flixborough and the North Sea oil accident were both in industries where there is legislation about design and maintenance standards; Battersea fun-fair was not. If at the end of the interview he has not produced any constructs with a legislative tone to them, we know he has training needs in this area. If his constructs indicate that he knows who to blame for the accident, but not how to prevent it, we make further inferences about training needs.

Or, in the interview itself the interviewer can probe further, by getting the interviewee to choose between the two ends of a construct against some provided criterion:

Interviewer: You drew a distinction between accidents due to designer error, and accidents due to people putting pressure on the driver. Which sort, in general, are easiest to prevent?

Interviewee: Accidents where people put pressure on the driver.

Interviewer: Why?

Interviewee: 'Cause you can keep people away from the driver, and if they know why they're doing it they'll see the sense.

The interviewee is displaying a touching faith in human nature which he will have to be trained out of before becoming a good safety manager.

The interrogation of constructs may suffice to get a picture of training needs—remembering that with Grid what he doesn't say is as important as what he does, given the lack of suggestion from the interviewer. It is possible to go further and to draw up a matrix, with the elements at the top and the constructs down the side; the interviewee is asked to rate each element on each construct, as in Figure 5.1.

Here we are getting close to a 'map' of this man's perceptions of accidents. The map can be interrogated, by the trainer or by the man himself, looking for errors, contradictions, overlaps, etc. New elements and constructs can be added as they come to mind.

	Aberfan	Staines Trident	Titanic	Seveso	Flixborough	North Sea blow-out	Harrow rail crash	Battersea fun fair	Birmingham bombings	
methods of transport	—	+	+	—	—	—	+	—	—	not methods of transport
slow build-up	+	—	—	+	—	—	—	—	—	quick build-up
designer error	+	—	+	+	+	0	0	0	0	people stressing driver
straight after error	—	+	—	+	+	+	+	—	+	lack of maintenance
chemical plants	0	0	0	+	+	+	—	—	—	rail travel
long term effects	+	—	—	+	+	—	—	—	—	no long term effects
recent	+	+	—	+	+	+	—	+	+	long ago
British	+	+	+	—	+	+	+	+	+	foreign
easy to prevent	+	+	—	—	—	+	+	+	—	difficult to prevent
likely to recur	—	—	—	+	—	+	—	+	+	unlikely to recur
killed people	+	+	+	—	+	—	+	+	+	killed no-one

Fig. 5.1   Start of a Repertory Grid of accidents

The trainer may supply some constructs to see if the manager can work with them.

In the Grid shown, for example, some inferences about training needs can be made from looking at the way elements are rated on constructs. Does he really think that the North Sea oil blow-out will have no long term effects? Does he think that the Staines Trident disaster was easy to prevent? (The hazard had been identified a long time previously, but attempts to get it recognised were fruitless.) [7] The Grid can also be examined for patterns: for example, the construct 'Likely to recur/unlikely to recur' is used in almost the same way as the construct 'Killed no-one/killed people'. The interviewer presents this information to the interviewee and asks whether these two constructs mean the same thing, or whether he can think of an accident that killed people but is likely to recur. The manager here responded with the element 'Birmingham pub bombings', which has just been written into the Grid at the point where we stopped to take a picture.

A Grid built up like this can provide a powerful diagnosis of training needs for all concerned; the very act of going through a Grid interview is an educational experience for the manager concerned, and he is put in a much better position to organise his own learning. Grids can be done before and after training to measure change and learning.

This brief account covers the highlights of Grid; more is to be found in the references given [8, 9, 10] though these are mostly about clinical work; work in industry proceeds apace. Almost anything can form the elements in a Grid interview—people, events, objects, activities—and the interview can take many directions. It is therefore wise to seek some advice and training before going in for Grid technique in any depth, but the training is well worth while, as Grid can be used in so many situations besides training needs analysis.

H   Summary

In these two chapters we have examined ways of carrying out a training needs analysis. The depth to which one wants to probe, the coverage one wants to give, the type of training need to be investigated, all influence the choice of technique. The end-point is always the same, however; a statement of what people need to do better, expressed in measurable terms. The nearer one comes to this ideal with training needs analysis, the less trouble one runs into with later evaluation of training. There are some other common threads running through these chapters: the need to think about behaviour and performance first, and to translate into training needs, or training courses, at the last minute; the requirement not to find out about things beyond your control; the need wherever possible to get the manager participating in discovering the need, rather than having it thrust upon him unannounced; the need not to generalise, not to evaluate, not to be surprised, not to condemn. So many training problems fall into place once training needs analysis is understood.

I　Discussion questions

1　'Information about people's training needs should be fed back to them as soon as possible.' Do you agree? Why?

2　Imagine you are about to send a manager to a foreign country, where none of your staff has ever worked before. (Think of a specific country.) How would you discover any training needs he might have in respect of this assignment?

3　In a meeting a manager shows a behaviour ratio:

$$\frac{\text{giving information}}{\text{seeking information}} = \frac{16}{48}$$

Name three sorts of meeting in which this would be *prima facie* desirable behaviour, and three sorts in which it would be undesirable.

4　You probably assumed that the manager in the previous example was male. Does your answer change at all if the manager is revealed to be female? Should it?

J　References and further reading

[1] P. B. WARR, M. BIRD and N. RACKHAM. *The Evaluation of Management Training*, Gower Press, 1970.

[2] R. M. GUION. *Personnel Testing*, McGraw-Hill, 1965.
A very thorough book covering all aspects of testing in industry; written for people with some expertise, but containing sound guidance on the organisational issues involved in a testing programme.

[3] K. M. MILLER. *Psychological Testing in Personnel Assessment*, Gower Press, 1975.

[4] S. FINEMAN. 'A Modification of the Ghiselli Self-Description Inventory for the measurement of the need for achievement amongst managers', *International Review of Applied Psychology*, vol. 25, no. 1, 1973.

[5] S. FINEMAN. 'The Work Preference Questionnaire: a measure of managerial need for achievement', *Journal of Occupational Psychology*, vol. 48, 1975.

[6] S. FINEMAN. 'The influence of perceived job climate on the relationship between managerial achievement, motivation, and performance', *Journal of Occupational Psychology*, vol. 48, 1975.

Don't be put off by the titles of the learned journals in which
these tests appear; their appearance in these journals is, in fact, a
guarantee that the tests have been properly designed and
standardised. If you wish to experiment with the tests the best
method is to get in touch with Dr Fineman himself, who at the
time of writing was at the School of Management, University of
Bath.

[7] G. PETERS. 'The Crash of Trident Papa-India', in V.
BIGNELL, G. PETERS and C. PYM, *Catastrophic Failures*,
Open University Press, 1976.

[8] G. KELLY. *The Psychology of Personal Constructs*,
Norton, 1955.

[9] D. BANNISTER and F. FRANSELLA. *Inquiring Man*,
Penguin, 1971.

[10] L. THOMAS and S. HARRI-AUGSTEIN. 'Learning to
Learn: the Personal Construction and Exchange of Meaning', in
M. HOWE, *Adult Learning*, Wiley, 1977.

6 Your training options

A Background to training design

As a result of the training needs diagnosis the trainer should have a clear idea of the needs of his managers, expressed in terms of what they need to do differently. Now the trainer's job is to give managers the experiences that enable them to learn the new knowledge or skills. Most people know about the standard range of courses and seminars available, but a course may not always be the right answer. How does one decide the kind of experience which will help managers learn?

To answer this question we return to Chapter 2, and the three essentials of managers' learning: practice, feedback, and a non-threatening environment. Suppose we have identified a group of training needs in the area of negotiation skills; our managers needs a better grasp of strategy, an ability to think before they speak, an ability to offer the other chap a bridge always, and the ability to summarise what has been achieved speedily. Not too unusual a collection of requirements!

Most of these new behaviours involve *doing* something as well as *knowing* something. Therefore the trainer concludes that the training must involve active participation in negotiations, because skills need practice. This is the first question to ask when outlining training options: are we concerned with skill, with familiarity, or with working knowledge? This training must increase negotiating skills, so the trainees need to do some negotiating. If the training need were greater familiarity with the Health and Safety at Work Act, the trainees could sensibly take a more passive role.

The second question the trainer must ask is this: what is the minimum time we can spend in training that will allow each trainee to perform each skill *twice*? The reason for this question is simple, and relates back to the need for practice and feedback. Suppose the trainee comes on the course prepared to say the first thing that comes into his head during negotiations. (This, remember, is one of our training needs.) He takes part in an exercise during which he realises for himself—or the trainer makes him discover—that he says the first thing coming into his head, and that this is undesirable. He makes plans to overcome the problem, and tries out his new intentions in a second exercise, during which he finds out that he is now able to hold his tongue a little.

The first exercise generates feedback; he listens to the feedback; the second exercise gives him chance to practise, and generates more feedback. If the exercise can be repeated a third and fourth time, so much the better. Yet this simple point in training design is missed so often by so many training designers: look at all the courses in public speaking, appraisal interviewing, selection interviewing, etc., where each person takes part in one exercise only. The best these courses can do is give the trainees an appetite for further learning, which is then disappointed when they discover that they must spend the rest of the time watching other people perform.

The trainer's question, then, is about the minimum length of time necessary to get a sample of the appropriate behaviour; arrange feedback to the trainee; get the trainee to try the behaviour again in a risk-free environment, and give feedback on that; and round the cycle as many times as necessary to get from the starting behaviour to the desired behaviour. If this seems to be recommending much longer times spent training than are normally allotted, then we must disagree. The key lies in the training needs analysis, and the precision with which it is done.

Let us return to our original list of training needs in negotiating skills. It would have been easy at some stage in the training needs diagnosis to cease thinking with such precision, and to talk of 'Negotiation Training'. Forget that Manager A needs a grasp of strategy and an ability to offer the other chap a bridge; Manager A needs Negotiation Training. But it is quite easy to design a series of short exercises—each lasting maybe no more than fifteen minutes—which will give Manager A practice in offering people a bridge; and in less than a morning give Manager A—alone or in a group of similar managers—half a dozen chances of practising this skill. Presented instead with the statement 'Manager A needs negotiation training' one cannot be sure what he needs to do better, so one does not know how long he's going to take practising doing it better. If you containerise your training needs, you invite packaged training programmes, and the trainer settles into an easy job as a course administrator.

The length of time for training is therefore determined by the need for practice and feedback, and this is influenced by the type of skill to be learned. A small, precise skill that can be isolated from context—like our negotiation skills—may be reducible to short exercises measured in minutes; others, like the ability to take over someone else's project half-complete in the knowledge that you yourself will be retired before it's finished, need by their very nature to have a longer practice time. This is one factor that divides on-the-job training from off-the-job; short discrete items of learning are taken off-the-job, long complex ones need learning on-the-job, but with support.

The trainer must also ask himself whether the training need he is servicing is for *new* knowledge or skills, or for a vocabulary for understanding *old, unverbalised* knowledge or skills. Sometimes one is confronted by what look like needs for skills that would take a very long time to learn, but on deeper probing it becomes apparent that the real need is for people better to understand and control what they already know but have not formalised. In this case lectures and short seminars can be positively helpful.

A further question for the trainer trying to satisfy training needs is: how am I going to ensure that the trainees are in a low risk environment in which they feel free to experiment with new ways of doing things? Of course, the most risk-free environment is probably a course full of strangers using pseudonyms, and the low risk element in most external courses is what makes them attractive in servicing training needs that might not be thought suitable on other grounds. The risks in on-the-job training are greater; first because it is real performance in the real work environment, with the possibility of genuine disaster if things go wrong, and second because the learning happens under the eye of one's boss, and in years to come he may remember where the bodies are buried. Good on-the-job training tries to reduce these risks where possible, by taking the learner off-line sometimes, by giving him a 'Dutch uncle' or other figure as counsellor/trainer, and by more subtle methods which we shall look at later in this chapter.

We can summarise the trainer's questions thus:

1 Surface knowledge, deep knowledge, or skills?
2 Minimum cycle time for practice with feedback?
3 How many cycles needed—i.e. gap between present and desired performance?

4   New learning or rehearsal/structuring of old learning?
5   How to ensure low risk learning environment?

The answers to these questions should enable him to choose one
or more of the training methods outlined below.

B   Training methods

The methods most commonly used in training managers include
some old ones and some new ones and some old ones under new
names. Later chapters will cover the important ones in detail.
They include:

1   *Active courses.* Trainees participate in off-the-job activities
in which they take part in live exercises which comprise the main
part of the training course. Nearly all management skills can be
taught by this method; at its best it is a powerful vehicle for
learning, with lots of opportunity for practice and little chance of
people dropping out. Badly planned, it can be a big failure and
in extreme cases can do people damage. Courses vary in the
actual content of the exercises, the degree of structure, the
participant mix, the length of time, etc. They can be internally
organised or run outside the firm for mixed groups. Examples:
Interactive Skills training, Coverdale training, T-groups, Action-
Centred Leadership courses.

2   *Seminars.* This is a portmanteau label applied to many
kinds of activity. The typical seminar is a one or two day meeting
held off-line, at which guest speakers hold forth for part or all of
the time. Usually some time is spent in general discussions,
discussions in syndicates, and perhaps an exercise or two, but
most of the time the participants listen to the speakers. Seminars
usually concentrate on one limited topic of current management
interest; they can be organised in-house or publicly, and the
market in public seminars is an active one—it is often more
convenient to send one or two managers to a public seminar than
to organise an in-house one. As with active courses, when they
are good they are very very good, and when they are bad they are
horrid; many seminars centre on topics that should really be
treated on an active training course (e.g. interviewing skills,
salesmanship, leadership) giving participants the illusion of
having learned something but no opportunities to practise.
Successful seminars provide managers with knowledge that they

can go away and use. Many examples could be quoted; most of the professional and semi-professional bodies in management (the BIM, the IPM, the Industry Training Boards) organise seminars; so do consultants (e.g. PA, P-E, Eurotech) and management schools (e.g. Brunel University, London Business School). This is perhaps the most volatile part of the business education market, where a lot of money is spent and a lot of caution needed.

3 *Correspondence courses.* A somewhat neglected area of management education until the Open University demonstrated what could be done and revived people's interest. Many professional qualifications useful to managers can be acquired through correspondence courses, in areas as diverse as accountancy and personnel management, engineering and law. For professional qualifications it is easy to tell how good the correspondence college is by the level of qualification it prepares people for; it is more difficult to judge between colleges when they offer courses in skills such as report writing, salesmanship, or problem analysis. A good correspondence college will make enquiries about the person's present level of education, why he wants the course, how long he has to spend per week in studying, etc., and will not try to use the course as a vehicle for selling expensive textbooks or equipment. In selecting a course to give someone a professional qualification, the trainer is advised to seek the counsel of the appropriate professional body, who will be able to recommend a number of approved courses; where the course does not lead to a professional qualification the trainer must first ask whether this is something that can be studied through the post (one doubts whether 'salesmanship' can, for example) and must then judge by the helpfulness of the course organisers, the amount of information they reveal and the trouble they take in matching requirements. The Open University is a different kind of creature; their admissions policy and the length of time they take to go through the study programme mean that trainers are unlikely to find themselves recommending an OU degree course to meet a manager's training need. However they should be prepared to respond with help and support if a manager decides on his own account that he would like to try for an OU degree, and many firms make special arrangements for managers who do this.

4 *Programmed learning.* Programmed learning teaches by dividing what is to be learned into small chunks, and presenting

these chunks in a logical order to the learner; each chunk requires him to respond in a way that tests his knowledge. If he gets the answer right he goes on to the next chunk; if he gets it wrong he may stay with the same chunk or be passed into a short remedial loop until he does get it right. For example, an extract from a programmed text in statistics looks like this:

The *mean* is the arithmetic average of all the scores. It is calculated by adding all the scores and dividing by the number of separate scores.

Tick which one of these words is the same as the term *arithmetic average*

median   mean   tangent   mode   score

If the learner ticks the right word—in this case *mean*—the programme passes him on to the next frame:

The *mode* is the most frequently occurring score—the one that is à la mode, in fashion. It is found by arranging all the scores in ascending or descending order and discovering the one that occurs most often.

In a normal distribution, do the mean and the mode coincide? Tick one answer

yes, always   no, never   sometimes

And so on.

For programmed learning to be successful, the designer needs a very full knowledge of what has to be learned, and of the right order for learning the concepts. There are problems in selecting the range of alternative answers, and in designing the way the programme branches; also, the text has to be presented in such a way that people are prevented from seeing the right answer, which means one question to a side of paper, or computer controlled presentation, or some similar device. All these problems of design mean that the trainer will probably not be able to design his own programmed text, nor find it economical to do so, unless he has a very large problem to overcome. However, if there is a lot of technical training to be done thoroughly, and it is material that can be learned sitting at a desk, and is unlikely to change quickly, then the trainer should think about getting a text designed for him; many of the procedures a manager has to know are amenable to presentation in this form, and it is a very efficient way of learning. Its disadvantages are in the large amount of preparation time needed, from skilled people, and in fact that it is quite difficult to alter a programmed text once it is in use, so that material which dates quickly is not suitable. As a technique, though, it is designed specifically to meet the criteria of practice and feedback, and its privacy makes it risk-free; it is worth more consideration from industrial trainers than it has had in the past. Examples are difficult to give, but the interested reader will find the book by Kay, Dodd and Sime a good introduction to the subject. [1]

5   *Coaching programmes.* The term *coaching* has recently come into fashion to describe something that good managers have done with their subordinates for a long time; built on-the-job learning plans with their subordinates, perhaps ancillary to the annual performance appraisal, with frequent progress checks and counselling meetings. The manager's own experience is utilised; he teaches by both precept and example; and the subordinate stays on the job instead of going away to expensive courses. A good coaching programme is a splendid way for the professional trainer to reach many more trainees than he ever could through giving courses; if he can equip himself with a network of managers, all coaching their subordinates as part of the routine and coming to the trainer when they need help, he has introduced an element of gearing into his training influence.

Coaching works by the manager identifying a training need (with or without help from the trainer or the subordinate) and expressing it in terms of what the subordinate needs to do better. This discovery may take place at the appraisal interview or at any other time. The manager then enlists the aid of the subordinate in (a) accepting that there is a training need, (b) making plans to overcome it by planned experience, and (c) arranging to keep records of progress and to discuss these in regular meetings devoted solely to the purpose of coaching. Some skills are needed by the manager—skills of spotting training needs, turning the training needs into planned experiences, and selling the idea of learning in such a way that the subordinate is not offended or frightened. A trainer setting up a coaching programme has very much the same set of steps to go through—convincing managers that they could help by coaching their subordinates. Then they must be equipped with the necessary skills, including the skills of creative listening and counselling, to put the coaching programme into operation. This is not always easy, as managers have to be convinced that the learning process will inevitably involve making mistakes, asking silly questions, etc., and a firm effort is needed to make sure that all sides know why and how coaching works. The Training Services Agency in conjunction with the Air Transport and Travel Industry Training Board made a pair of films on coaching [2, 3] which form a good introduction to the subject.

6 *Learning projects.* These are closely allied to coaching; a training need is identified, one which will take a long time to service and which is best dealt with on the job. A special project is selected which, with suitable guidance, will teach the trainee the necessary skills and knowledge. The project may occupy part of his regular job, or it may replace his regular job for a while.

Projects differ from coaching programmes in a number of—mainly administrative—ways. Coaching is in the hands of the line manager; a man doing a project may be assigned to someone in the training department, or to a different line manager, for the advice and counselling that accompanies the project. Coaching often results in a mix of activities, whereas the project is one specific, and maybe major, activity; it may even be an activity specially devised for the project programme, as when a team of managers is put to work as a task force with the twin objectives of solving a company problem and developing the managers themselves. Some firms make a point of using projects as part of their graduate training programme; for example, one firm gave two of its graduate trainees the job of closing a factory—everything from planning the redundancy notices to selling the last of the assets. Other firms use projects in the early stages of inducting graduates—giving them a project to do which allows them to find their own way around quickly and ask lots of naïve questions.

There is a fine balance, in a project, between the intrinsic needs of the project and the learning needs of the manager doing it, and care must be taken to balance the two. It is made more difficult when projects are used as a laying-on of hands preparatory to promotion, instead of a vehicle for learning; take care that they are used for learning, not for glory.

7 *Secondments and job-swaps.* These are projects conducted in another firm. They come in two forms; the organisation can lend a manager to another organisation for a while, out of charity and the goodness of its heart, or two organisations can swap managers for a time. As an example of the first kind of

secondment, IBM (UK) has lent promising managers with development potential to organisations solving inner-city problems, or to help plan the marketing of Job Centres. No financial return accrues to the organisation; the manager returns having learned something, and the company is pursuing its goal as a good corporate citizen. Examples of exchanges between firms are more widely known.

As with projects, only more so, the difficulty with secondments is to keep the learning objectives in sight and not let them be swamped by the demands of the job and the glamour of having been involved in a (necessarily) rather rare form of training. They also present problems of career management which we shall consider in a later chapter. Also there is a temptation to think that because A and B have changed places the good work has been done and learning will automatically follow; this is an incorrect assumption, and the learning needs managing and control from an authoritative source.

8   *Sabbaticals.* Sometimes one cannot point to a specific training need, but one knows that the manager is stretched, that he needs time to think and ponder, that he has been under short term pressure for so long that he has lost touch with his inner self. In these cases the trainer may think of a sabbatical of some sort; that is, a length of time spent without formal pressure in a learning environment. Sabbaticals vary in content: a trip abroad visiting other firms, management schools, etc.; time spent in a library amongst experts and other managers, but no courses to go to; time spent on courses that have no immediate relevance to the job in hand. One or two firms have arranged with the older universities that short courses will be put on by the dons in the summer—nothing to do with business, covering subjects from archaeology to Zoroastrianism, the courses to be attended by middle managers who have run hard for too long and need time to reflect and get back into the habit of learning. A sabbatical is not a holiday, and should not be confused with one; nevertheless it is one of the few occasions in the trainer's life when he dispenses with specific learning objectives and instructs managers just to go away and think for a while.

9   *Self-development systems.* These are packages prepared for a manager by an expert inside or outside the firm, wherein are instructions for the manager to follow; if he follows them, he will learn something. Self-development packages come in all shapes and sizes, for all sorts of purposes. They are a good

alternative to coaching if the trainer cannot get his managers to coach; they are good for training managers in far-flung outposts. One self-development system, for newly created managers, gives the manager a list of places to visit; for each place it gives him a list of questions to ask people or information that he should be finding out, for example:

> What is your breakage rate? How does it compare with the firm's average? If you are different, why?
>
> Ask the foreman about the most difficult problem he has had to cope with this week.
>
> What stocks do you carry of chemicals A, B, C and D? What are the arrangements in case of failure on the part of the supplier?
>
> How much does it cost you to recruit and train a new milkman?

Other self-development packages concentrate on development of interpersonal skills, self-motivation, etc. A good self-development programme has a lot in common with programmed learning, only it requires action at the end of each frame instead of a tick in the box. Because trainees can proceed at their own pace, and no-one need know about their mistakes, self-development programmes offer advantages which the trainer may care to think about.

We are aware that this list of training options is incomplete; we have omitted the long term training programmes, for instance, because we are trying to concentrate on programmes that the trainer in the organisation can control himself. We have probably missed some fashions and fads, too. But the basic principles underlying most of the training options are set out above: on-the-job or off-the-job, self-controlled, manager-controlled or trainer-controlled, long term or short term. These considerations then interact with the business considerations—how urgent is the need? how long can we spare him for? how much can we afford? At the end of this process we hope that a training option will have been selected that stands a good chance of meeting the diagnosed training needs.

C Summary

After the training needs diagnosis the trainer has a statement of what people need to do differently. The statement is interrogated

—is the training need for knowledge or skills? how long will it take to practise the new behaviour thoroughly? how can a low risk learning environment be created? Taking these things into consideration the trainer has a choice of training methods: courses, seminars, correspondence courses, programmed learning, coaching, projects, secondments, sabbaticals, and self-development packages. He must match the training need with the training method, taking into account the business pressures.

D Discussion questions

1   What in your opinion (or you can do some research) are the training needs of married women hoping for a career in management after having raised a family? What would be the best way to meet these needs (a) resourced by the woman herself before returning to work, and (b) resourced by her employer after engaging her?

2   If you could leave your present employer for six months (return entry guaranteed) to work elsewhere, where and as what would you learn most?

3   What are the opportunity costs of sending a middle manager in the Sales division on an external course lasting a week? Can you calculate the opportunity costs for a coaching programme in the same way?

4   'My training options are limited first of all by the availability of suitable hotel accommodation, second by the fact that the MD insists on a course dinner on Thursdays with a speech from him or one of his side-kicks, and if you come down to basics I'm limited by the fact that I'm usually forced to have coffee at eleven, tea at three-thirty, and take an hour and a half for lunch.' We can all sympathise with that speaker; please list as many similarly frivolous limitations on your training options as you can think of, and then make plans to overcome some of them.

E References and further reading

[1] H. KAY, B. DODD and M. SIME. *Programmed Instruction*, Penguin, 1968.

[2] Film 'I Owe You' distributed by the Training Services Agency.

[3] Film 'Received With Interest' distributed by the Training Services Agency.

7   Internal training courses: knowledge-based

A   Background

We have stressed before the importance of distinguishing between training in knowledge and training in skills; the two are often confused. A knowledge-need is expressed as: he needs to know X, Y and Z. A skills training need is expressed as: he needs to do X, Y and Z. Training needs expressed as: he needs to be X, Y and Z, are almost certainly skills needs expressed with less than complete precision. Much of a manager's job consists of skill rather than knowledge, but there are times when genuine knowledge needs are expressed to the trainer: product knowledge, technical briefings, legal briefings, export intelligence, and so on. Knowledge needs can be satisfied with the more formal teaching methods such as lecturing, case studies, films, and programmed instruction. These methods are examined in detail in this chapter; first, though, we must consider the strategy of organising knowledge-based courses.

It is safe to assume that the trainees are more motivated to attend a knowledge course than a skills course; there is less risk of self-exposure, and attendance on a knowledge course rarely carries the stigma of having been sent 'for improvement' which some skills-based courses have. However, though one can assume a higher initial motivation, one cannot take it too much for granted; dull lectures that go on for too long can soon dispel the goodwill. Indeed, it is easy for the professional trainer to forget that the managers sitting in front of him usually have no more than ten minutes at a time uninterrupted behind their desks, and to sit for eight hours absorbing information is sheer purgatory. A variety of training methods is essential therefore; centring on lectures perhaps, but with films and group discussions and individual exercises to break the rhythm and exercise different channels of perception. A variety of lecturers is also useful if the course is much longer than a single day.

It helps a great deal if at the beginning of the course two things happen. First the trainees should be encouraged to test their own state of knowledge somehow. This can be done formally with a quiz of some kind—in which case the trainer will find the results useful for on-course adjustments and for post-course evaluation; more informally the trainer can lead off with a short session in which he invites the trainees to consider a problem, or to shout out answers to a question of the 'How many can you think of?' variety. Knowledge of the gaps in one's knowledge—provided that the gaps are not enormous—is a motivator. And the second preliminary is to give the trainees a full outline of the structure of the course—what is the body of knowledge to be acquired, how they are going to approach it, and what the end-point of the course will be. One cannot always do this on skills courses, but on knowledge-giving courses it is essential.

Where the course starts from, and how fast it moves, depends on the topic and on the skill of the trainees in acquiring knowledge. The training needs analysis is essential here. However, a good rule of thumb is to mix formal instruction, e.g. lectures, with opportunities for rehearsal, e.g. small group discussions. The speed of moving from lectures to discussion and back again can be gauged by thinking about the number of new concepts that the trainees will acquire in a lecture. They come to the lecture with some concepts already formed; for example, sales managers come knowing about the company's existing product range. The lecturer then builds new concepts on top of these pre-existing concepts; let us imagine that he gives the managers a presentation about the company's new product range. It would be unwise for the lecturer to go on to build a further set of concepts on top of these *new* concepts without first giving the trainees an opportunity to consolidate those new concepts; so before telling them about the new marketing strategy to go with the new products our lecturer would be wise to give the sales managers the chance to discuss the new products in small groups, or to see a film show about them. The basic principle 'Build new concepts on old concepts, and don't build new concepts on new concepts' is a good guide to planning the pace of the course and the amount of information to be conveyed each session.

When material is prepared, for use in lecturing or other formal instruction, it is fatally easy for the trainer to plan, and to judge himself, in terms of the amount of material he has got through. One must always keep in mind the objective of the course, which is to get information into the minds of the trainees, not out of the mouth of the trainer.

B Lectures

Studies of the use of lectures [1] make it clear that the lecture is as good a way of imparting knowledge as any other, but that it is not good at stimulating independent thought or changing attitudes. Lecturing to people about problem-solving techniques does not make them any better at solving problems (with some exceptions at the very top of the intelligence scale); lecturing to managers to get them to be more democratic is unlikely to change them. But given a body of information to impart, lectures can be very efficient; so why do so many people shudder at the very thought of a lecture based training course?

Probably because lectures are easy to do badly. They can be dull, boring, infuriating; they encourage trainees to be passive; they often present material in unorganised, unassimilable chunks. To plan a good set of lectures we need to know something about how material gets forgotten, because the lecturer's task is to beat this gremlin.

Forgetting happens through four separate mechanisms, any one of which can ruin the lecturer's work for him.

1 *Decay of the memory trace.* There are two sorts of memory—short term and long term. Short term memory covers the ten to fifteen seconds after one has first perceived the information, and the short term memory is limited in what it can take in—about seven unrelated digits is the limit for most adults, for example. An attempt to overload the short term memory will ensure that only a certain amount of information is actually processed; reading a long list of strange names to someone and asking him to recall them will get some from the front and some from the back and very few from the middle. So, the first message to the trainer is: don't overload the short term memory. Don't read out long lists; don't present slides covered with information and expect them to be remembered. The second rule is to allow the information time to be transferred from the short term to the long term memory. We have all felt the failure of this process when we have been given a telephone number and are about to write it down when something else—a knock at the door perhaps—interferes. When we try to recall the number, it has gone completely.

Once in the long term store, memories decay very slowly, if at all; but long term memory operates in different modes and we may find it easy to *recognise* familiar information although we

cannot *recall* it unaided. Over a long time, memories are
'organised' too; strange happenings may be remembered as more
straightforward, one occasion may be imposed on another, the
unfamiliar may change to make it more like what went before. In
most cases the trainer need not worry about the long term
memories of his trainees—though it is legitimate to wonder a
little when people start to reminisce about *very* old good old
days; the main concern should be to avoid overloading the short
term memory and making sure that information goes from the
short term to the long term store, and this is achieved by pacing
the information carefully—not too much and not too fast—and
by using more than one sense modality—speech and vision, and
touch and taste and smell if possible.

2   *Interference* between the material to be learned and the
preceding or following material. This is most likely to happen
when the material to be learned (the 'primary' material) is
similar to the preceding or following ('secondary') material, but
different in some way. For example, if the primary material is a
briefing on the Sex Discrimination Act, and the secondary
material is a briefing on the Race Relations Act, the two are
likely to interfere with each other. Part of a lecture can interfere
with the rest, if, for example, the lecturer is trying to make a
point clear and the trainee starts to take notes part-way through,
the very act of note-taking can interfere with learning the
lecturer's point. Interference is reduced when there is plenty of
time to consolidate important points before going on to the next
one, and where an effort is made to ensure that the material in
one lecture will not be confused with the material in the
surrounding sessions.

3   *Trying to learn too much* is another cause of forgetting. It
is quite common to find that trainees remember the beginning,
the end, and any high spots of a lecture or of a training course,
but the material in the middle is missing so that when they come
later to try to organise the material for themselves they find they
cannot. The trainer controls this partly by pacing, and partly by
trying to prevent the trainees from going at the course material
like a bull at a gate. We have all seen the trainee who arrives on a
course, looks at the programme, snorts: 'What, no work after
nine-thirty? We're all expensive chaps on this course, and I
would have expected to be working until midnight at least'. This
may satisfy his self-esteem, but it will certainly stand in the way
of acquiring new knowledge.

4 *Repression* is what happens when people forget unpleasant things that have happened to them, or things that they are ashamed of. It is quite common to find that one's memory of a personal tragedy fades and becomes unreal: 'I can remember it happening, but it's like watching a film and seeing it happen to someone else'. At a deeper level, most people have repressed memories which they cannot access at all; where this happens on a limited scale it is an admirable example of the body's coping response. For the loss of a little information we remain reasonably stable people. The trainer should not treat every example of memory loss amongst his trainees as repression, but there will be times when memories are imperfect because the associated events were so traumatic—accidents, strikes, tough negotiations, redundancy, etc. It is unlikely that anything the trainer teaches on an ordinary knowledge-giving course will be material his trainees will want to repress—this is our profound hope; but discussions asking trainees to talk about their previous .experience may bring to light one or two cases of inexplicable forgetting. If this does happen the trainer should not press hard; repression happens for good psychological reasons and a training course is not the time or place to strip people down and start rebuilding.

A good trainer will design his lecture material in advance so as to minimise, by proper pacing and presentation, the likelihood that the material will be forgotten. He must also plan to fight the next gremlin that besets lectures and lecturers; the boredom and passivity of the trainees, which can quickly lapse into sound restful sleep.

Who has not struggled with the problem of holding an audience's attention after a heavy lunch? We find this problem so difficult that we try to design courses using anything except lectures and films after lunch; but on a really bad day the eyes can glaze over straight after breakfast. Things that help are:

1 *Showing the relevance* of the lecture, both to the plan of the course and to their jobs as managers out in the field. For example: 'After this morning's discussion on Saudi Arabia we are now going to turn our attention to Iran, the last of the Middle Eastern countries on our list; then after we've reviewed the Middle East we can turn our attention to Nigeria and the other African countries we are likely to find ourselves exporting to. It's interesting that we should be discussing Saudi Arabia at this moment because some of you may have seen in the Company

Newsletter that the Chairman is going out there in a few days to examine the possibilities of a market research study . . .'. Here the trainer begins by relating the current lecture to the preceding one, and then to the plan of the whole course; then he reminds them why they are on the course at all. The way *not* to do it is to begin: 'Now we come to Saudi Arabia, which as you all know is very relevant to your jobs, and the first thing to say about Saudi Arabia is . . .'. Don't *tell* them it's relevant; *show* them.

2 *Showing the benefit* of the lecture, which must be done with care as one must not arouse fear of failure. The implication behind '. . . the possibilities of a market research study . . .' should be enough for most sales managers, though if one were lecturing to a non-sales group one might go on to add '. . . which, if it were successful, could be a quantum jump in the company's activity'. Again, the key is to mention how the knowledge to be imparted could benefit the trainees, rather than to assure them that they will find this knowledge useful.

3 *Question them* during the course of the lecture, asking them to draw on their own experience as it relates to the content of the lecture. 'Harry, you were out there for a while last year, weren't you? Did you find it easy to get along in English?' is a better way of keeping their attention than: 'Well, we're half-way through, has anybody got any comments or questions they'd like to put forward?'

4 *Get them talking* with one another, and with the lecturer, sharing questions and answers, experience and ignorance. A skilled lecturer knows that the best way to deal with a really obnoxious person in the audience is not to be drawn oneself, but to wait quietly until one of the other course members is drawn to reply; but this line is only open if the lecturer has already encouraged discussion. This tactic is also used when the questioner is not obnoxious, but merely puzzled, or lost, or seeking reassurance; if other course members answer this may seem more genuine than if the trainer answers, and it gives the others a chance to rehearse their knowledge and build up a feeling of group cohesion.

5 *Be enthusiastic* about the material. This is not merely evangelical advice; there is clear scientific evidence to show that people learn more from a lecturer who conveys enthusiasm about his material than from one who gets through the same amount of material but without enthusiasm. How one becomes enthusiastic about a topic one doesn't like, or which one is lecturing about for

the thousandth time, is a personal matter; it helps to re-read
one's lecture notes even if this is the thousandth time, it helps to
get eye contact with the trainees, and it helps to remember that
though this is the umpteenth time you have explained this bit of
information, for each trainee it is the first time he has heard it,
and it may be the last time. You may have second chances, but
he hasn't, and a really bad trainer can actually send people away
worse off than when they arrived.

Assuming that there is a formal body of knowledge to be
imparted, the lecturer is faced with the task of organising it for
himself and for the notes which may accompany his lecture.
Over-preparation is the secret of many good lecturers; the ones
who speak without notes may be able to do that because they
spent a lot of time preparing the notes which they now feel able
to discard. Material can be organised in at least three ways: in a
hierarchical arrangement, in comparison tables, and in a
hypothetico-deductive narrative. For example, if the material
includes a lot of classification and sub-classification, a
hierarchical presentation would be appropriate; if the material
includes concepts which must be examined and compared with
one another then a comparison table is appropriate; examples of
problem-solving, and knowledge in action, lend themselves to the
hypothetico-deductive narrative. Of course, all three might be
mixed within one lecture or one course; once the principles of
each are grasped the planning of lectures and lecture notes is
much simplified.

1   *Hierarchical* forms are used when a great deal of diverse
material is to be understood; when it is best understood by
expressing it as a series of classifications; and where the trainees
will be better equipped to remember the information and absorb
new information if they remember the classification system as
well as the material itself. The bare bones of a lecture using the
hierarchical form look like this:

A:
_____
  (i) ....
  (ii) ....
 (iii) ....
B:
_____
  (i) ....
 (ii) (a) ....
     (b) ....

    (iii)
    (iv)
  C: _____
    (i) ....
    (ii) ....

and so on. The export sales managers on whom we eavesdropped earlier were studying material that had been laid out in a hierarchical form: A was Europe, B the Middle East, and C Africa; within the heading A came (i) France, (ii) Germany, and (iii) Italy, and so on. Hierarchies can be divided and subdivided without limit, though it is important to retain homogeneity within the labels used; it would be wrong to give the export managers a further category D, standing for Congo, which was then divided into (i) Congo—Kinshasa and (ii) Zaire. This breaks with the previous headings, which used capital letters to identify continents and small Roman numerals to indicate countries. It is easy to see how this rule operates for continents and countries, less easy to draw up homogeneous classifications in some other areas of management knowledge, and this is important because this system is most likely to lose trainees when they try to follow jumps between different levels of classification. People also get lost in classification systems like this:

Personnel Problems
A: Group problems
    (i) union problems—official
                 —unofficial
    (ii) problems outside union members—unorganised staff
                                   —lower managers
                                   —middle managers
                                 —senior managers
B: Individual problems
    (i) personal domestic problems—family
                         —financial
    (ii) problems with other employees—subordinate
                                 —colleague
                                 —peer
                                 —manager
                                 —other

because they expect the classification system hanging underneath the heading B to be the same as the system following A. The two could be the same, of course, but there is no reason

why they should be, and the lecturer should be alert to ensure
that this kind of misunderstanding does not happen.

Obviously, any hierarchical ordering of the lecture material
should be obvious to the trainees while they are absorbing the
material; a chart or overhead projector slide permanently
displaying the system is a vital part of the lecture itself.

The question arises: given a bundle of disparate material
which can be classified in a number of ways, which one is the
right way? There are four main ways of organising the average
management trainer's material: by the concepts involved, by the
constraints involved, by the techniques used, and by the problems
to be solved. For example, suppose the lecture is about a new
range of cosmetics to be introduced by the firm, and the trainees
are sales managers. The trainer could organise his material by
the *concepts* involved: eye make-up, lipsticks, foundation cream,
perfumes, deodorants, etc. Under the first head he would list the
new forms of eye make-up, under two sub-heads: eye shadow and
mascara. Under the second head he would list the new lipsticks,
and so on. Or, he could choose to list the material by the
constraints affecting it: allergy-free make-up, low-allergenic
make-up, and make-up untested for allergic effects. He could
choose another constraint entirely as the basis for classification,
and list the good according to whether they were cheap, medium
range, expensive, or very expensive. As a third option, he could
organise the material according to the *techniques* involved, in
this case classifying how the goods are applied: with a
powder-puff, with the fingers, with a sponge, with a roll-on
device, with an aerosol, etc. Or he could list according to
problems to be solved: young spotty skin, dry skin, old leathery
skin, unsavoury armpits, and so on.

The sales managers will probably find the hierarchy of
concepts most useful to them; it is likely to match the way they
already think about the products. The trainer would therefore
organise his material around the concept hierarchy, and deliver
his presentation; later, after the managers have had time to
discuss the new products amongst themselves and work out some
of the implications for their own operation, the trainer would
review the material introducing briefly the next most important
hierarchy—the hierarchy of *problems*. However, when the sales
managers themselves come to brief their beauty consultants on
the new product range, it would pay them to present the material
first of all ordered by *problem*, because it is as problems that

customers present themselves for counselling; mostly they do not know what product they want to buy. The consultants' knowledge is later reinforced by taking them through the concept hierarchy. If the presentation were being made not to sales managers, but to product presentation managers, the first hierarchy to show them would probably be the *techniques* hierarchy, as so much depends in the cosmetic business on the way goods are presented and used; the research and development managers might be more interested in the division into different degrees of allergy-production.

If we have laboured the point about different kinds of hierarchy, we make no apology; too many lecturers know only one kind of hierarchy, the concept hierarchy, and they use it exclusively when the managers listening to them would get a much better grasp of the material if only it were presented classified according to problem. Listing the thirty-seven different ways of doing manpower planning may be a good way of lecturing to manpower planning experts, but with managers who don't recognise any way of doing manpower planning it is better to start with what they know—a discussion of different kinds of manpower problem, leading to a classification of problems, leading to a discussion of solutions and then, maybe, a classification of solutions. The point is to start with a classification system that they will recognise.

Having expounded the system one way, it is often wise to give the trainees an insight into the other ways they could order their new information. In order not to cause interference, this should not happen immediately after the first run-through of the hierarchy; one or two exercises and discussions to let the material settle, and then a new look.

2 *Comparison tables* are a useful way of presenting information when the similarities and differences between different concepts are to be examined in detail. Students of A-level chemistry will remember the hours spent drawing up compare-and-contrast tables between different kinds of organic compound: ketones and aldehydes, ethylenes and acetylenes, ortho-, para-, and meta- forms. A comparison table partly completed is a good draw for the audience's attention, if they are asked to suggest more parameters on which the concepts are compared; so the trainer should prepare his own completed table, but keep it in reserve until the audience have had their attempt at completion.

A partly completed comparison table might look like Figure 7.1, which is the basis of a lecture/discussion with personnel managers trying to get to grips with the anti-discrimination legislation in the UK. Even with a topic on which it might be thought few UK personnel managers would have much to contribute, it is worth getting them to assist in drawing up the table, for experience of only one side of the comparison enables one to suggest divisions that might occur. In discussion it is well

Anti-discrimination legislation

USA	UK
1 Legislation prohibits unfair discrimination on grounds of sex, age, and race.	1 Legislation prohibits unfair discrimination on grounds of sex and race but not age.
2 Onus of proof is legally on employer to prove his innocence.	2 Onus of proof is legally on employee to prove employer's guilt.
3 Quotas for proportion of minority group employees on payroll.	3 No quota system is proposed.
4 'Positive discrimination' in hiring and promotion is encouraged.	4 'Positive discrimination' in hiring and promotion is disallowed.
5 'Positive discrimination' in training programmes is encouraged.	5 'Positive discrimination' in training programmes is encouraged.
6 Guidelines exist on use of some psychological tests for purposes of selection and promotion.	6 No guidelines exist on use of psychological tests for purposes of selection and promotion.
7	7
8	8
9	9

Fig. 7.1 Comparison table, partly completed, on anti-discrimination legislation in the USA and UK

to let the suggestions come free-wheeling, but the lecturer may have organised the different parameters on his ready prepared chart, dividing them into (say) legal differences, practical differences, differences in testing procedure, differences in case law, for the sample table given above.

At the end of a lecture or discussion, trainees can be asked to draw up their own comparison tables, thus testing the knowledge they have absorbed and giving them an opportunity to organise it.

3 *The hypothetico-deductive narrative* is another way of

presenting information. We apologise for the title; polysyllabic though it is, it explains the order in which information is set out. The lecturer aims to take the trainees through the process of analysing data, forming hypotheses, testing the hypotheses, and formulating an explanation. Well done, it has all the excitement of a good detective story; audiences have been held spellbound by a good narrative for the whole of a morning. One such story was told by Don Bryant, of the Tavistock Institute, about labour turnover in lumber camps.

He began by setting out the different grades of people employed, and putting them into the context of the camp, the camp town, the local and provincial politics. Then he presented the figures for labour turnover in each grade: the problem as it had been presented to him. Next he went into the figures a little deeper, analysing the cost of recruiting and training each type of grade, and showed how this changed the nature of the problem; the costliest turnover was not in the grade with the highest numerical turnover. Then he described the jobs done by the people in each grade, and the results of exit interviews with leavers, and told how he had formed the hypothesis that the high labour turnover amongst skilled log-cutters (the costliest problem) was due to the de-skilling of their job by the introduction of computer-controlled sawing patterns; previously it had been left to their discretion how they cut the log so as to get the best return. He then described various 'natural experiments' looking at job satisfaction—as evidenced by the amount of skiving off to watch the television, etc.—when the computer had broken down. The audience was presented with his figures, which strongly supported his hypothesis, and were asked for their suggestions for upgrading the skill level of the job; after a long while someone suggested the obvious, that they should engineer a computer breakdown from time to time. Bryant agreed that this was the only practicable way of giving the men a skilled job back, even on a spasmodic basis, and said that this was what had actually happened; he presented the labour turnover figures for a period when the computer had been taken off-line for short random periods each day. Even when the men knew what was happening and why, they still showed a lower turnover and higher satisfaction.

To compress Bryant's story into so small a space is to do it less than justice, but it illustrates the progress of a hypothetico-deductive narrative, thus:

1 State the background.
2 Give the presenting problem.
3 Give the surface information.
4 Analyse this information more deeply.
5 Use this analysis to form a hypothesis.
6 State how the hypothesis is to be tested.
7 Narrate the testing of the hypothesis.
8 If hypothesis disproved, return to step 4.
9 If hypothesis upheld, discuss further hypotheses or remedial action.
10 If remedial action taken, discuss its outcomes.

All through the narrative the scientific method is being applied; all throught the narrative there are places to stop and question the trainees, or even give them the problem to analyse. When trainees have been presented with a large body of new knowledge, which they will have to apply themselves, a narrative describing the knowledge in action, solving problems, is a great help in putting things into perspective.

These three paradigms for organising lecture material help in the lecture presentation and in the lecture notes. Notes can serve a number of purposes; to give the bones of the lecture, to give the whole of the lecture, or to go further than the lecture. Most trainers prefer to hand out lecture notes at the very end—with the possible exception of a chart of the lecture structure if they choose so to present it—because there is nothing so distracting to a lecturer as watching his audience follow him in his notes to see how far he's got and whether he is departing from the text. It is worth telling the trainees if they can expect full notes, so they they do not try to capture everything themselves. Notes can sometimes contain copies of the slides and flip-charts, if they were used ready prepared.

Opinions differ on the use of slides (including acetate foils for overhead projectors) and flip-charts. One battle is fought between those who say the lecturer should come with slides ready prepared to save his audience's time and trouble reading his bad handwriting; the other side reply that an intelligent audience might feel insulted at the implication that its learning processes are sufficiently predictable to be drawn in advance. There is some evidence that a wandering audience's attention will be captured if the trainer pays it the compliment of writing specially on the flip-chart for it; it is our experience however that the different schools of thought are so firmly embedded in their respective organisations that the trainer who wants a hearing had better conform. Even if he does come with ready prepared flip-charts, however, he should not commit the error of reading the charts aloud for the assembled throng; the charts should amplify his words (by providing diagrams, etc.), or summarise them, but not duplicate them.

Any *examples* to be used in the lecture should be prepared in advance. As the trainees are taken through a hierarchy, or asked to amplify a comparison chart, the trainer will stop frequently to give instances of what he means, and if he relies on the spur of the moment for these examples he will undoubtedly dry up. We spent a week with a trainer in the travel industry, training sales supervisors; though full of job knowledge at lunch and tea time, when in front of a room full of trainees the only example of a difficult sales situation he could think of was a disabled old lady wondering if she would be able to get to the toilet during her journey. She was a well worn incontinent grandma by the time the course had finished, and it brought home the lesson that small examples, and the opening and closing phrases of the lecture, should always be available on a sheet of paper easily to hand.

Finally, how can the lecturer tell if his audience is following him? He can test at the end of the lecture or the course, but that may be too late. The following list of clues to an audience's state of mind can be used while the lecture is in progress, in time for corrections to be made:

1   Do the course members arrive on time, or drift in late?

2   Do they slump in their seats, or do they look alert?

3   When they talk amongst themselves, as they come into the room, are they talking about the course material, or about wine, women and song?

4   If they have freedom to choose where to sit, do they go to the back or come towards the front?

5   Do they ask questions of the trainer?

6   Do they ask questions of each other?

7   Do they answer questions readily, or do they look taken off-guard?

8   Do their lecture notes look a random hash, or do they appear to have some organisation—not necessarily the lecturer's own—behind them?

C   Discussion groups

These are often used in conjunction with lectures, as a way of getting the trainees to rehearse and organise what they have heard. They vary in length, composition, and task, from ten minutes tackling a single question to a whole day analysing a case study. Well planned, discussion groups counteract the passivity of lectures, bring out doubts and questions that people might have felt inhibited from voicing in the lecture itself, help to get a cohesive group established—and give the poor lecturer's voice a rest.

The kind of question people are asked in discussion groups affects the way they rehearse their knowledge—analytically, synthetically, free-wheeling or tightly focused. Questions can be categorised thus:

(a) *think of as many as possible*, e.g. 'Think of as many potential safety hazards as you possibly can.'
(b) *what's the answer?* e.g. 'Here are the consultant's notes on the Scientific and Universal Manufacturing Co. What would you recommend the managing director to do?'
(c) *how would you test?* e.g. 'Draw up a list of criteria that any system for identifying management potential must meet.'
(d) *what are the merits of?* e.g. 'Here is a proposal for a piggy-back advertising campaign giving away three of your products with every bicycle purchased. Comment on the merits of this proposal.'
(e) *what's the difference between?* e.g. 'How would this new pay bargaining structure differ from the old one as far as its effects on the Payroll department are concerned?'
(f) *what are the similarities between?* e.g. 'Here are some samples from someone who would like to be our supplier. They are 20 per cent cheaper than the products we already use: are they as good?'

Each of these questions uses the newly acquired knowledge in a different way, and the skilled trainer knows how to balance the tasks given to discussion groups so as to allow all appropriate types of rehearsal to take place. All the questions can be prepared in advance, and it is unwise to rely on the spur of the moment for inspiration; some require a good deal of information to be prepared in advance so that they can be used as case studies. It is never wise to put people into groups and say: 'Now discuss what you've learned for half an hour'. Always give them an objective to work towards, and a criterion for the completion of the task.

There are books of case studies ready prepared [3, 4] which the trainer may browse through for inspiration in preparing a long project; alternatively he can seek material from within his own firm. An interested line manager may be willing to be interviewed for case study material, and again· to review the range of possible answers; he may visit the course to take the case study himself, and if he is open minded enough to admit that there are other ways of solving the problem than the one he chose this makes for a very interesting session. Case study material shoud be updated for changes in money values, societal changes, and legal changes; there is one large consultancy in the UK still running case studies in which the shop-girls earn £9 for a 40-hour week! This destroys credibility, and gives trainees an excuse for holding the learning at arm's length if they disagree: 'It was too unrealistic, it wouldn't be like that today'.

When assigning people to discussion groups, it helps to put all the noisy ones in one group and all the quiet ones in another, if numbers allow. Thus the noisy ones cannot monopolise the proceedings as they would otherwise, and the low contributors are given a chance; these behaviour changes often last beyond the confines of the individual discussion group through to the rest of the course. If the trainees have been split into a number of groups, time should be allowed immediately afterwards for them to come together and share ideas under the guidance of the lecturer, who will have to work hard to ensure that all groups get equal time and there is some time left for general interchange afterwards.

D Tapes, films and video cassettes

These media are best used in support of a lecture or other formal input of knowledge; they are much less effective when used instead of a lecture. Used on their own, without prior lecturing or discussion, they can rapidly lose the trainees' attention—tapes especially are unable to give an advance picture of the layout of the information, so that it is easy for people to get lost in hierarchies or comparisons; narratives come out slightly better. Films vary greatly—we are not here concerned with the inspirational or attitude changing film, discussed in the next chapter. A bad film shows a lecturer lecturing to a non-existent audience; a good film uses voice, picture, diagrams, colour, and maybe music to make its points. For putting over pure knowledge, a film that the trainer can stop for a while, to discuss a point with the trainees, and then pick up again, is better than one telling a continuous narrative.

Tapes and video cassettes, which have a number of limitations when used with groups, can be used profitably by individuals taking advantage of technology to learn at their own pace. If after a lecture they are free to follow it up by browsing in the cassette library, all the better; they can wheel backwards and forwards, stop, take notes and run on to the end at their own pace. Doing this with a group means that very quickly the pace will be wrong for everyone.

An oft-heard objection to these techniques is their expense. Few companies can afford to have films custom made; so they must be bought or rented from a maker of training films. Inevitably the film maker chooses one industry to make his film in; inevitably the cry goes up after the film has ended: 'But we're different from that: there are no lessons in there for us.' This objection, if foreseen, is fairly easy to deal with; the difficulty is that film makers must choose topics of common management interest to make their films about, so that in-depth analysis and presentation of a new product, for example, is just not possible.

Planning a training course from scratch, the trainer cannot rely on finding a film for every need; he must go to the film library and see if there is one that fits. He must also plan the course so that minimum disruption is caused to course members by the hardware and preparations necessary for setting the film up; and he must have at least one course of action prepared for when the film breaks down.

E   Programmed instruction

In the previous chapter we stated that the trainer with a massive training programme, needing to cover lots of managers with essentially the same information, should consider having a programmed text designed to do the job. We also said that it was a job for experts; the task needs to be analysed so closely, and the thought processes of the learner understood so well, that the amateur might make mistakes or miss opportunities.

Programmed instruction has sometimes failed when used with industrial managers; in these cases the problem seems to be that they were not given a sufficiently comprehensive picture of where the procedure was taking them before the program came into operation, and the chunks of knowledge were so small, and tested so frequently, that managers felt their intelligence was being insulted and they were being prevented from taking an overview—that they were concentrating on the trees at the expense of the wood. These are valid points, and should be discussed with the designer of any programmed text the trainer may contemplate commissioning.

Though the design should be left to the experts, the place of programmed learning in a knowledge-based training course is something the trainer can decide. One good use is before the course—send the text out to managers a few weeks before they are to come on the course, with instructions to go through it before arriving. This has the twin benefits of evening up the base levels of knowledge of the trainees, and also priming them with something to talk about; indeed, some texts actually finish by asking the trainee to name three issues he wishes to bring up when he sees the trainer.

Actually doing a programmed instruction text on the course may seem a little wasteful—why pay people to sit in hotel rooms working out their answers when they could do it as easily in their office—but there are good reasons why PI is useful on courses. It can get people away from a group atmosphere, towards relying on their own thinking; useful when the course members are many in number and dominated in discussion by one or two noisy individuals. Some managers spend most of their working days meeting people and have forgotten how to concentrate alone on a problem for a long period of time; doing a programmed text reminds them what learning is all about, it throws them onto their own resources instead of allowing them to spend all their time reacting. A programmed text may be useful in setting the trainees up for a particularly important discussion; if the Marketing Director is taking an afternoon out of his busy schedule to come and address the course on the latest sales plan, then a text to familiarise the trainees with the sales plan helps ensure more concentrated questions. Programmed texts are also useful it the course members have drifted away from each other in their levels of knowledge—usually for good reasons—and need to be brought back to a common level of knowledge before the next part of the course can begin; they are also useful to have around if some of the course members would otherwise be at a loose end while others receive individual attention from the trainer(s). Some firms with multi-national technology and multi-national management systems have a programmed text available in a suite of computer programs which can be called up using a desktop computer terminal; with a quiet moment to spare one simply plugs into the last frame one was at and carries on from there.

F   Trainee talks

A good way of rehearsing knowledge and getting a discussion started is to ask the trainees themselves to take over the role of lecturer. This is best done a little way into the training course, when they have absorbed some knowledge and would feel moderately confident about public exposure. Experienced managers, for whom the lecturing has often been a clarification of what they already knew in parts, can use these talks to marry their own experience with what they have learned on the course; and the informality and sense of participation makes this a good way of filling the after-lunch or late evening spot.

Obviously it is best to give people a little time to prepare their talks, and not to press if someone seems very unwilling; also the gap between what they are asked to talk about and what the trainer has been talking about previously should not be so great as to be daunting—this exercise is for rehearsing knowledge, not revealing ignorance. One person only can give a talk or a short series can be requested; in either case comments from the rest of the trainees prove useful, but the comments and questions should be restricted to the content of the lecture, not to the lecturer's style.

G   Course design

With knowledge of the objectives of the training course, and familiarity with the training methods available, the trainer can now design the course proper. From the inside, course design feels more of an art than a science; one sketches programmes until they look right, and then tries them out. Part of the art,

Seminar One	*Seminar Two*

Seminar One

Day One

0900—0930	Introductions
0930—1100	The Act
1100—1115	Coffee
1115—1230	Our company's response
1230—1400	Lunch
1400—1530	Syndicate work: identify areas where our company is vulnerable
1530—1545	Tea
1545—1630	Syndicates report back
1630—1800	Accidents
1800—1930	Dinner
1930—2100	Film and discussion

Day Two

0900—1030	Our safety record
1030—1045	Coffee
1045—1230	Impact on collective bargaining and part-icipation procedures
1230—1400	Lunch
1400—1530	Syndicate work: identify the implications of the Act for the company
1530—1545	Tea
1545—1700	Syndicates report back and general discussion

Seminar Two

Day One

0900—0930	Introductions
0930—1100	The legislative context
1100—1115	Coffee
1115—1230	Counting the cost
1230—1400	Lunch
1400—1530	Syndicate work: identify up to three areas known to you or in your control where health and safety could be at risk
1500—1515	Tea
1515—1600	Syndicates report back
1600—1730	Looking after yourself
1730—1930	Dinner
1930—2100	Film, personal note-taking, and discussion

Day Two

0900—0945	In small groups, plan to interview the safety manager
0945—1045	Interview the safety manager
1045—1100	Coffee
1100—1230	Watching slides and film clips to identify the safety hazards
1230—1400	Lunch
1400—1500	Syndicate work: making action plans to implement on arrival back home
1500—1530	Report back in general session, to safety manager
1530—1545	Tea
1545—1700	Individuals make notes of their action plans. Suggestions for further reading. Discussion

Fig. 7.2   Two-day seminars on safety and health at work

though, lies in paying attention to the various rhythms in the learning process; the requirement to establish new learning and consolidate it before going on, the requirement not to overload people's memories, the need for variety of presentation, the need for relaxation, and the knowledge that some of them will go to sleep after lunch unless you physically take their chairs away.

Let us compare two two-day seminars on safety and health at work, designed for junior managers, to be run in-house by someone from the training department. Comparing the two seminars in Figure 7.2 it becomes obvious that the second is more likely to achieve its objectives than the first, especially if the objectives are directed towards getting the trainees to take action themselves.

In Seminar One, after the initial introductions we have a talk on the relevant Act of Parliament; compare this with Seminar Two, whose title suggests that the legal requirements will be discussed as they relate to the company. In the first we have a session on the law; in the second a session on how the law affects our business—much more likely to get attention. After coffee both seminars have a further talk; in the first one, a senior manager relates the company's reponse to the Act, thereby setting up the Act as a challenge and making the trainees think about strategy when (being junior managers) they ought to be thinking about how the Act affects themselves. The comparable session in the second seminar covers the costs—business and human—of poor safety and health precautions, and is given by a trade union representative who is there in his capacity as an expert in these matters, not speaking on behalf of his union. Both seminars use group discussions as an antidote to the after-lunch sleepiness, but in the first seminar they go on too long and the title is too general; the second seminar takes less time and asks them to think about areas they can affect themselves. Both seminars fill the time between syndicate report-back and dinner with a talk from the company doctor, but in the second seminar his talk is given a personal reference—looking after one's own health and safety. The two seminars differ in the way they handle the after-dinner film; though it is the same film in both seminars, after it is shown in the second seminar trainees are asked to take ten minutes or so to make personal notes of what they have learned before participating in a general discussion.

Both seminars have a visit from the safety manager on the

morning of the second day; in the first one he lectures—which must be getting a bit dull by now—whereas in the second one the trainees spend some time in small groups planning to interview him, and then they question him; a more lively approach that will hold their attention better. The first seminar has another lecture after coffee, again at the level of company policy which, while important, should not be the cornerstone of such a seminar for *junior* managers; the second group are shown a series of short films and photographs in which they have to identify the safety hazards. In the first group, the safety manager leaves after coffee; in the second group he stays to hear the comments people make about the film clips, to add his own anecdotes and stories which will help the participants remember. Both seminars have syndicate work in the afternoon, but the second group is under more pressure and is given tasks of greater personal relevance; the first group reports back to the trainer, while the second has the safety manager present (who therefore helps to ensure that the good resolutions made on the course are put into practice back home). Both seminars finish with a general round-up, but the second one makes space for the trainees to write down for themselves what each is going to do better.

An overall comparison of the two seminars shows that the second has more variety of teaching techniques; uses tasks and lecturers which emphasise the relevance of the subject matter to each person concerned; makes a determined attempt to bridge the gap between 'course' and 'real life' by the presence of the safety manager and by asking trainees to write personal memoranda; and gives the trainer slightly more opportunity to alter the course programme to fit the requirements of individual trainees. Before being totally satisfied with the course design, however, the trainer should run a pilot programme (if this is a course that will be repeated many times) and discover what further alterations are necessary.

Much of the remaining skill in course design is the ability to put oneself in the shoes of the complete novice, to guess at the best way to make him hungry for new information; and having experienced this, to know how one's course should be modified when the trainees already have some knowledge. We learned this the hard way with a series of seminars on the identification of management potential. When this seminar is given to a group of people who already know something of the problems and techniques available, it is appropriate to progress from broad manpower planning considerations to the methods available for diagnosing effective management performance in a particular firm; then to move to the range of techniques available, and finally to consider some of the more promising techniques in detail. When given to people without experience in this field, however, the seminar must be changed so as to catch their attention early, and to uncover for themselves some of the problems which the more experienced people have already grappled with: so we begin by presenting the range of techniques, some of which will be familiar to everyone present; demonstrate one or two of them; then, having established that it's no good choosing a technique until you know what you want it to look for, we introduce the methods of diagnosing management effectiveness. Then we look at some of the techniques in more detail; and we treat manpower planning issues as part of the final discussion, when someone is certain to ask a question which provides the opportunity to mention manpower planning. Had we started the novice group with a review of background considerations, probably several steps removed from what they thought the problems of identifying potential were, we would have lost them by the middle of the first day. It is important to begin the course with material that is fairly familiar to the trainee; this implies that when teaching a technique the trainer must ask himself whether the trainees are familiar with the technique itself, with the problems the technique is intended to solve, or with the deeper background. Then he must start with what is familiar, and fill in the gaps as they arise.

H   Summary

New knowledge can be imparted by a variety of techniques, the chief of which is the lecture. Discussion groups, tapes, films, video cassettes, programmed instruction and short talks by the trainees can all be used with lectures to build up a varied programme in which the trainees are not too passive; some of these other techniques, like programmed instruction, can be used on their own. The amount of information imparted at a time is governed by the need to let people rehearse new knowledge before building on that knowledge with additional information. By correct pacing and planning the flow of information the trainer can help keep forgetting to a minimum.

I   Discussion questions

1   What are the problems most likely to be experienced by a foreigner with moderately fluent English listening to a lecture in English; watching English management films; and taking part in discussions? What can the trainer do to reduce problems?

2   Some lecturers like to prepare full handouts covering their chosen topic so that during the lecture itself they can concentrate on one or two aspects or highlights. Audiences who like this feel it makes the lecture more participative and responsive to their needs; audiences who dislike it say that it seems unstructured and gives them no guide to taking notes. Under what circumstances will they be right?

3   'Programmed instruction doesn't always succeed with the British, because they feel it's somehow immoral to be forced into a position of getting the answers right—it's like looking them up in the back of the book.' Thus said one well known psychologist; do you agree?

4   You want to show your trainees a film about industrial espionage, so as to increase their security awareness. The only film you can find is set in a firm making aircraft (if the reader's firm actually does make aircraft, please substitute textiles). You know that some of your trainees will object to the film because, they say, the problems of your own industry are unique and cannot be represented in a film set in a different industry. Find twenty separate arguments—logical and psychological—with which to respond.

J   Further reading

[1] D. A. BLIGH. *What's the Use of Lectures?* Penguin Education, 1972.
A very clear book setting out the arguments for and against using lectures, giving clear hints on how to structure and deliver a lecture, and advice on what else to use. Not specifically related to the industrial context, but losing nothing thereby; an excellent book.

[2] M. J. A. HOWE (ed.). *Adult Learning*, Wiley, 1977.
A mixed bag of contributions to the topic of adult learning, written by specialists with laymen in mind. Chapter 6 and 7 have advice on learning strategy, useful (when translated by the

trainer) for the manager who has forgotten how to cope with formal tuition; Chapter 9 is a good summary of programmed learning; Chapter 12 is an invaluable guide to the layout of material (a great obstacle to learning when wrong, but something nobody thinks about usually).

[3] R. McLENNAN. *Cases in Organisational Behaviour*, Allen and Unwin, 1975.

[4] *Bacie Case Studies*, British Association for Commercial and Industrial Education, 1970.

These are two books of case studies which the trainer may find useful when preparing course material. The first contains complex material about sophisticated organisational problems, often taking several pages to expound; the second consists of many short cases, of varying degrees of difficulty, with full guidance to the trainer on how to conduct case study exercises. Many people find that in browsing through books of case studies they think of many other incidents known to them which could easily be turned into a case study.

8 Internal training courses: skills-based

A The essentials revisited

Learning a skill requires that three things be present: opportunity for practice, plenty of feedback, and a low risk environment. If these are not present, skills will not be learned; yet the great problem of designing skills-based courses is the provision of a rich environment for all the trainees. The many courses in interviewing or public speaking which assemble a group of trainees around a flip-chart and television camera, giving each person one, or at most two, chances to perform in front of the camera while spending the rest of the time watching the others, provide a shockingly impoverished training environment; yet many trainers think this is the best that they can do.

In Chapter Six, reviewing the trainer's options, we advised that the length of time spent in training was dictated by the length of time taken to practice each skill, with feedback, and the number of times the trainee would have to go through the feedback loop. The key to getting a rich training programme, with lots of practice for everyone, is to break up the skills into mini-skills; statements of what the trainee needs to do better at the end of the course. Thus, it is better to say: 'In a group Joe needs to listen more, to support other people more, and to allow his ideas to be taken up and modified by other people,' rather than saying: 'Joe needs training in teamwork.' It is easy to design exercises for the first statement, exercises which give lots of practice and feedback; much more difficult for the second. Rackham's books [1, 2] are full of examples of how this can be done.

In the first part of this chapter we discuss the different kinds of exercise that can be used for skill improvement, with examples. Then we look at the different ways feedback can be provided, and go on to examine the general problems of course design. Before doing so, though, let us state a personal prejudice. We believe that it is nearly always better for a trainer to design exercises using material from his own firm, rather than to buy exercises in. The increased credibility is usually enormous; it is useful for the trainer to get to grips with organisational problems in depth, which is what he needs to do when designing exercises; from time to time courses have produced solutions which the organisation can implement; and one is insuring against the objection: 'This is only a course; it's not like this in real life'. There are good reasons for buying exercises in if the course is about skills or problems which the organisation has not experienced yet; or when the trainer has a group of trainees some of whom might already be familiar with the material and he wants to use something equally unfamiliar to all. Exercises which require people to take a deep interest in something—like role-plays, for example—lose greatly when taken from a different industry.

B Exercise design

1 *Individual exercises* are, as their name implies, done by the trainees working alone; though they may meet as a group later to discuss the exercise. Some examples of individual exercises to increase skill are:

(a) *language laboratories*, in which trainees work through a series of exercises recorded on tape, while connected through headphones to a tutor in the central point. Though each trainee works alone in a soundproof booth, the tutor monitors each one's progress and can intervene, through the headphones, to correct grammer or pronunciation. The language laboratory principle is only useful for speech skills, but if a group of managers must be trained or refreshed in their foreign languages this is a very efficient way to go about it.

(b) *interactive computer programs*, in which the trainee sits at a computer console and a program stored in the computer types out questions for him. The computer is programmed to store and/or analyse the answers, and to adjust its questions accordingly. The range of skills that can be taught this way is enormous—thinking and reasoning skills are especially good material. For example, one computer program presents the trainee with a range of possible answers—red, blue, green, and yellow—and asks him to predict which one the computer will choose next. The trainee then discovers if he is right or wrong, and the game continues until either the trainee is guessing right all the time or the computer asks for his estimate of the likelihood that each colour will come up. At the start of the program, for instance, the colours are programmed to appear in the ratio red:blue:green:yellow::50:30:10:10, and it is an interesting phenomenon that most people who have spotted the approximate ratios will guess 5 reds to 3 blues to each green and yellow, whereas if they wanted to maximise their correct guesses they would predict red every time. The computer is expecting this, and goes into a little programmed learning routine about probability until the trainee understands; then the level of sophistication increases, until finally the trainee is being asked to make complex interpretations of data and complex decisions. Many other technical skills are amenable to computer-programming, if the size of the training need justifies it or if there is a systems analyst looking for a little job enrichment.

(c) *in-baskets* can be used to teach both technical and interpersonal skills, though not the face-to-face kind. A typical in-basket instructs the participant to imagine that he has just been promoted to position X (say Plant Manager). He comes in to his new office for the first time on Saturday morning, in a hurry because he has to leave in ninety minutes to catch a 'plane to Aberdeen where he will be in continuous conference for the next four days. As it is a Saturday there is no-one else in the office, and the switchboard is not working; therefor he cannot talk to anyone. In his in-tray he finds the pile of papers which forms the contents of the bulky envelope he is now handed; his task is to work through it as if he were X, dealing with the items as best he can.

In-baskets vary according to the job to be done and the skills to be exercised, but most would contain some of the following types of item:

management information, e.g. manager's manual, day-to-day planner, organisation chart, building plan, welcoming note from predecessor giving thumbnail sketches of the new manager's team, budget statements;
queries demanding an immediate answer, e.g. a request to substitute constituent X for constituent Y at a point in the plant's process, a note from a gatekeeper hoping that the manager will support him for having reported people who were leaving early because of fog;
queries he must see the need to delegate, e.g. requests for him to

do things next Monday, letters to him as Plant Manager that should have gone to Sales or Legal department, notes which he can give to a subordinate to deal with;
items he should not bother with, e.g. long questionnaires from a maker of office furniture on how they can improve their marketing, yesterday's newspaper.

In-baskets can be of varying degrees of difficulty. The more complex ones expect the manager to see the hidden implications of an apparently innocuous memorandum; or to put several pieces of information together to reveal a more serious problem, or a greater opportunity, than was apparent from looking at any one. Technical, administrative, financial and interpersonal skills can all be exercised, depending on how the items are written; getting a line manager to collaborate in writing some of the items—and providing a list of sample 'good' and 'bad' answers—is an education for all concerned.

Incidentally, it was through the involvement of line managers that we had our prejudices about writing the exercises in the organisation's own language confirmed. We had designed an in-basket for plant managers in one firm, and (with their permission) showed it to a manager in another firm for whom we were also designing training, hoping that this would inspire him to produce some useful in-basket items. There was therefore a fair degree of similarity between the items in the two in-baskets—both for plant managers, roughly the same level and financial responsibility—but the answers differed enormously. A right answer in firm A was often less than good in firm B, and vice-versa; and there were good organisational reasons why this should be so. Off-the-peg in-baskets are a bad idea; designing your own is fascinating.

Because of the concentration which the in-basket demands, and the effort the trainee puts into it, it is worth planning interviews with each trainee after the in-baskets have been marked. Feedback can be given, and the answers he gave, and his reasons, discussed. If individual feedback is just not possible, then in-baskets should be returned marked and commented on, and a group session in which the items are discussed one by one, and the answers, should be held; the more participative this can be, the better.

(d) *book reviews* are used to practise skills of abstraction, and skills of processing unpleasant information. Books, papers, reports, etc., are given to the trainees, who have to prepare a précis to a given purpose: e.g. 'Study this ITB document and see what implications there are for the Managing Director'. This is followed by a review and a further practice session. It is surprising how few adults have any skill in précis, so that the review can be largely vocabulary-enhancing, concentrating on methods of skipping, page lay-out, marking documents, etc.

Slightly different, but more germane to many managers' training needs, are the skills of looking at information one doesn't like, or presented in unpalatable form, while taking it in the understanding what it says. This skill is a clear differentiator between effective and ineffective managers wherever one looks. The products of Marxist bookshops serve for this exercise with most managers: *The Hazards of Work*, [3] a virulently anti-capitalist guide to safety and health at work, presents some irrefutable and shaming examples of safety hazards ignored for profit and/or comfort. Given to production managers, with the brief to review it on two sides of A4, it separates those who are totally put off by the book's politics from those who can nonetheless understand its message; a review and discussion with the trainer brings home the need for this skill and some advice on how to develop it. Suitable books exist for just about every organisation and profession.

(e) *mathetics* is a much neglected approach to teaching those skills whose performance can be broken down into stages. Its strength can be demonstrated by teaching someone to make origami figures—the ones made from paper folded and re-folded. The *usual* way is to start with a blank sheet of paper, and tell him how to make his first fold; then the second fold, and the third, and so on until the figure is completed. Then a second piece of paper: how much does he remember himself? when does he get lost? how many times do you have to remind him? It is a simple matter to count the number of tries he must make before succeeding in making a figure himself.

Teaching the mathetics way, the trainer begins by handing the trainee a paper almost completely folded, but with the last step missing. He tells the trainee how to complete the last step. Then he gives him a piece complete except for the last two stages; tells him the next move to make; and the trainee completes it for himself. Next a piece of paper complete except for the last three steps, and so on until one starts from a blank sheet. Usually one finds that the number of tries needed to learn the procedure is much shorter, and that forgetting happens less. The reasons are obvious when one experiences the method; the satisfaction of completion every time is a great reward, and the fact that one learns only one new step each time but rehearses all the others means that a lot of practice is achieved.

The mathetics approach has obvious uses in non-managerial training in industry—training an airline reservations clerk to fill in a ticket, for example. It can be used when training managers in skills that involve *procedures*—many financial skills, diagnostic skills, data-preparation skills, etc. The trainer must prepare according to a slightly different schedule, but the resulting improvements in training time and trainee motivation will be worth it.

2   *Structured group exercises* form the basis of many skills training courses, especially those concerned with interactive skills. The basic idea is that a small group of people—two, three, up to eight in number—have a common task to do. The task itself may practise some of their technical skills, and performing the task with other people practises their interactive skills. The balance between technical content and interactive content has often been the cause of controversy and argument.

It is quite common for the trainer to assign the task to the group but to take no part in the actual group process himself; especially when the members' interactive skills are being exercised it would be inappropriate for the trainer to take over the leadership or assume a key position. The trainer may well take part in the review which follows the exercise, in which technical and interpersonal points can be discussed and feedback given.

Among the many examples of group exercises which managers find themselves taking part in are:

(a) *brain-storming groups* where the group is given a problem and told to think of as many possible answers as they can, according to certain ground rules. No idea may be criticised, by its producer or anyone else; all ideas are welcome, however outrageous or stupid. Ideas are written down by a scribe as they appear. When the group dries up for the first time, a short period of silence is imposed, followed by a second round of ideas. *Then* a group evaluation of the ideas follows, with special efforts made to get the odder ones examined before they are thrown out. Brain-storming is useful for developing technical abilities, and the ability to produce and pay attention to novel and startling ideas. It is useful early on in a training course, to get people limbered up and to emphasise the risk-free atmosphere; where the topic is one of live concern to the organisation there is occasionally the additional benefit of an idea which works.

(b) *synectics groups* form a problem-solving team brought together for that purpose, and designed with problem-solving in mind. Some of the ideas used in these problem-solving groups are adaptable for use on training courses. Typically the group is given a problem to examine, but there is one ground-rule; nobody must criticise an idea before he has previously stated three things about it that are good. From the ideas point of view, this makes sure that uncertain, half-formed, wavering ideas are given the chance to grow a little before being stamped on; from the interactive point of view, it gives people practice in listening to others' ideas, supporting and building on them.

(c) *general discussion groups* where an issue is presented for discussion: 'What will the competition be doing in five years' time?' or 'What are the qualities necessary for leadership in a nationalised industry?' and so on. Usually the content of the discussion is less important than the interactive purposes; it is this sort of discussion that is used, with varying degrees of success, to practise chairmanship, teamwork, participativeness, supportiveness, etc. The success of the exercise depends on the feedback mechanism used—the tighter and more objective the better—and on the personal learning objectives of the people taking part. 'Have half-an-hour's discussion about Concorde, and it will help Joe practise his chairmanship', is less effective than a short session beforehand in which specific behavioural objectives are set for the exercise, e.g. 'Joe is going to try to make sure that no proposals get lost, that agreement is specifically sought rather than taken for granted, that all items on the agenda are included, and that Malcolm does not interrupt Henry; Henry is going to practise his supporting behaviour, and is going to try to cut down the amount of gratuitous information he gives people; Malcolm is going to cut down on his interrupting, and try instead to bring more people into the conversation . . .'. With objectives as tightly set as this, general discussion groups work well. Slacker individual objectives mean that learning is harder for everyone to assess.

(d) *planning groups* may tackle a task for its technical content, its interpersonal content, or both. A great variety is possible:

'Plan a town; plan an office; plan to launch a new product; plan to interview the R & D Director when he visits the course on Thursday; plan a menu for the course dinner . . .'. Skills to be exercised here include chairmanship and/or group leadership; sequencing skills; skills of extracting information; the ability to see the consequences higher up the organisation, and lower down, of particular decisions, the ability to see things from someone else's point of view, and technical skills such as information processing, critical path analysis, etc.

(e) *information extraction groups* are given the task of interviewing X to discover what he knows about an issue, what his problem is, and so on. Usually the group is given enough time to prepare amongst themselves before calling X in, though some will go ahead and bring him in without planning. This is especially useful for practising skills of planning and job assignment, and skills of extraction of information and summarising. Such groups are a useful preliminary to an interviewing training course, for example, to bring home the need for careful preparation beforehand and co-ordinated interpretation afterwards.

(f) *physical task groups* are given a real live task to perform— making and selling widgets, sorting through newspapers, fixing a machine. Technical skills may be addressed here, but more often the objective is to learn about and practise working under pressure, against the clock, in a confined space, or with an ambiguous task to perform. Where the task is itself unimportant, e.g. making paper aeroplanes, the trainer has to work doubly hard during the review sessions to make sure that the lessons have gone home and have been generalised; it is easy for people to get caught up in the details of the task, maybe refighting some battles during the review period, and they may need help to see that the lessons are transferable. This help is not always easy to give, especially when trainees have had a hard time during the task and would prefer to forget it and the fools they made of themselves; physical tasks should therefore be used with care, and where there is an opportunity to concentrate on something outside the task itself. For example, the manager of the task could be appraised on his performance, and the group's attention directed towards the process of appraisal; the group could be asked to do the task again and improve on their performance, after which the trainer leads into a discussion of standard setting, how people's ideas of standards differ, and how this relates back to the daily business of coaching subordinates and trying to improve their performance.

From these examples of structured group exercises it is possible to see that most of them could be used for technical training, or interpersonal skills training, or both. The dichotomy between 'task' and 'process' is seen at its clearest in programmes like Coverdale training, where managers are given paper hats to make, Lego-brick towers to build, and holiday brochures to sort through. The belief is that a task which is in itself unimportant will allow managers to concentrate on the group processes and improve their interactive skills without the distraction of technical demands. Though a plausible assumption, it has not always been proved in practice; we have seen a number of unpublished studies comparing nonsense tasks with job-relevant tasks, and the general consensus is that it is possible to get just as much learning (as measured by behaviour change during the course) with job-relevant tasks, and that furthermore these tasks do not antagonise managers as much as being asked to make paper aeroplanes. The occasional content-free task is useful: it emphasises the low risk atmosphere, it may entice people to try totally new ways of behaving, it isolates 'process' for a length of time no greater than managers find convenient to deal with. In general, though, it is safe to use tasks with a certain degree of job-relevance even when the course is purely directed towards interactive skills.

3 *Unstructured group exercises* are often used in management training, but represent very difficult and dangerous ground for the amateur. Most people have heard of T-groups; there was a vogue for this type of training for managers in the late 1960s and early 1970s. Encounter groups, and sensitivity training, have come along since then, with a deliberate attempt to reduce even further the structure and assumptions people bring to a training course.

An unstructured group exercise may be planned for a short time, say half an hour, but most of them are intended to take hours or even days to complete. Typically they begin with the group arriving in a room with tables and chairs, and a 'trainer' who welcomes them with the minimum amount of information and then gives them a task description which is as indeterminate as possible: 'Your task in these five days is to discuss the reality of the here and now'. He then retreats into a corner, though still watching the group, and will not be drawn to say more.

What happens next is fairly predictable. There is a long silence, punctuated perhaps by attempts to ask the trainer questions, which he ignores. Then one or two people in the group say 'Well, we'd better make a start on this—anybody got any suggestions how we should tackle it?' and the task is repeated. One or two people may volunteer their opinions about the reality of the here and now; others will suggest that the group ought to have a chairman, and maybe a secretary also. In the early stages of the group this faction wins, and various formal or semi-formal attempts to get to grip with the 'subject' are made. Gradually the group members come to rebel against the formal framework, which doesn't seem to be getting them anywhere, and the conversation becomes more wide ranging; subgroups form; attempts are made to get the trainer involved, which he usually refuses, and so on. The end result of this fragmentation process is that people begin to talk about themselves, their relationships, their problems, and how they see each other. By subtle comments and interjections the trainer can influence the way this stage progresses, forcing people to confront difficult personal issues, provoking emotional catharses, or calming the situation down. It is not uncommon for T-groups to be a deeply emotional and personal experience.

After the initial phases—trying to rely on the trainer, and being rebuffed—the group may be given things to do by the trainer; discussion topics or exercises. Some trainers use very intimate exercises, encouraging group members to touch each other, to try to communicate without using words, to play children's games; at the extreme there are the training groups whose members are encouraged to do their work in the nude. It is important to make clear that most of the T-groups which managers and management trainers are likely to encounter do not go to these extremes.

The lack of structure, and the emphasis on the 'personal' or 'process' rather than on specific content, are the unique features of T-groups, and they have attracted attention and controversy since their inception. Most trainers have heard stories of participants being badly damaged by T-group experience; they may also have met managers who say that their T-group was the most fundamental thing that ever happened to them. More puzzling than that are the reactions of participants who say: 'It taught me a lot, but I didn't learn anything until six months afterwards'. Studies of managers' reactions to T-groups, and evaluations of their behaviour change, have been bedevilled by the large number of variables involved: in-house groups may be different from stranger groups, volunteer groups different from conscript groups, groups run by one trainer different from groups run by another. This has led to wide variations in the proportions of people described as 'hurt' or 'helped' by their T-group experience. A study commissioned by the Training Services Agency [4] examined the T-groups run by five reputable training organisations for UK managers, and concluded that on a short term basis about 5 per cent of the participants had been hurt by the programme, and about 30 per cent had been helped; but that some of those deemed to have been hurt had recovered, or even moved into the 'helped' category, when followed up after seven months. The study makes the point that damage is most likely to occur when:

Trainee is taciturn and serious; shy and timid; introverted and self-sufficient.

Trainer is assertive, aggressive, uninhibited; spontaneous; impulsive and lively; sensitive and open.

Group culture is focused on social interaction (the here and now); relatively intimate; relatively confronting; relatively person centred; and relatively less structured

and that positive outcomes are most likely to occur when:

Trainee is self-sufficient; conservative; somewhat tense and apprehensive; somewhat controlled.

Trainer is a social engineer, i.e. personally and socially supportive; having a low anxiety level; somewhat relaxed; with low involvement.

Group culture is highly structured; low level of intimacy; little confrontation; little focus on social interaction (in the here and now); low level of intra-group support but little rejection within the group.

All the studies of the outcomes of T-groups regard as positive outcomes statements like 'improved relationships', 'coping better', 'emotionally more stable', 'more trusting and adaptable', and so on. Few if any ask questions about improved work performance, especially the 'how many more widgets out on the back of the lorry today?' type of question. Trainer and trainee must approach T-groups as *personal* training, not *management* training; not just about work relationships but family and social relationships also. If the trainer still wishes to use T-groups, or to investigate them further, then we suggest the following policy guidelines:

1   They should never be run by amateurs. The professional trainer who has himself attended one or two T-groups remains an amateur for this purpose.

2   They should be run by people with industrial experience who are anxious to help industry work better. Eschew the nude Marxist meetings eating macrobiotic foods in a deconsecrated church.

3   Participation in a T-group should be completely voluntary. Indeed it should be rather difficult to get admission; and nobody should be allowed to nominate another person, or himself, on the grounds that he is sick or in need of treatment.

4   The trainer should make the purposes of the T-group clear in advance. The length of time involved, the other people involved, the personal rather than business orientation of the training, and the degree of confidentiality of information, should all be made clear well in advance.

5   A decision must be taken, on professional advice, whether to send people to 'stranger' groups or to run groups in-house. If the latter course is advocated people in direct reporting relationships to each other should not be assigned to the same group.

6   Participants should be known to the trainer who nominates them, and should be screened with a questionnaire and/or interview. People who are ill, or have domestic problems, should not take part.

7   A follow-up counselling service should be provided for those who need it.

8   No-one should have access to T-group data who could be in a position to use those data to influence the careers of the trainees, and the confidentiality of the information must be respected at all times.

In summary, it is better for the amateur trainer, including people who have run training courses for years, to keep off unstructured exercises unless they are very sure of themselves and their purposes. Nearly all the training needs managers present can be dealt with without venturing into the seductive realms of unstructured group exercises.

4   *Role play exercises* are a popular way of teaching interactive skills. Participants—usually two, but sometimes more—are given a sheet of paper containing brief details about a person and the business issue he is involved with. For example, participant A is given a character sketch of Joe, the supervisor; the group Joe manages; and the recent behaviour of Fred, a member of the team whose attitude to safety has been somewhat lax lately. A recent incident in which Fred disregarded the warnings on some cyanoacrylate glue and stuck his eyelids together for four days is described. Participant B is given a character sketch of Fred, including the recent incident, and details of a domestic problem which has been on Fred's mind for a while. After A and B have read their role descriptions and planned their tactics, they meet for a discussion, taking the parts of Joe and Fred. In conducting the discussion they learn—one hopes—some counselling and problem-solving skills, as will the trainees who are not taking part in the role play but are looking on.

Role play runs the gamut of effectiveness from excellent to detrimental. When it is well done, it reduces the participants' risk, by giving them small circumscribed parts to play, and mini-problems to deal with, in a situation that is obviously off-line. It is badly done when the emphasis moves from learning to performance, i.e. when people are judged on how well they play parts; when the observers have no guide to observing, and when the trainer selects role plays which are irritatingly different in work content from the jobs the managers have to do in real life.

There are at least four ways in which role plays can be scheduled:

(a) *A is Fred and B is Joe:* the most common form, outlined above. Most often this is done with two participants—counselling, performance appraisal, selling, selection interviewing, etc.—or with a small group of participants acting as a team—a problem-solving task force, the members of a board, a pair of negotiating groups. Because it is the most common form it is the most open to abuse; during the review comments can be heard: 'It wouldn't be like that in real life', or 'This is an incomplete role description and I did my best'. These comments indicate one of two things: either the experience has proved thought provoking for the trainees, and they are trying to hold the learning at arm's length because of its implications for behaviour change; or the task was not relevant to their jobs as managers and they genuinely can't see the point. To avoid this latter difficulty role descriptions should always be adapted for one's own firm: job titles, amounts of money, and organisational expectations should be adjusted. It's no good giving a pair of local government administrators in Harrow a role play written for production line foremen in Detroit.

If the role play has observers, then they should be briefed for particular things to look for, and encouraged to report these in the review session. It is unhelpful to hear comments like 'I thought you played it very well', and 'If I'd been doing it I wouldn't have said that', which the unbriefed observer will volunteer; much better if they have been given a schedule of specific skills to observe—questioning, listening, summarising, asking for the order, and so on.

(b) *real life counselling* removes the need for some of the unreality which people may find unhelpful in role plays. Used specifically for teaching counselling skills, it involves taking a trainee who has a genuine work problem (or, sometimes, a personal problem) and inviting him to be counselled by another trainee or group of trainees. Care must be taken to see that no-one is pressed into revealing details about himself that he would rather not uncover; and again the observers need a careful briefing. Well done, though, this is a way of getting over points which are very difficult to instil otherwise—points about listening, about the speed counsellors should adopt, and about the fact that one can only counsel the person who comes with the problem, not the other people involved.

(c) *reverse role play for attitude change.* If one of the aims of the training is to make people more sensitive to other people's feelings, and more sympathetic towards them, the trainer can take advantage of role play as a vehicle for inducing attitude change. If, for example, managers are to be trained in handling the problems caused by making people redundant, and it is thought that the present management team is too unsympathetic to do this with finesse, then a manager may be asked to role play the part of someone who has been made redundant discussing the matter with his boss. This will make him much better at dealing with redundant workers himself. Similar considerations apply to salesmen (make them role play buyers), to selection interviewers (make them role play applicants), to managers doing performance appraisal (make them role play appraisees), to finance managers (make them role play the merchant banker), and so on. This is a powerful weapon for changing attitudes that have become entrenched—racial prejudice, anti-feminism, and so on.

(d) *forcible character change.* Sometimes on an interactive skills course a trainee arrives who is obviously fearful, unwilling to experiment, a little scared of putting a foot wrong. One way to get him to shake loose and to demonstrate that this is a low risk environment is to give him a role play exercise with deliberate instructions to change his style: thus, 'Interview this salesman as if you were Robin Day', or 'Make a ten-minute presentation on the new product, but make every mistake in the book'. Useful tips may arise during the conduct of the actual role play, but the chief advantage is its unfreezing quality.

5   *Group to solo exercises* are a way of geting more people involved in the conduct of an exercise than is allowed by, for example, two-person role play. The trainer is constantly faced by the problem of organising lots of practice for everyone, and some role plays and group discussions allow people to opt out. The *group to solo* method of exercise design tries to overcome this problem, by getting everyone involved in the preparation of a task as much as possible, but selecting at the last minute only one or two to take part. Some examples of this method in action are:

(a) *the tape-stop exercise.* Trainees sit around a tape recorder on which is played a conversation between various people— customer and sales manager, consultant and client, manager and employee with a grievance, etc. From time to time the tape is stopped, just as the key person is about to give a reply; the trainees' job is either to write down what they would say next if they were in that position, or to say aloud what they would say next should the trainer actually point to them. For example, here is an excerpt from a meeting between consultant and client:

Client: I'm not at all happy that you want me to feed these results back to my group. I think you should do it—you're the ones who did the survey, after all.
Consultant: They'd have much more credibility if they came from you.
Client: I don't agree. I think you're trying to duck out of presenting unpleasant information.
Consultant: . . . .

The trainer stops the tape and points to one of the listening trainees, who must respond quickly and directly (not 'I would say something like . . .'). The trainer can either stop to discuss that reply there and then, or he can re-start the tape, see what the consultant actually did say, and carry on. This is more immediate than getting people to write their answers down, but has a less complete coverage. When people are asked to write down what they would say, there is a splendid opportunity for content-analysing the responses later and presenting group or individual feedback on that basis. The group of novice consultants trained using the tape quoted above had their answers classified into Reflective and Directive—reflective answers pushing the problem gently back at the client, directive answers telling him what to do—and this provoked a useful discussion of consultant style as well as indicating what kinds of assignment would suit each consultant.

Professionally prepared tape-stop exercises are available for some kinds of job—chiefly in the sales area—but it is quite easy to design one's own. The amateur designer always begins by looking for tremendously important interactions to get on tape, and of course is disappointed; in fact the daily bread and butter of the job is the best basis on which to design a tape-stop.

(b) *the appraisal module* described more fully in our book on performance appraisal [5] is another example of group to solo exercise. In front of a group of trainees someone does something appraisable—gives a short talk, mends a fuse, sews on a button. Then everyone prepares to appraise the performance. One person is selected by the trainer to perform the appraisal; the rest look on. Then everyone prepares to appraise the appraisal, and one is selected to do it; after which there is a group review. This basic module is adaptable for all sorts of appraisal problem— looking at objective-setting, appraisal for improvement, appraisal on someone else's performance, etc.—and something of the strength of the group-to-solo method may be estimated from a comparison we made between managers trained by this process and comparable managers trained by role play; eighteen months after the training the group-to-solo trained managers were much further ahead than the others in clearing their backlog of appraisals, and their subordinates' satisfaction with the appraisal interview was on average one point higher on a five point scale.

(c) *controlled pace negotiation* is an exercise devised by Neil Rackham [6] which exploits some of the group-to-solo features and in addition slows down the pace of the exercise to give people time to reflect. The trainer divides the trainees into two groups, A and B. He visits group A and presents them with a problem— a minor problem, such as there not being enough cups of tea to go round, or a major problem, such as the extent to which group A managers should carry group B's problems (A being Sales and B Production, say). The problem should be genuinely relevant to the parties involved. After the trainer has stated the problem each person in group A has three minutes or so to write down the message he wishes the trainer to take to group B. When they have finished, as individuals, they must choose as a group which message they wish the trainer to take. They are not allowed to composite the various messages—just choose one. The trainer leaves them, delivers the message to group B, and goes through the same process there. Thus a gradual interchange of messages between the groups builds up.

While the trainer is out of the room, the group can discuss strategy and tactics if it so wishes. Alternatively the trainer may set it the task of categorising its own message against a simple list of categories, and categorising the message it last received. The review of this exercise is therefore open to conduct on various levels—at the individual level, looking at individual people's negotiating style; at the group level, looking at tactics and strategy; and examining the way a message which is categorised by its senders as a helpful proposal is seen by its recipients as a territorial threat.

6 *Films* are also useful on skill improvement courses for helping with the vocabulary problem—both technical vocabulary and behavioural vocabulary. Some of the recent crop of deliberately funny training films are great ice-breakers, and by restricting themselves to a few points reiterated many times manage to convey clear messages. Other films by their sheer dramatic force make a considerable impact—the film *Who Killed The Sale?* is excellent in this respect, making as it does the point that everyone in an organisation, not just the sales force, is responsible for selling the company and the company's products.

The examples above of the sort of exercises trainers can use for increasing skill cover most management training needs. Another way of classifying exercises is by their pacing (self paced or group paced; quick, normal, or slow); their structure (highly structured to completely unstructured); the content-process balance (all content, all process, some of each); the number of people involved; and the convergence-divergence of the group tasks. Using the examples given above, the trainer can draw on the experiences and expectations of his own organisation to produce a veritable library of exercises for different management skills.

C   Feedback systems

No exercise is complete without feedback; indeed it is often difficult to describe an exercise without describing also the feedback processes involved. There are three potential sources of feedback on a skills training course: the trainee himself, the trainer, and the rest of the group. The trainer must go out of his way to ensure that feedback happens; that it is accurate; that it is timely, and that it is rich. It is never enough to put people in a small group discussion or other exercise and trust that they will somehow extract their own feedback and improve their performance; their capacity for self-deception and for forgetting will win every time. The big problem is getting feedback on interpersonal skills courses; here the problems of accuracy, richness, and acceptability become acute. Examples of the way feedback can be given are:

(a) *by the trainer*. Some form of behaviour analysis (see Chapters 4 and 5) is the trainer's best way of ensuring coverage and objectivity. Against the objective of the exercise the trainer decides the appropriate B/A categories to enter on his form (see Figure 4.5). In an exercise designed to improve problem-solving skills, for example, the trainer might choose:

> caught proposals
> escaped proposals
> supporting
> building
> disagreeing/criticising
> giving technical information
> seeking technical information
> giving people-information
> seeking people-information
> hypothesis-testing

as categories to analyse into; in an exercise designed to improve skills on consultancy, for internal consultants, he might choose:

     reflecting back
     directing
     seeking information
     giving information (asked for)
     giving information (unasked for)
     defending/attacking
     admitting difficulties

Feedback is then given individually or to the group, as part of the review of the exercise or as part of a special stocktaking exercise part way through the course. It is important for the trainer to avoid giving the impression that he is simply imparting his feelings about people's behaviour; therefore he should be ready to show people how his behaviour analysis works. It is also important that people take their feedback and work with it; a small amount of feedback, worked over into performance improvement plans for the rest of the course, is much better than a large chunk of information which is greeted with a blank stare.

   (b) *by the group*. If as in some role play exercises there are two trainees working while the rest of the group observes, the group is a potential source of feedback. Again, the problem is to make the feedback objective and opinion free; the trainer may brief the group to watch for particular things and actually to count what goes on. For example, they could be briefed to look for:

     who interrupts whom, and how often?
     who makes most proposals?
     who disagrees the most?
     what is the balance of technical and people matter in the
       conversation?
     who closes the interview, and how?

The trainer must then structure the review so that the objective feedback is extracted from the observers, not their subjective opinions about who won and what they would have done in the role players' places. Trained groups of observers—as used on management assessment programmes, for instance—can achieve a very high level of reliability and can make useful suggestions for performance improvement based on their observations; untrained observers can be worse than nothing, because they can actually get it wrong. The worst case is where the trainer leads the observers into producing negative criticism of one trainee, after which it is someone else's turn in the hot seat; some public speaking courses are like this, and in one case the trainer only realised the seriousness of what he was doing when the trainee wet himself with apprehension. Briefed to be objective, and given particular hints on looking for skills as well as deficiencies, the group observers can do a good job; but they must be managed with care.

(c) *from the trainee.* The best source of feedback is the trainee himself; then he can leave the course managing his own learning instead of relying on other people. Much good management training is designed to help managers monitor their own performance. There are several ways of doing this; mnemonics and other devices are useful for keeping a crosscheck while learning technical skills. Two useful techniques for learning to monitor one's own interactive style are:

(i) *prefacing games*, usually used in conjunction with some form of behaviour analysis. A small group of trainees—four to six—is given a trivial or silly task to discuss: solving a crossword puzzle, designing a menu, designing a new pet animal. They must discuss the subject, with the caveat that no-one may make a contribution unless he first prefaces it with the category-name into which that contribution will fall. It is surprising how quickly this teaches people to monitor their performance; the game is good fun, too, which is why we suggest frivolous tasks to perform. Variants on the prefacing game include the suffixing game, where the speaker must first categorise what the previous speaker said before making his own contribution, and games where people draw cards with the category names on and they have to suit their behaviour to the category on the card.

(ii) *spot the game*, played by people with a working knowledge of the 'games' outlined by Eric Berne. [7] In his book Berne lists various games which people use amongst themselves: e.g. 'Wooden leg' is played by people saying 'I'd like to help you but I've got this wooden leg', or in real life 'I'd love to visit your Glasgow office but my doctor says I mustn't travel at the moment'; 'Lunch bag' is played by people saying 'See how hard I work, I bring my lunch in a bag and eat at my desk', and so on. Given in the context of organisational politics, or the problems of persuading people to do things, an account of the games people play is very illuminating and a real help with vocabulary in a normally fuzzy area. The 'spot the game' exercise is played after the talk; in a large room with a clear space for people to circulate freely the group members are each given a card with the name of a game, and a personal score card. Their task is to engage each other in conversation, playing the game written on each person's card and trying to guess the game that the other one is playing. Each pair continue to talk until they have guessed each other; then they swap game cards, mark each other's score cards for a success, and go to find other partners to converse with.

People also learn to monitor some aspects of their behaviour after they have seen themselves on video tape. CCTV needs very careful handling and editing if the trainer is to use it for giving detailed feedback about personal skills; but at a superficial level there can be few people who are not made aware of mannerisms—head nodding, um- and er-ing, speaking with hands in front of mouth—when they watch themselves on TV. Some trainers use video equipment instead of planning feedback, not realising that people need help in using this kind of information; it is not enough to watch oneself doing a counselling interview on telly for planned behaviour change to occur. The consequence of this is that to use TV for intense feedback needs more resources than the average trainer can give; but people who have never seen themselves on the screen before will usually pick up some useful information.

D Course design

The maxim that one establishes new learning and consolidates it before going further bears repetition again in the context of designing skills courses; the trainer, having reviewed the options he has for exercise design and feedback, may feel that the course has designed itself, but there are one or two points about overall course design that are best made by dissecting some actual courses. As well as the rhythms dictated by speed or presentation of the material and people's ability to assimilate it, the trainer must also grapple with the problems of group dynamics which must arise on any course longer than a single day.

A group of people assembled together over a period of time go through some fairly predictable stages. At the beginning, they show behaviour indicating a need for structure—they choose chairmen, seek objectives and terms of reference, conduct themselves formally, etc. Then as they settle down they move into a more informal phase, with people showing less need to depend on structure; as people vary in the speed with which they can shed their need for structure, there is often a fight for leadership of the group at this stage, as the leader who helped them through the first stage by offering some structure is deposed by a more informal type. Round about this stage—about Tuesday evening in a week-long course—open fights and arguments may erupt, and there is a great deal of tension. This is usually resolved by the group adopting a new way of operating, with some insights into the strengths of its members, and allocation of roles according to the needs of the task; but under severe external threat the group is likely to revert to the formal procedure, and even to the first leader.

Because of this natural course of group dynamics it would be possible to put people in a group together and do nothing with them for a week, after which some would undoubtedly say that they had learned something and would work better in future. People cannot bear to see something they have suffered for set at naught, so they are likely to say that any painful experience, especially if it appeared voluntary, has done them good. If they know that it has cost the firm a large sum of money to organise the training, their feeling of flattery will make them even more compliant.

A genuine trainer will try to train in spite of these human tendencies; a charlatan will sell them back to you at a high price. The first question in course design, therefore, is this: do we need group training at all?

Consider the following brief to a trainee. 'You are the Managing Director of Bloggs Helicopters, serving the North Sea oil rigs on the accompanying map. At midnight one Saturday you receive a call at home from the duty manager, telling you there has been an explosion on X Rig. Seven men are known to have been killed, and a large number are thought to have been injured by blast or by burns. It is thought that a further explosion may occur any time in the next four hours . . .' The brief goes on to say how many helicopters are available, how many pilots, where they are, what first aid is available, how fast people die of burns, etc.; most of the options available—who to send, in what machines, at what time, carrying what facilities, and where they should land— carry advantages and disadvantages, the weighing of which includes guessing or drawing conclusions from sparse evidence.

This is an interesting exercise for examining and teaching decision-making under stress. The designer promptly ruined it by making it into a group exercise in which the group was the

Managing Director, thus introducing into the situation an element—group behaviour—totally alien to the brief. We asked how the designer would react to the trainee who said to the rest of the group: 'Shut up and get off my back'; the trainee would lose points. Maybe a strong minded trainee will teach him that skills can be learned alone, even interactive skills.

Consider now this three-day programme for middle managers, there to learn interpersonal skills (especially delegation and teamwork), decision-making under pressure, communication (especially listening skills), and public relations skills. The course begins with the twelve participants in two groups of six, in a leaderless discussion exercise. In this exercise they each take the part of a product manager; each participant has a brief, supposedly prepared for him by one of his subordinates, about the new product he would like the company to promote. The products are all different; the exercise allows each trainee time to absorb his material, then to lay it on one side and make a short presentation to the group; when all presentations have been made the group must decide which one product will go forward. Each participant has two objectives; to make sure that his own product is accepted and to make sure that an agreed solution goes forward. While this goes on the trainer makes notes on a behaviour analysis form for feedback to the group later; at the end of the exercise he conducts a review, pulling out the lessons of committee work and working to a departmental brief, but does not refer to his B/A notes.

After coffee the trainees form the same groups for another discussion exercise; they are given an article criticising their company which appeared in the underground press, and told to compose a joint rebuttal. Again the trainer does behaviour analysis, but refrains from mentioning it in his feedback, which concentrates on the problems of processing information one doesn't like, and on the company's future public relations plans.

At this point the trainers—there are two involved—have quite a lot of behaviour analysis material for each participant. In the afternoon they review what they have learned by observing the trainees, while the trainees themselves work through an in-basket exercise lasting an hour and a half. This is an individual exercise, of course, and needs no supervision or observation. After tea the trainees form into new groups, assigned by the trainers, where their task is to brain-storm ideas on a problem currently confronting the company. While this goes on, the trainers and four senior managers conscripted for the purpose are busy marking the in-basket exercises, taking two exercises each; after dinner feedback interviews based on the in-baskets are conducted in two shifts, six people being interviewed while the other six watch a film, and then vice-versa.

Looking at the afternoon session here we see some good points of course design. The individual work makes it difficult to go to sleep, and helps break any distracting patterns emerging in the group; then the trainees reassemble in different groups, selected so that the high contributors are in one group and the low contributors in another. An early group mix based on contribution rate is sound practice; it rescues the low contributors, who would otherwise have sunk lower and lower on the horizon, and it ensures that the noisier ones are amongst their own kind where, after shouting all at once for a while, they have to shut up and listen. The trainers' absence during the brain-storming exercise is not very important; behaviour analysis of a brain-storming meeting is not very informative, but the exercise is nonetheless useful. The evening feedback interviews are very helpful, for a number of reasons; early feedback on a training course is better than late, because it tells one where and how to improve in time to do something about it, and feedback from a line manager (who has, of course, been trained to do the job) helps to emphasise that this is a real event and not just playtime.

The second day begins with group feedback from the trainers, on the behaviour they have observed on the previous day. They explain the behaviour analysis system they have been using, and show group profiles and give out individual profiles. Each person studies his own profile and is asked to name one or two areas in which he would like to improve his performance; this can be as open or as private as the trainee desires. The rest of the morning is spent in exercises to improve listening ability, summarising ability, and the ability to spot false arguments—the latter using a transcript of a discussion in which three managers try to pull the wool over one another's eyes. Each exercise is followed by a review with the trainer, who uses his behaviour analysis sheet as part of the material for the review. The afternoon is spent in a controlled pace negotiation exercise (see page 144); as part of the exercise each team has to categorise on a behaviour analysis sheet the contribution just arrived from the other group and its own contribution, and the difference in categorisation of the same contribution is the starting point for the review. The evening is spent with the trainers reading aloud short problems of the kind any manager is likely to find in his in-basket; after each reading the participants have to note down answers to questions like: What is the main problem here? What would you say if you were X? Under what conditions could this fail? and so on, after which they discuss their answers as a group.

The design of the second day provides variety and a change of pace, as well as starting the process of individual feedback at the end of each exercise. Personal skills and technical skills are nicely mixed—indeed the content of the problems in the evening session is selected to address the skills which the trainers have observed to be lacking. No attempt is made to make the trainees feel gloomy or to foment discontent within the groups.

The third day is spent in a series of very short exercises which the trainees selected some time on day two to give trainees practice in the areas in which they said they would like to improve. Until the middle of the second day, this part of the course was completely unprogrammed, and the trainers brought with them far more exercises then they would actually use; as things turn out, they may be helping some people develop more supporting and building behaviour (using synectics exercises, prefacing games, building-only games) while at the same time helping other people listen better (using various listening and reviewing exercises) and helping others plan better under pressure (using games where information has to be bought, company strategy exercises, etc.). By this time there may be four or five separate groups scattered over the training centre, all doing different things; some with a trainer doing behaviour analysis, some doing their own, some sitting and thinking for part of the time. The trainees come together for lunch and for an end of course round-up in which each one writes down three things he will try to do differently when he gets back to work, and shares as much as he feels like with the others present.

Many of the features of good course design are visible here; the change of pace, the rich feedback, the obvious relevance of the exercises to problems with the job, the involvement of line managers, the opportunity to follow one's own learning needs once they have been established. Some exercises are done under time pressure; others are not. Groups are mixed early to cope with the special problems of high and low contributors. The trainers confine their feedback to what they have observed, and encourage others to do the same; no ego trips for prestige performers, no deliberate stress, no staying up late to get things finished. There is more responsibility placed on the shoulders of trainee and trainer because of the unplanned nature of the third day; the trainees respond well because they see that the day has been planned to meet their needs, but this is no place for a trainer who cannot adapt.

Longer courses follow the same design philosophy, but it is very important to build in good natural breaks where people get out of the training centre altogether; after ten days' solid training one can easily forget whether it is nine in the morning or the evening. Long courses probably have more opportunity to adapt to trainees' needs, but it is not a good idea to leave a blank space on the timetable covering most of the course; some people will find this lack of structure disturbing. Fill the blanks with innocuous labels, and they will be content.

Most courses should start easy and get harder; an early failure is discouraging, especially for people unfamiliar with the context of the training. Feedback should be given as early as is consistent with getting a reliable sample of results, and should emphasise things that are done well in addition to things that are done badly. Courses with lots of group exercises should give participants time to make private notes on what they have learned.

If there is a golden rule for course design, it is this: to look at each exercise, and each component of the exercise (e.g. time allowed, group structure, report-back system) and to ask oneself 'What will each participant experience by doing this, and by doing it this way? and how will that experience translate into learning?' Using this question sorts out the exercises which are there for tradition's sake, or because the trainer likes to teach them, or because they fill the time slot, from the exercises which will actually help managers learn.

E Summary

Skills courses are based on intensive practice with feedback, and the trainer's job is to design exercises giving these things. Individual exercises, structured and unstructured group exercises, group-to-solo exercises, films and talks and role plays can be used, assembled into a cumulation of activities that unfreeze the trainees, give them feedback, and get them generating their own feedback and learning plans.

F   Discussion questions

1   A large organisation ran courses for teams of salesmen and sales support staff. The object of the course was to make a new sales plan to cover the next year or two. The course had a number of special features, for example:

(a) no one was told how long it would last. In practice the time varied from four days to a fortnight, but they did not know this.

(b) the course took over the facilities of a complete, isolated hotel. The switchboard was instructed that no outside calls were to be accepted from, or for, course members.

(c) no timetable of activities was issued. The trainer had a list of activities people were to go through, but he did not reveal this. However, if he thought people were going too slowly, he would make them work through mealtimes. They were also kept up late at night until he said they had 'finished'.

(d) among the 'ground rules' was the *yes/no rule*—that questions were to be answered with either 'yes' or 'no' but never 'I don't know' or 'perhaps' or 'it depends'. Recalcitrant course members were sometimes made to undergo prolonged periods of yes/no questioning by the trainer—up to an hour and a half.

(e) course members were to plan their next year's activities, but were not allowed to bring files with them. If they ran seriously short of information the trainer might be persuaded to ring up for it.

(f) part way through the first week their managers and other senior executives would appear in the course room, and observe progress. No communication between the groups was allowed.

(g) recreation was rare, but took the form of violent physical exercise.

(h) people were allowed home once they had finished the sales plan.

Questions
(a) What is the effect on the group dynamics in a course like this of not knowing the duration of the course?
(b) Nobody left the courses. Why?
(c) The end product was a sales plan. Bearing in mind the quality

of the information available and the pressures, do you think it would be a good sales plan? If not, how long do you think it would be before it was discarded?

(d) Though no-one was enjoined to secrecy after the course, they were never mentioned in public to people who had not attended them. 'Insiders' were reluctant to hear criticism of the course and its design. Why?

(e) Some people attending the course suffered severe psychological damage as a result. What sort of people would be most likely to suffer, and what sort of damage would they show?

2 Some management trainers believe that in order to learn more about the 'process' of groups, trainees should be given exercises with little or no important 'task' content. Do you agree? What is your evidence?

3 A trained observer using a pre-planned observation schedule, and an untrained observer with a blank sheet of paper, both watch a group discussion. List the differences you would expect to find in (i) what they observe, and (ii) how they feed back their observations to the group.

4 Why do so many trainers, given the task of training managers in good teamwork, assemble together a team of complete strangers for the actual training course? Is it possible to teach such trainees skills that will improve performance in the home group? What sort of exercises, and what sort of feedback strategy, would be appropriate?

G Further reading

[1] N. RACKHAM, P. HONEY and M. COLBERT. *Developing Interactive Skills*, Wellens Publishing, 1971.

[2] N. RACKHAM and T. MORGAN. *Behaviour Analysis in Training*, McGraw-Hill, 1977.

These books contain full accounts of the approach to interactive skills training, depending upon behaviour analysis, outlined in this chapter.

[3] P. KINNERSLEY. *The Hazards of Work*, Pluto Press, 1973.

Vehemently anti-capitalist book which has many good points to make about the country's poor record on health and safety at work. Useful material to use in helping managers process information they don't like; it has equally useful stable-mates from the same publisher on different business topics.

[4] C. L. COOPER and D. BOWLES. *Hurt or Helped? A study of the personal impact on managers of experiential, small group training programmes*, Training Information Paper 10, Training Services Agency.
A useful follow-up study of managers who have been through some of the more reputable small group training programmes, with good guidance for the trainer who might want to use such programmes himself.

[5] V. STEWART and A. STEWART. *Practical Performance Appraisal*, Gower Press, 1978.

[6] N. RACKHAM. 'Controlled pace negotiation as a technique for developing negotiating skills,' *Industrial and Commercial Training*, vol. 4, no. 6, 1972, pp. 266-75.

[7] E. BERNE. *Games People Play*, Penguin, 1970.

[8] A. BLUMBERG and R. T. GOLEMBIEWSKI. *Learning and Change in Groups*, Penguin Modern Psychology, 1976.
Written from an American point of view, this is a good outline of small group training theory and practice as it is used for promoting personal growth (not necessarily increased business effectiveness). There are good summaries of the main works in the field; ideas which the skilled trainer could use; and morbidly fascinating insights into what happens in some of the more remote outposts of these techniques.

[9] C. L. COOPER and I. MANGHAM. *T-Groups: A Survey of Research*, Wiley, 1971.
A detailed and scholarly survey of research into T-groups, looking at both business and personal growth; worth having for a specialist look at this type of training.

[10] M. L. BERGER and P. J. BERGER. *Group Training Techniques*, Gower Press, 1972.
A very variable collection of accounts of different people's experience in group training, and worth reading for its variability alone; some of the contributors adopt a very controlled and systematic approach to training, others less so, and the contrasts are interesting to observe.

[11] J. McLEISH, W. MATHESON and J. PARK. *The Psychology of the Learning Group*, Hutchinson University Library, 1973.
A clear account of the processes which take place inside a small group, with some good ideas for exercise design. Not specifically

directed towards industry, but easily adaptable.

[12] BOB HOULTON. *The Activist's Handbook*, Arrow Trade Union Studies, 1975.

Any trainer who thinks that group processes, influencing skills, leadership, etc., must be explained in jargon and high-falutin words should read this book and be ashamed. It—and its companions in the same series—are models of how to put over complex or sophisticated information clearly, without patronising, with the right pacing and well chosen exercises. If trade unionists can be taught this well, why can't managers?

9 Good housekeeping for internal courses

By the time the trainer has designed a course, from the initial training needs diagnosis through to course design and getting timetables drafted, he can be forgiven for forgetting what it will be like to be on the receiving end. Yet the best way to decide the kind of accommodation required for the course is to think about the trainee—how is he going to feel, what is he going to need to learn comfortably? If the accommodation is not right; if tea and coffee never turn up on time; if the hotel receptionist doesn't know who he is, the course secretary spells his name wrong and there doesn't seem to be anywhere for him to sit; then it doesn't matter how brilliant a course one is running nor how expensive the speakers are—the trainees will not give their undivided attention. If there is any element of stress on the course, any suggestion of assessment, any requirement for the course members to take personal risks, then unless they feel thoroughly confident of the trainers' abilities they will stay inside their shells. Consciously or unconsciously they say 'If he can't manage syndicate rooms that will take a flip-chart and six people, then he certainly can't counsel me about my delegation problem.' Unfair, but true. So, put yourself in the shoes of the trainee experiencing your course, and ask what he's likely to need.

We assume in this chapter that the course is being held in an hotel, because these are usually the most troublesome; but many of the remarks apply to purpose-built conference centres and company's own training establishments also. The following are the most important items to consider.

1 *Comfortable travel.* The trainee wants to arrive relaxed, without having to rush or to waste time. The trainer should therefore look up times of trains (and flights if necessary) for the beginning and end of the course, and plan the start and finish times accordingly. He should include this information in the joining instructions, as well as a map for people driving themselves. On large courses it is worth asking whether a number of people will be arriving by the same train or flight, and arranging to have them met; in remote locations (or for late

evening arrivals) the telephone numbers of local taxi firms may also be included. Remember that on Sunday in the UK British Rail often experience delays because of engineering work, and allow for this by suggesting that people arrive for dinner and have informal introductions afterwards.

2   *No domestic worries.* The trainee wants to be sure that his spouse can get in touch in case of emergencies. If the trainer includes with the course joining instructions a card which the trainee can leave at home, giving the name, address and telephone number of the hotel, the estimated times of arrival and departure, and information about when the course will be working (messages taken for transmission at break times) and when people will be off-duty, the spouse's worries will be minimised. On strenuous courses, or courses where people are expected to be on their best behaviour, trainees who are ill, suffering from domestic problems, or taking maintenance doses of drugs should perhaps be excluded, or at any rate given the opportunity of personal or medical counselling before taking part. A surprisingly large number of drugs react with alcohol, or with certain types of food; pressure to drink and to over-eat is always present on hotel based courses, however much the trainer tries to stop it happening, and someone on a maintenance dose of tranquillisers (undetectable to the outsider) may be made seriously ill by a couple of gin-and-tonics before lunch and the cheese board afterwards. Deliberate stress on courses is hardly ever a good idea; some courses outside the scope of this book, e.g. assessment programmes, carry an inevitable amount of stress which the course manager should always have under control; but any abnormal amount of mental or physical stress should be covenanted for by the trainees beforehand.

3   *Welcome.* The hotel should be expecting him and make him feel welcome. The receptionist should have a list of names of trainees, should know the name of the organisation, and should know the first set of directions to give the new arrival: 'The porter will take you to your room, and then Mr Jones (the trainer) will be expecting everyone to join him in the upstairs bar for drinks any time after six-thirty.' If it can be arranged the trainer himself or an assistant should be in the reception area waiting to welcome people, though if arrivals are scattered and there is much preparation to do this may not be possible. The cold, uninterested stare from the receptionist who's never heard of your organisation is not a good way to begin things.

A welcoming touch to greet the trainee as he arrives in his room is also appreciated; a note from the trainer giving basic information, where the first meeting is to be held, times and places of meals, how to get room service, is appreciated; a small plate of fruit or personally chosen paperback for light bedside reading is another small gesture which makes people feel welcome. This is especially so where people have come from overseas and are still adjusting to the new language and etiquette.

4   *Bedrooms* can spoil everything if they are wrong; a trainee with a splitting head because he hasn't slept is going to get a marked disbenefit unless things can be put right. Bedrooms should be quiet; not over the kitchens, nor over the bar, nor giving out onto the main road a few feet away. This needs checking at the time of booking the hotel—for big courses the trainer might even stay there a night without revealing himself, to see if there are prominent central heating noises in the early morning or noisy domestics who think that everyone should be up with the lark. If bedrooms are to be used for study purposes then it is worth contemplating taking out any televisions provided, especially if the rooms are booked *en bloc*; it is difficult to study with the noises of a familiar programme filtering through the walls. Bedrooms used for study also need plenty of working light, and a chair at the right height to reach the working surface.

A telephone in the bedroom is useful, but brings in the problem of private calls and expensive surcharges. It is not unusual to find hotels charging fifteen pence for the first unit (for which the Post Office charges three pence at the time of writing) when the calls are made from the bedroom; if such a scale of charges operates, people should be warned to make calls from call boxes as much as possible. A decision should be taken about whether all calls are charged to the trainer's account, or whether some are to be billed separately.

Private bathrooms are obviously the best option, but in some conference centres and company accommodation they do not exist; in that case the sexes should be assigned different lavatory and bathroom facilities. It's solitary enough being the only woman on a course (still the case for most management training courses) without having the men glaring at you for having monopolised the bathroom and made it smell of scent.

On long courses, courses with lots of people, and courses in remote places, the careful trainer will bring with him spares of the toilet equipment that some people are bound to forget—toothbrushes and toothpaste, aspirin, Alka-Seltzer, earplugs, safety pins, needle and thread, and razor blades.

5 *Working rooms* must first of all be big enough. Err on the side of generosity; there is nothing worse than sitting for eight hours in a strange chair and feeling that if one moved one's elbows three other people would fall over. If people are going to be relaxed and chatting, then easy chairs in a small circle; if they are taking notes or watching films, then a table or tables, with chairs of the right height, and room to move about.

Working rooms should be quiet—again a job for the trainer to check when booking the hotel. Rooms near the bar or kitchens can give problems (noises of people glassing up; Musak; kitchen noises and aromas). So can rooms in a suite of conference rooms where the adjacent rooms are to be used by someone else; check that next-door will not be having a film show when you are asking yours to pay attention to the problems of inflation accounting. Signs of workmen should be viewed with caution when the trainer is making arrangements—does this mean that the road outside will be dug up during his talk, or that workmen will suddenly appear and start painting the windows?

Rooms also need to be temperature controlled and air conditioned. Too cool is better than too warm, always; a state of temperate immobility is very sleep-inducing after lunch. Now that smokers are in a small minority on most management training courses some trainers ask people not to smoke during conference sessions, and it is surprising what a difference this makes—much less eye strain and feeling of puffiness round about four o'clock. If there is no air conditioning then the windows will need to be opened (special attention to outside noises, proximity of aircraft flight paths). Check that the air conditioning doesn't make so much noise that people cannot work.

Flip-charts, blackboards and overhead projectors need to be positioned so that course members can see them easily and the trainer doesn't fall over them. If he is to write on it during the course, the overhead projector needs to be to the right of the trainer's chair (for right handed trainers). The trainer should check to see that there are enough power points for the equipment he wants to bring into the room, and that trailing wires that can be tripped over are kept out of the way. If films or slides are to be shown then a proper black-out should be possible; some hotels have two levels of lighting, only one of which can be switched off easily. Pens and markers for the various bits of equipment need checking each time they are put out; colours like orange and pale green are difficult for colour blind people to see if the ink is not strong.

Most hotels will hire this sort of equipment, but at enormous cost, so it is worth querying what their charges will be before committing oneself. Similarly one sometimes sees 'purpose-built' conference centres with special furniture and layout; check before committing to one of these that the special furniture allows for left handed people and the special layouts allow for wheelchairs and people with sticks.

The same considerations apply to syndicate rooms; they should be big enough to do everything that syndicates will expect to do—will the room take six people, their chairs, a table, and a flip-chart? Do the rooms need to be close to each other for the trainer to move quickly between them? Are the rooms quiet?

6   *Security* of personal belongings and company information. Trainees should be asked not to discuss confidential company matters in public areas where they can be overheard; even if no secrets are transmitted, it is bad public relations. Some hotels, knowing that the course breaks at six with no evening work, will allow the conference room to be booked for an evening function. The possibility of this happening should be checked at the time the booking is made; if the trainer does not object, then trainees should clear their belongings out and take them to their rooms, and the hotel must be sure to remove signs of the previous occupation before the course resumes. If the rooms are to be left empty, they should be locked against other hotel occupants walking in and gaining company information or private property. The trainees also must feel that any messages from their office will be passed on intact by the hotel telephonist; we treasure, in a black museum, the manager of a conference centre who presented us with the message, 'Please ring IBM'.

7   *Privacy* is something the trainees need, and should respect in others. Some hotels mix conference participants with the rest of the guests; this may cause no trouble at all, but could give offence if the conference holds a noisy end of course dinner, with speeches, three tables away from the honeymoon couple and the businessman who's come to get away from it all. If there is any suggestion that the two life styles won't mix—even if the course

meals need serving noticeably quicker than the rest of the guests'—the trainer should consider asking for separate facilities.

8 *Administrative support* as much as necessary, depending on the length of course and the type of manager taking part. Will people need things photocopied? complicated messages sent and received? information obtained? travel booked? meetings set up? It is not fair to place a large administrative burden on the hotel staff unless they have been warned to expect it; most will be happy to run off a few copies on the hotel copier, or to book the occasional train ticket, but for long or large courses it is worth taking a secretary to the course and setting her up in an office with typewriter, copier, and a direct line telephone. Even her presence at the beginning and end of the course makes a difference.

Some organisations cope with the problem of administrative support by keeping on their books one or two retired but sprightly managers whose job it is to act as course manager on training courses. It is their responsibility to set up the equipment, to take messages, to chase the hotel in case of trouble, and to pack up everything afterwards. This is a solution with much to commend it; it relieves the trainer of chores at the beginning and end of the course, which is when he wants to chat to participants; it gets the bulk of domestic worries taken care of; and it is enjoyable for the course manager, who may meet old friends and keep in touch.

9 *Notes and jottings* that the trainee may take need a folder or binder to keep them in. It is courteous to warn trainees, at the beginning of a lecture, whether or not they can expect full notes to be given them; then they know how much to jot down. Ring binders are most commonly used; they should contain spare paper, and the trainer's notes should be ready punched with a compatible hole punch. As all binders look alike, they should have sticky name labels on; colour coded labels help people find their own one more quickly, if the binders are ever to get jumbled together. The trainer needs a large supply of spare paper, pencils, erasers, rules, ring binders, and a hole punch. Colour coded paper to distinguish one set of notes from another, or cardboard tabs, are useful when people accumulate lots of notes.

10 *Food and drink* should be in moderation, unless you're designing a rich holiday instead of a training course. On long courses a course dinner may be promised for the last evening,

with the guarantee that the boat may be pushed out then; until then, meals after which people are expected to work should be plain and frugal. Table d'hôte menus are quicker for the hotel staff to serve; and people drink less if the trainer provides sherry and vermouth before lunch, and carafes of wine with the meal, than if they go to the bar. It may be more convenient for the hotel to send round a menu card during the morning coffee break, on which people mark their choices, thus cutting out waiting time at lunch; if this happens, make sure either that the menu comes round during coffee or that the session after coffee will not be disrupted as one person after another drops out temporarily to consider what he will have for lunch.

11 *Relaxation and a change of pace* should be planned into any course lasting a week or more; even one-day seminars get boring if the pace never varies. It is not a good idea, no matter how expensive the trainees are, to work them from eight-thirty in the morning to eleven at night, day after day without a break. People easily get immured inside a hotel so that they forget what the outside looks like; an afternoon off, a planned walk, a guide to the local amusements and an instruction not to return until dinner time—these do managers an immense amount of good. Seaside hotels in the winter season are usually good places to hold conferences, because of the facilities and the greater helpfulness of the staff; being able to tell the course members to go for a blow along the pier is another advantage the trainer should consider.

Besides getting out of doors, trainees need a change of pace in their work. Training centres that have a library or journals room are useful here; a whole day to gather information at one's own pace is an enriching experience for many managers. If this cannot be done, a break in the pattern of formal instruction and the opportunity for personal counselling interviews with appropriate specialists could be provided.

12 *Methods for handling complaints* should also be made clear to the trainee; if he has any complaint about the hotel, it should be funnelled through the course manager, or secretary, or trainer, who can present it to the hotel manager. Thus the trainer knows if the hotel is delinquent in any way, and the hotel knows whom it has to deal with.

13 *Farewells* should be handled with as much tact as the welcome; people must feel confident that they have enough time to catch their trains and planes, that they have time to pack in

the schedule, that taxis have been booked; and the trainer should make sure that each is bade farewell personally. When the trainer disappears to put away the equipment, and nobody seems to care, people go away with a rejected feeling.

Looking at the course from the trainee's point of view gives an idea of what to ask of the hotel or conference centre; but the trainer should not ignore his own personal and organisational needs. For example:

1 *His accommodation* needs choosing with the same care he gave to the others—maybe more. He will need a larger room because of the greater quantities of material he needs to keep, though if there is a lot of equipment the hotel should be asked for an ante-room or broom cupboard. If there are to be a number of courses at the same hotel it should be possible to keep some equipment there from course to course to save it all having to be taken home. If equipment, etc. is to be kept in the trainer's own room, he should be careful about lending people the key to go and get goods from the room; besides being an elementary safety precaution if anything were to be mislaid, this also ensures that (say) other course members' papers are not seen by people who should not be looking.

2 *His relationship with the hotel* must be clear to all concerned. He and the hotel staff should know who is the course members' channel for complaints or special requests. The trainer concerned with any one course should have some authority with respect to the hotel management, even if the hotel has been chosen by someone other than the trainer himself and this third party is also paying the bill; for there are few things worse than finding one's course ruined by slovenly service and the hotel unprepared to do anything about it because they see the trainer as too junior to matter. As a strategic point, it does not pay to commit oneself to a long series of courses with an hotel if one is in doubt about the hotel's standards and conscientiousness; if people notice that courses get a more off-hand treatment than ordinary guests they become discontented. Beware, too, the hotels with a record of insurance fires and the ones where the staff are obviously on the fiddle—cash down and no receipts for drinks bought out of hours is a good indicator of one level of fiddle.

3 *Who pays the bills* must be made clear at the time of organising the course. There are two questions here. The first is

whether each trainee pays his own bill and puts it through his own departmental budget, or whether all room bills are put on the trainer's budget. This is an internal matter of whose budget bears the cost of training, and the important thing is to make sure that no cross-departmental rectifications are needed later. The second question is whether trainees are allowed to charge minor personal expenses—telephone calls, drinks, laundry, etc.—to their bill and have it paid for in the same way as accommodation. Whatever the policy is, it should be made crystal clear to the participants on their joining instructions and again in the welcoming speeches, and the hotel staff should not be authorised to waive the rule without the trainer's permission. People sometimes grumble if the organisation places them in an hotel where telephone calls cost pounds and drinks need to be paid for by cheque, so a small overnight allowance may help.

    4   *The trainer's own pacing* needs care and attention. During the course he needs fresh air and exercise as much as the others, and probably away from their company. He should try to programme this in without it looking too obvious—people do not like to feel deserted—but he should be prepared to discard the leisure at a moment's notice if a crisis erupts.

    More important is the pacing between courses. It is easy to become a professional course runner, an in-house prestige performer spending three weeks out of four away from home. This is not healthy. At the end of a course the trainer needs somewhere to unwind, someone to listen to his successes and failures; better to drop in at the office rather than take a solitary drive home. This is especially true for trainers who work solo and who lack feedback on their performance—except for the seductive feedback on how they performed as an entertainer, which may actually be misleading. Debriefing for the solo trainer is essential; for trainers who work in pairs there is more on-course feedback, and a review immediately after the course may not be a good idea provided that the two know they will meet again before long.

    The deadliest trap is that of becoming nothing but a performer. The preparation that goes into a course and the follow-up afterwards are just as important and should take just as much time. Preparing new course material is time consuming—reckon a ratio of eight to one for the preparation of lecture material, and longer perhaps for some exercises. The trainer also needs to get involved with the rest of the firm, visiting managers, spending time on working parties, maybe splitting his time between the training job and a line function. If he doesn't do this he will become stale, like an old fashioned music hall comedian doing the same old act in front of ever-changing audiences. Management training has more than its share of Archie Rices already; by careful self-management the reader should avoid this fate.

Summary

The housekeeping associated with a management training course is dull routine, but important for the confidence of the participants. The trainer should choose accommodation with care, looking at things from the point of view of the participant and what is necessary to make him comfortable; he should delegate as much of the work as possible to an administrator, secretary, or course manager; and he should pay attention to his own housekeeping and self-management if it appears that he will be involved with a number of training courses.

Discussion questions

1   Look at the programme for your last course. What would you do if you had a power cut: (a) between 0900—1200, (b) between 1200—1500, (c) between 1500—1800, (d) between 1800—2100?
2   Some in-house and public courses ask participants not to smoke in the lecture rooms. Do you think this is a good idea? If you agree, how would you get it implemented? If you disagree, what would you do if you were asked by a non-smoker to prohibit smoking?
3   What are the special dietary requirements of: (a) Muslims, (b) diabetics, (c) Orthodox Jews, (d) Vegans, (e) people taking Tryptophan?
4   You are the only trainer present on a residential course. What would you do if someone knocked on your door at three o'clock in the morning complaining of: (a) sharp pains in the chest and left arm, (b) pain in the abdomen, (c) sudden vomiting and diarrhoea, (d) violent pains in both eyeballs? If you can't answer, and you're likely to find yourself in this situation, buy a book on first aid. And always make sure you know where to contact a doctor in emergencies.

10 Choosing external courses

A How they fit the training strategy

We have all experienced the glossy brochures and single mailing shots landing on our desks advertising the latest course or seminar. 'Dear Executive,' they begin, assuring you that with your vital job (whatever it is) you can't afford to miss the very latest on Product Liability, or Exporting to Pago-Pago, or Undiscovered Tax Havens. You are assured of high quality speakers, comfortable accommodation, and the opportunity to share ideas with other go-ahead managers with problems similar to yours. The brochure may be informative, or persuasive, or both at once; the training may or may not work. In this chapter we attempt to review the range of external courses available, and to guide the trainer who has to choose one for his managers.

The first danger point comes when the brochures land on the trainer's desk. An internal training course is designed with reference to diagnosed training needs; knowing what you want to achieve, you set out to achieve it. Getting a package of brochures is a little like inertia selling; the goods come to you without your having realised you are interested in them. The trainer who has done a good training needs diagnosis has no problems; he looks at the brochures, decides which courses fit his known needs, and rejects the rest. If he has no training needs diagnosed, he may judge the courses on their superficial appeal and the number of prestige names they muster. A well thought out brochure may nonetheless do a service to the trainer with a training plan, by bringing to his attention areas which he did not realise were possible training needs, or drawing attention to problems he did not know he had; nonetheless the caution remains—a good shopping list is the best protection against impulse buying.

Managers can impulse buy too, if they are allowed; brochures are sent to line managers as well as trainers, and the manager may book himself on a course without consulting the trainer. This is something on which organisational policies differ, and no harm is likely to come from a manager booking himself on a technical course; if they wander into more outrageous realms of interpersonal skills training problems may result.

Before selecting an external course, the trainer should be very sure that the needs cannot be resourced internally. There are a number of reasons why the external course may have more to offer than the internal alternative.

1 *Greater knowledge* on the speaker's part than any in-house speaker might bring. Some technical courses, briefings on new research or legislation, or product or marketing up-dating fall into this category.

2 *Greater skill* on the part of the external trainer than can be mustered in-house. This is often a factor where the training needs require a good deal of skill in actual training techniques— some interpersonal skills courses, for example—and the training department's own resources are limited to technical training. Political reasons sometimes dictate that external courses be used if, for example, a very senior manager feels uncomfortable being taught how to negotiate by someone many years his junior.

3 *Greater credibility* of the outside course or speakers. Every organisation has its Cinderella functions—personnel, finance, engineering, sales . . . they each qualify somewhere in British industry. When training needs in the Cinderella area manifest themselves it may be politic for the trainer to arrange outside courses, using speakers with lots of cachet, in order to overcome the credibility gap.

4 *Small number of trainees* making it impossible to justify running a course in-house. Some training needs are best met in groups of a certain size, and the course falls flat if the numbers are smaller. Small firms are very vulnerable to this factor; if they sent all their managers on an internal course there would be nobody minding the shop. For some of them this means that they never get tailor-made training, which is a pity.

5 *Association with other managers* from different firms. It is a sad fact that many managers, questioned about the benefit they received from external training courses, place 'opportunity to meet managers from different organisations' at the top of the list. This is an argument for getting a lot of managers together, serving them meals at regular intervals, and leaving them alone to talk. However on courses where they actually learn something substantive they also benefit from chatting to other people, finding out what other people's problems look like, discovering they are not alone. We have seen a number of mutually helpful

long term relationships started between managers in different companies as a result of their meeting on external courses.

One or more of the considerations, taken in the light of his training needs diagnosis, could influence the trainer to choose an external course. Now he has the range of course offerers to go through to sort out what he wants. We have been on both sides of the external course market—buying and performing—meeting just about every type of course offerer, and having seen the business from both sides we beg to offer the following personal account of the types of organisation offering external courses.

B   Who runs courses?

1   *Educational establishments* such as the business schools, polytechnics, and staff colleges. What sets them apart from most of the rest of the course running world is that they have a commitment to research, and maybe to teaching university students as well as managers. Many of them are funded only partly by what they earn commercially, and are helped by research grants, grants associated with their university status, and so on.

Among their advantages they usually have well thought out programmes, put together with some care, and very often they select their students rather than taking all comers. They tend to offer long courses—weeks or even months of concentrated study, or long courses taken part time. This enables the trainee to take a long look at his job and the demands made on him, to examine the theory as well as the practice, the long term as well as the immediate. Personal relationships with tutors also have time to develop—relationships which may persist long after the trainee returns to work. There is interaction with other courses—business or university courses. Facilities for learning are often excellent—libraries, computer terminals, opportunities to visit local firms. There may be access to recent research results; there certainly should be an atmosphere of research into problems rather than the production of instant solutions.

Among the drawbacks one sometimes sees with these establishments is their consciousness of their own prestige, making them rather stiff and unresponsive to external needs; they may prefer to work at board level with blue chip companies and be less concerned with the training needs of supervisors, production managers, or managers in small firms. This trend is diminishing, we think, but some business schools in the early 1970s were notorious for their social climbing. Some establishments have an outdated philosophy that equates management with military leadership; other establishments are vulnerable to left wing anti-business influence. They can rapidly become ivory tower unless the staff make positive efforts to go out into industry for part of their time; one way this shows itself is that some organisations plan their courses according to what the staff can teach, not what managers want to know. A final drawback—not the fault of the establishments but something the trainer should be wary of—is that these establishments are sometimes used not for training at all, but for laying on of hands; the Crown Prince in a firm is identified, and sent to a business school as an accolade rather than to learn.

The main thing for the trainer to bear in mind when considering such establishments is that they are not there primarily to teach managers; they have other things to do as well. If the establishment already has a research competence in the required area, and a reputation for good teachers, and if the trainer wishes his trainee to take a long, considered look at the problem, then the business school/polytechnic/college is probably a good idea; but the trainer will probably have to take what's offered, and if it does not fit his requirements he may find them unresponsive. It is important not to be put off by self-puffery or claims to be long established; this may indicate a dyed-in-the-wool conservatism. And with long expensive courses there is no substitute for a visit to the course, and a follow-up chat with some people who have already been on the course and have tried applying the lessons back on the job.

2   *Research institutes*, semi-academic bodies, etc. These are bodies not completely attached to a university or other seat of learning, and dependent wholly or mostly for their income on what they can earn by teaching and funded research. The Brunel University Management Programme is perhaps the best known of the entirely self-financed programmes, and the Oxford Centre for Management Studies is familiar to most trainers, though funded in some part by grants from the University Grants Commission.

In their favour it seems that they are much closer to the market than many of the business-school-type institutions, able to respond more quickly to demands from companies and able to organise special events for companies as a matter of routine. The product is often more varied—one- or two-day courses as well as some lasting for several weeks—and there is a greater tendency to use outside speakers rather than relying on the institution's own staff. This is a good thing if it brings to the trainees experienced practitioners from within industry who can convey what they are doing; it has the corresponding drawback that speakers may repeat the previous material, leave bits out, and so on. Compared with the more overtly commercial course running organisations, these types of institution usually have a more selective mailing list and sift the applicants for particular courses so that unsuitable mixes do not occur. They also bring to the trainees new research results, new findings; often presented by Young Turks rather than by venerable prestige performers, but none the worse for that. Some have library facilities also.

Drawbacks include the academic style of presentation and environment, if people are expecting something plusher. Highly specialised research institutes may give seminars that are intellectually very demanding, often without the speaker realising it; it is vital for the trainer to check the level of experience people are expected to bring to the course if the subject matter is very technical—manpower planning, for example, or hazard analysis, or epidemiology. Some specialised institutions are more committed to their research programme than to teaching, and this can cause difficulty if the trainer is trying to get a special course planned.

3   *Commercial businesses* sometimes run courses for outside people, usually to familiarise them with the commercial product. Best known amongst these are the familiarisation courses run by computer manufacturers for other firms' senior executives, and the product launch seminars run by everyone from drug companies to motor manufacturers. Overtly or covertly they are doing it to sell something—which is not to exclude an element of genuine philanthropy which appears from time to time—and so most trainers ignore them when making training plans. Yet they have a number of advantages: cheapness, quality of presentation, closeness to the market, and the opportunity of listening to other managers' questions as they contemplate purchasing. The obvious disadvantage that they are trying to sell something can be seen by everyone; a more subtle disadvantage is that they are trying to sell *their* product, so that a trainee totally unfamiliar with that type of product (e.g. computers) may believe the

features of this one manufacturer's product to be a necessary requirement for all such products.

If the trainer knows exactly what he wants—a mixture of familiarisation with the product range, and risk free practice as a buyer—these courses may meet his requirements exactly, especially if he can send the trainee to more than one course. Obviously as the course organiser is not running courses for a living the trainer cannot expect much responsiveness to his own needs, but this is often balanced by the attention given to individual trainees once on the course.

4 *Outward Bound* type courses are offered by a small number of organisations who arrange physically challenging activities for managers and others—usually in lonely places, for several days at a time, with a fair degree of physical hardship.

In favour of these courses the first thing to be said is that they are different. Different from all other types of course, and different from the manager's normal working day; they are therefore often more enjoyable and interesting, and certainly more memorable. Managers presented with daunting physical challenges—the need to scale up a sheer rock face, or to drive oneself beyond the point of exhaustion—find that they can do it, and this gives them a new sense of their own competence, a confidence in themselves that several years on the production line may have eroded. Also their attention is directed towards their physical health and fitness, and it is no bad thing if they decide to stop smoking and take more exercise.

Their disadvantages must also be carefully weighed. The improvements in performance resulting from these activities are often difficult to predict; a better sense of personal well being is all that can be expected. This may be very useful indeed, but it is all the trainer should expect; there is little transfer of training between managing a mountain rescue team and managing a typing pool. The philosophy that equates management with leadership in battle predominates, and we believe that management is different. Also, stressful courses are dangerous in that there is the temptation to put an artificially high value on something for which one has suffered, so that people may claim to have learned a lot while their performance shows no change; the publicity given to some of these establishments is also unhelpful, along the lines of 'If he crossed the Antarctic on a unicycle then he can imbue me with the qualities necessary to be a good manager'.

Trainers should use these courses in the same way as they would a sabbatical; not in the expectation of a specific improvement in managerial performance, but in order to bolster self-confidence. They should also be careful of creating an élite of managers who have been on such a course, and should not press people who have doubts about their fitness to take part.

5 *Consultancy organisations* usually have training departments which offer public courses and seminars. There is a wide range of choice here; as wide as the quality of consultants, and as wide as the areas in which they specialise or wider.

Consultants are usually close to the problems of business—if they were not they wouldn't survive. They react quickly to new training needs in the market, and the speakers on their courses usually have a wide range of experiences they can talk about—other people's problems and solutions. At best, the case studies used by consultants are the finest available. Usually they offer a good level of creature comforts—maybe too high if they use hotels rather than their own accommodation. The good ones are flexible enough to meet just about every client need—small seminars, unusual topics, odd timings—because that is what they are in business for. It must also be said that there are far fewer bad consultants around nowadays than in the late 1960s and early 1970s, when ITB money encouraged a lot of small get-rich-quick 'consultants' to offer their services; they were suffering before 1974, but the recession brought about by the oil crisis eliminated many of the charlatans. As with masseurs and osteopaths (and psychologists!) there is no licensing body covering management consultants; anybody can call himself one, and lots of people did. The good ones—not necessarily the biggest—have come through the recession improved; a little more responsive to clients' needs, a little less inclined to pontificate.

The negative side of using consultants' courses is that some of them will distort your problem until it fits a course they happen to be running in four weeks' time, or until it fits a packaged consultancy solution they have to offer. They may try to sell a knowledge course when what is wanted is a skills course, for instance. Some consultants use the training department as a place to break in new consultants before letting them loose on the client; not only does this make for inexperienced trainers, but it results in a lack of continuity in the management of training, with no-one seeing it as their responsibility to up-date the training material. (One consultancy is still using a case study in which the ideal solution, which includes making people redundant, takes no account of trade union reaction.) Life as a consultant tempts one to expediency rather than research when problem-solving, so that the long look at a problem may be missing from the training. Some consultants who have made their reputation marketing a particular solution find that the problems for which their solution was devised have changed, but they feel they dare not change their product in case this looks like admitting inadequacy. The trainer should beware in any case of consultants who seem solution- rather than problem-oriented, and if they boast that people have been using their package since 1955, ask them about updating and research. Beware, too, the tie-in sale; the course which is really paid marketing for their consultancy service, or the course which is a trailer for another course.

6   *Industry Training Boards* vary so widely in their quality that it is difficult to generalise. We have often asked managers (line and training) in small businesses to state whether they get any help from their ITB, and the answers run from high commendation to total disdain. Even within individual Boards much seems to depend on the quality of the local adviser. They are, of course, industry specific—though not all industries have them—and this is a major advantage; the ITB staff get a feeling for the problems of the industry as a whole, and can cross-fertilise well. It is also the ITB's job to do research into training problems which may be highly industry specific but which no one organisation could fund—the training of airline pilots, for example, or managers coping with North Sea oil exploration. They are also cheap to use—a benefit for the trainer and his budget, though with some loss of prestige compared with expensive outside performers. They have a duty to be responsive to the needs of the market and to cover all the training needs that they possibly can, so they have much less opportunity to pick and choose. If you have a good ITB, then, or a good adviser, you have the best of many worlds—industry base, responsiveness, practitioners with a research base as well; some of the best people we know in training work with ITBs.

So, unfortunately, do some of the worst. The ITB provides a more sheltered environment than a company training department; mistakes are less easy to spot, objectives easier to fudge, the opportunity to wait for the market to come to you instead of going to the market. Many of the people shaken out of the small consultancy market by the oil crisis tried to find refuge with the ITBs.

If you have a good ITB adviser, it's like having your own consultant on tap. Let him know how much you appreciate him—it's a lonely life for many of the field training advisers—and make sure you use him. If you think your ITB adviser is not giving you value for money, let him know, and let him know why, and give him a chance to improve, as you would an ordinary employee; and don't damn the whole ITB because you happen to be badly served. Because he costs little, it is easy to push him around; if you treat him like an unpaid servant, never contacting him unless you want something done and that right now, you'll get poor service. Treat him as a consultant, as a regular sounding board, as someone useful for an off-the-record chat, and his performance could improve; if after that he's still only interested in the number of classroom hours your managers put in, show him the door.

7 *Professional and quasi-professional bodies*, such as the Institute of Personnel Management, the British Institute of Management, the Institution of Civil Engineers, etc., run courses at a variety of levels. Some of them are licensing and/or certificating bodies, running their own training programme or allowing other people's training programmes to be accredited for their own purposes. If this is what the trainer requires—a secretary wants to do an IPM diploma, for example—he has little choice about the type of training, he must take what is recommended. But he needs advice about whether the end product will really be useful; there are all sorts of bodies offering diplomas that don't mean much. Beware the kind of body that offers posh diplomas, with distinctions, to senior managers as a come-on to get more people enrolled.

Besides their function in licensing and certification, these bodies often arrange conferences and short courses. Usually the subject matter will be chosen by the course runners rather than by the clients, and it may be highly specialised; a good thing if you want it, but disturbing to come across by accident. Some of the very old bodies have become a little conservative and unadventurous, relying on years rather than on competence; some are more preoccupied with labels than with function. However, if the body is a standard setting body the courses it offers should be treated with respect.

The annual conference deserves a book—a more light hearted book—all to itself. All human life is there: meeting people, food and drink at the company's expense, lectures and discussions and films and free samples and bookstalls and people you haven't met for donkey's years. It is important to know why someone is going on a conference—as a jolly, as a reward, to give a paper, to learn, to meet people, to promote your company—and to set objectives to meet those expectations. If the purpose is earnest learning, then the trainer should discuss with the manager beforehand which papers he is going to listen to, and should probably arrange for a report to his fellow managers on return; but if he's going as a reward for having sold more widgets than anyone else, don't be hypocritical about it—give him his rail ticket and the following day off to recover.

8 *Course running organisations.* Usually the most obvious and noisy of all organisers of external courses, these are small companies who arrange seminars using freelance speakers on a range of management topics. Often their seminars are conducted in hotels; some will arrange in-house seminars also, and some have an allied consultancy service.

Usually they are close to the market, actively listening for what the clients need. A high standard of accommodation and food is usually provided. The speakers too are often of high quality, and some seminars offer combinations of speakers that would be difficult if not impossible to arrange in-house; though there is the charisma problem—a famous name spouting nonsense is less likely to be hissed from the stalls. Most of these organisations have an active programme, with seminars repeated several times a year, often in different locations.

The disadvantages correlate with the extent to which they are in show business rather in management education. For example, nearly all these seminars are 'evaluated' by reference to how much people said they enjoyed the programme. This hardly matters if you are seeking to meet a technical training need, or a need that people know they have, or if you want an up-dating; but there are some courses—skills courses especially—where end-of-course happiness is unrelated to later behaviour change, and the ideal is to send the trainees away looking a little thoughtful. The trainer should pay particular attention to phrases like 'our courses are a success' and should think twice before using courses for interpersonal skills training which their givers evaluate by members' reactions alone. Being in show business too means that the pressure is on the lecturer for the quick answer, the devastating rather than thoughtful handling of objectors, for the *ex cathedra* statement rather than the admission of ignorance. Most of the organisations arranging seminars on a purely commercial basis make little attempt to see whether the speaker in one seminar contradicts a speaker in another seminar; there are honourable exceptions to this, but mostly quality control is left to the individual speaker. Speakers vary in their purposes too; some really want to teach, others see the seminar as a way into consultancy for the firms attending.

Before using one of these seminars the trainer should refer to his training needs diagnosis and make sure what he wants—knowledge, familiarisation, practical skills. He should read the course brochure with this in mind; there are too many courses with an unhappy mixture of knowledge and skills, and a two-day seminar of which the first day is instruction and the second consists of practical exercises needs examining very carefully to see if it is getting the best out of the participants. The trainer should also ask about the participant mix. We have seen personnel directors mixed with supervisors, on a course about performance appraisal which had a little bit of everything—manpower planning, management by objectives, and a couple of rather wooden role plays—and we have no hesitation in reporting that the mix did not work. In general, short seminars with good speakers lend themselves well to being told about things, and less well to learning how to.

All these providers of external courses have a purpose, and all can be misused. The training needs diagnosis is the key; without it one does not know what questions to ask to guide some of the very basic choices. Another useful tip is: never be afraid to ask. Ring up the person running the course and ask about it. If the course doesn't look as if it will fit your needs, but you like the speakers or the training method, ask if they can adapt it to fit your needs. Ask to visit, or to see the literature. Course runners are not 'take it or leave it' any more—or they will not survive long—and if you know what you want you should be able to get it.

C   Warnings

Now for some do's and don'ts, again taken from painful (and no doubt useful) experience.

1 *Read the brochure* properly before booking anyone on a course. The title is to catch your eye; the contents should tell you more. A seminar that examines one problem, or one solution, in detail may be fine if you want to know that one topic; don't send someone who has been led to believe that the seminar covers a range of topics. He'll grumble, and spoil the thing for the participants whose training managers can read.

2 *Beware silly hours.* Courses boasting that they keep managers up till three and four in the morning working on case studies and presentations are not worth the money nor the participants' effort. To repeat an old lesson: hardly anyone works better after midnight, and one of the first things to go is the ability to monitor one's own performance.

3 *Beware deliberate stress.* It interferes with learning, and plays about with people's dynamics so that they say they value the experience even when it was sheer hell. The wilder shores of interpersonal skills training are peopled with this sort of course.

4 *Keep away from director collectors.* By this we mean the kind of course which sets out to flatter the most senior manager present in the hope that he will send his subordinates. 'I did well on it, therefore we'll use it' is powerful motivation for managers choosing training, selection tests, appraisal systems, etc., and it should be avoided by all independent-thinking trainers.

5 *Beware the stab in the back.* The trainer will probably only see this if he goes on a course himself. On some courses, people with difficulties or objections are dealt with by making them look ridiculous in front of the rest, giving them impossible exercises, and manipulating the group to turn against them. This does not happen often, in our experience, but enough to justify the warning.

6 *Beware people who play the dissonance game.* These are the courses which set out to induce a feeling of frustration or failure early in the proceedings, maybe adding a little stress or sleeplessness to help things along, and then lift out of the trough later, sending people away convinced they have learned something because they have struggled so hard. Cashing in on cognitive dissonance reduction is an old con-man's trick; the trainer can spot it by looking at the pattern of exercises and activity (do they look as if they are setting people up for failure?) and by asking how the courses are evaluated (beware reliance on trainees' ratings of the course utility).

7 *Ask how the training is evaluated.* Most courses collect

sheets of paper at the end. If these are seriously referred to as 'evaluation sheets', beware. The course organiser needs to know how people feel at the end of the course, but the real test is how they perform when they are back doing their jobs. So: is there any formal or informal follow-up? Is there a session on implementation of new learning towards the end of the course? Is there any provision for trainees to monitor themselves? How has the training changed over the years? Has the training ever been the subject of a full evaluation study? (Quite a few of the more popular training programmes—Coverdale, Blake's Grid, Transactional Analysis—have been researched by ITBs, business schools, or by in-house work in the big organisations.)

8   *Ask what the fee covers.* Tuition alone? Accommodation? Travel between hotel and training centre? Literature? Follow-up work?

9   *Pay no attention* to the long lists of companies, usually found on the back of course brochures, saying: 'Among those organisations using our services are . . .' It only takes the relief storeman in Mac Fisheries Wigan Pier branch to attend a report writing course, for some course organisers to claim that 'Among those organisations using our services are . . . The Unilever Group of Companies . . .'. You'd have thought people would be aware of this dodge by now, but it still works.

10   *Ask if the speakers* advertised will really appear, or whether substitutes may be sent. Some consultancies are notorious for making last minute substitutes if there is fee earning work to be done.

D   Re-entry

Many external courses fail because they are never dovetailed into the daily work of the organisation. 'Right, you can forget all that high-falutin rubbish and do as I say,' appears to be the attitude of many managers receiving a subordinate back from a course. The trainer must take special care—much more than he takes with internal courses—to see that this does not happen. He therefore needs a policy about the use of external courses, which must be communicated to all managers; for example, he might say that all bookings for courses must be channelled through him. This helps save money being wasted, and gives the trainer an opportunity to go back to the manager to discover what the real training need is, and whether it could be better served some other way. This increases the administrative load on the trainer, of course, and may be unacceptable in some decentralised organisations; an alternative is to allow managers to book themselves or their subordinates on courses costing below a certain amount in money or time, but to require central sanction for greater commitments.

Then the trainer should be proactive in the choice of courses, rather than responding to salesmanship from course runners; he should know where each course fits into the training needs diagnosis and training plan, so that he can meet with the trainee before the course to brief him. This will probably not be necessary for short seminars, but it is vital that longer courses be preceded by some sort of briefing—what the course is about, what it is intended to achieve, what the trainee will be expected to do differently as a result, etc. Managers who have not been on courses for a while will appreciate being warned of the difficulty of sitting listening for eight hours at a stretch. The trainer may brief both the trainee and his manager, and anyone else involved.

Good external courses usually have something about implementation in their last part; the trainer should follow this up by arranging a debriefing session as a matter of routine when someone comes off a course. How it happens and who is involved varies; in small organisations it may be the trainer himself who does the debriefing, while large organisations must delegate this responsibility to the local manager. 'Tell us about your training course' at weekly meetings of the management team is a good idea, but the personal debriefing is better. The trainer may use administrative devices to encourage good debriefing: sending the trainee a request for an outline of his action plans (which, please, the trainer follows up in a few months' time); sending a routine form for the trainee to give a sketch of the training course and what he learned, who else in the organisation might benefit, etc.; sending the manager a request for similar details. Machiavellian trainers could so arrange things that the training costs remain charged to the manager's budget until debriefing has successfully been completed.

The trainer must not equate an ecstatic response to the training with the judgement that the course is worthwhile; only later behaviour change can show that. The purpose of debriefing is to remind the trainee that it is possible to apply the lessons he learned on his external course, and that such application is expected of him.

E Summary

The choice of an external course is dictated by a comparison of the internal training resources with the external ones, and by needs to mix with managers from other companies. Organisations offering external courses vary along a number of dimensions: ivory tower—real world, research approach—pragmatic approach, teaching the trainees—marketing consultancy, market-oriented—product-oriented. The choice must be made with care, and is aided by good diagnosis of training needs and an unwillingness to be misled by fanciful claims. All external courses need fitting into the training plan, and special attention must be paid to debriefing trainees so as to integrate their learning with the rest of the organisation.

F Discussion questions

At the beginning of a week-long course in teamwork the trainees were asked to write an account of a problem at work which they would like the course to help solve. One trainee, a graduate newly hired into the personnel department, wrote that her problem was a manager whose sole criterion in selecting people was their astrological sign. The problems were not shared with the rest of the trainees.

Later in the week it became apparent that the course was not doing all that it claimed: the group dynamics were being deliberately manipulated to make people feel ecstatic at the point where a trainer was taking orders for further courses; and that doubters who did not respond to the manipulation were deliberately made the butt of the other trainees' hostility. The trainee voiced her concern during the concluding sessions. When she returned to work the following Monday she was called in to see her manager, who wanted to know what other libels she had been spreading about him besides his dependence on astrology. As the course trainers had been the only ones to see the written problems, she deduced that the trainers had contacted her manager over the weekend; the training firm was attempting to secure a large order for in-house training from him. The manager admitted this.

1   Is there an implied commitment to secrecy from the trainer to the trainee? If there is, are there any circumstances under which

it should be broken?

2   The trainers on this course said that the people they most disliked training were the ones who had come to evaluate the training. Why do you think they said this? Could their view ever be justified?

3   Assuming that there are training needs which are best served by a series of courses, when, ethically, is the best time to make the follow-on sale?

4   Later research on this training course showed that while it was effective in some ways, other major assumptions made about learning in groups were incorrect. How do you think the designer of the training reacted to the research?

11 Coaching and counselling

A What is coaching?

Coaching is a training technique which utilises the boss-subordinate relationship as the vehicle for learning; the subordinate's performance is improved by his boss selecting certain job activities for their developmental content, supporting this with regular counselling interviews.

Coaching is therefore an on-the-job rather than off-line form of training, and has advantages which make it a likely alternative to courses. In the chapters on training needs diagnosis and the choice of training options, it was stated that training courses are a possible form of training when the knowledge or skill can be practised more than once within the time limits of the course. When this is not possible the training must take place in post. Circumstances indicating coaching rather than other training methods therefore include:

1   Where there is no way of simulating the training need in a course because of the complexity of the situation, e.g. learning how to close down a factory.
2   When it would take too long to simulate the training need on a course, e.g. the self-management skills needed by managers who must take over a project half-designed, manage it for their length of tenure, and hand it over to the next incumbent.
3   Where the trainer fears that there would be re-entry problems if the training were done on a course, e.g. the senior managers in a business they regard as unique—too small in number for an internal course, and likely to reject external courses as irrelevant.
4   Where there is a need to strengthen man-manager relations in general, and the coaching programme will help.
5   Where there is a history of courses having been misused—unfair report-back, jolly holidays, laying on of hands, etc.

A trainer facing such problems will find that coaching programmes (or projects and assignments) can meet his need, but he has to accept a change of role for himself. In coaching,

184

managers do the training; the trainer's job is to see the need for coaching, to equip managers with coaching skills, and to help monitor and control. Only rarely is it acceptable to use the trainer as coach, and his resources would be spread a little thinly. The trainer must also realise that learning is organised slightly differently in a coaching programme: in most courses the learning can be described as *teacher-objective*, in that it is the teacher who looks forward to what he wants people to have learned, and plans the experience accordingly. There is an element of this in coaching, but there is also a strong component of *learner-retrospective* learning—the kind where after the event the learner looks back and says 'Yes, I learned something from that'. A good coach tries to manage both types of learning, by selecting activities which he believes will teach the trainee something, and by giving frequent opportunities for the trainee to talk about his experiences so that he will realise what he has learned. Strategically, this means that the trainer must accept that many different activities could be used to achieve the same learning goals; if he has six manager-coaches all trying to improve their subordinates' ability to delegate, he must not expect them all to go about it in the same way. Tactically, it means that the coach must strive to adopt a counselling rather than a teaching style in the review interviews, never telling the subordinate what to do, always helping him discover his own solution. And, under this seemingly loose control there must be well defined training objectives, otherwise the programme will fall apart for lack of end-points.

What, in practice, does coaching look like? From the subordinate's point of view, the process has a number of stages:

1 *A setting-up meeting* between himself and his manager. At this meeting some training needs are established; the notion of meeting them by on-the-job training rather than by formal courses is agreed; and a plan of action drawn up containing a list of things that both parties will do, a set of success measures, and a review date for the next meeting.

2 *Activities* selected for their developmental opportunities are undertaken by the subordinate, who probably has a written record of his progress.

3 *A review meeting* is held, during which the manager-coach helps him review and consolidate what he has learned, gives

praise and encouragement where possible, and they jointly set further learning targets.

The second and third stages are repeated as often as necessary to complete the subordinate's progress. Now let us examine in detail what happens at each stage.

B   The setting-up interview

The difficulty with this is getting it started. Sometimes a subordinate will come to the manager with a problem which can be turned into a coaching opportunity; more often, though, it is the manager who would like to start a coaching programme but cannot find the right way to introduce it. Summoning the subordinate to his office and stating that they will now start coaching looks artificial or even threatening.

Some sort of pre-meeting document, completed by the subordinate, is a possible solution; it will serve to start the discussion. The manager could ask his subordinate to keep a diary, along the lines of the examples in Chapter 4, showing where most of his effort is going and how he is spending his time. A manager about to start coaching with a number of subordinates will find it helpful to compare the different diaries, though he should be careful about who else has access and should not make implicit comparisons between subordinates to their faces. Or he could ask the subordinate to fill in a Preparation for Counselling form, to be brought to the interview, along the lines of the one in Figure 11.1 opposite. Managers may invent their own Preparation for Counselling forms, or the trainer can be called in to help. Some coaches use the Performance Appraisal form, giving it to the subordinate to fill in for himself; firms whose appraisal systems are participative may well find that the best time to start a coaching programme is shortly after the performance appraisal interview. Where the appraisal system is in disrepute, or has been used as a spoken charge sheet, efforts should be made to dissociate the coaching programme from the appraisal system.

A more probing document with which to prime the setting-up meeting is the Job Climate Questionnaire of Stephen Fineman. This is shown in Figure 11.2 together with a scoring key. The questionnaire (without the key, of course) is given to the subordinate to fill in. (The manager may like to predict how he thinks the subordinate will fill it in, and ponder any differences before beginning coaching.) The questionnaire is scored by adding up the positive and the negative scores separately; an algebraic sum can then be taken, but for coaching and counselling purposes it is better to concentrate on the two scores separately. Someone with a high positive score overall, but who has one or two —3 scores, needs to have these low scores looked at. The outcome of the JCQ is more closely related to job satisfaction than training needs, though training needs can easily be inferred; the JCQ is therefore most useful when the trainer wants to use coaching to strengthen the man-manager relationship as well as to meet training needs.

Preparation for counselling form

1   What are the main activities you have undertaken in the last year?

2   Which was the most successful? Why?

3   Which was the least successful? Why?

4   Which aspects of your job interest you the most? the least?

5   Are there any skills you have which your present job does not fully utilise?

6   In what areas do you need training or other help to do your job better?

7   Where do you see your career going, ideally, in the next five years?

8   In your present job, what sort of things tell you that you are doing a good job?

9   How could your manager help you do a better and more satisfying job?

> The information appearing on this form is confidential

Fig. 11.1   Example of a preparation for counselling form

Other documents may suggest themselves; the simpler the better, as they serve to start a discussion rather than summarise a relationship, and we repeat our warning not to get carried away by pseudo-psychological tests that have no validation evidence. The need is for something that can be taken at its face value,

Job climate questionnaire—key

Below are pairs of descriptions with which you can describe the way you see the immediate environment, or climate, in which you work. The descriptions refer to various aspects of your job situation such as the amount of independence, the degree of formality, how much responsibility exists and so on.

Look at each pair of descriptions and decide firstly whether *Description A* or *Description B* is in general more indicative of your own view of your job situation. Secondly decide the extent to which this description applies—then place a tick in the appropriate box. If neither description is applicable tick the centre box.

Description A	Description A applies			Neither description is more applicable	Description B applies			Description B
	to a great extent	to a moderate extent	to a slight extent		to a slight extent	to a moderate extent	to a great extent	
1 I am allowed a great deal of independence in my work	+3	+2	+1	0	—1	—2	—3	I am allowed very little independence in my work
2 I always have to share the credit for the results of my work with other people	—3							I am allowed to take full credit for the results of my work
3 Personal initiative is highly valued	+3							Personal initiative is rather frowned upon
4 I feel I am able to set my own work pace	+3							I feel I am unable to set my own work pace
5 I always have to get permission from my superior before doing anything new	—3							I rarely have to get permission from my superior before doing anything new
6 It is easy to plan ahead in my work	+3							It is very difficult to plan ahead in my work
7 I feel that I work in a highly competitive department	+3							I feel that I work in a department that is not at all competitive
8 Most of the people around me are very decisive	+3							Most of the people around me are rather indecisive
9 The work allows me very little personal responsibility	—3							The work allows me a great deal of personal responsibility
10 The work gives me a sense of achieving something	+3							The work does not give me a sense of achieving something
11 How I progress in the organisation has very little to do with my own performance	—3							How I progress in the organisation depends very largely on how I perform

Description A	Description A applies			Neither description is more applicable	Description B applies			Description B
	to a great extent	to a moderate extent	to a slight extent		to a slight extent	to a moderate extent	to a great extent	
12 The work goals have very little challenge for me	−3							I am able to work towards very challenging goals
13 My successes are noticed far more than failures	+3							My failures are noticed far more than my successes
14 I can rarely find out how well I have performed at a task	−3							I can very soon find out how well I have performed at a task
15 I feel that I am able to stand out as an individual apart	+3							I feel very much like a small cog in a big wheel
16 Promotion is mainly on the basis of length of service	−3							Promotion is closely linked with good work
17 I am encouraged to improve myself through formal training	+3							I am not encouraged to improve myself through formal training
18 The support that I get from other departments is often inadequate	−3							The support that I get from other departments is first class
19 There are pressures on me to get problems out into the open	+3							There are pressures on me to 'sweep problems under the carpet'
20 Ambition tends to be frowned upon	−3							Ambition is strongly encouraged
21 Success in my work is highly rewarded	+3							Success in my work is hardly recognised
22 I can take no risks in my job	−3							I am able to take reasonable risks in my job
23 There is a great deal of novelty in my job	+3							There is very little novelty in my job
24 I feel that I work in a highly inefficient department	−3							I feel that I work in a highly efficient department
25 All-in-all this is a dynamic place in which to work	+3							All-in-all this is not a very dynamic place in which to work

British senior managers' mean score   16.2
British junior managers' mean score   14.6

Fig. 11.2 Job climate questionnaire, with key (Fineman)

without offending either party, and which the manager can use to lead into a discussion about coaching.

A pre-coaching document of some kind also serves as a check on the success of the coaching, if it is re-administered at a later stage; this is another reason for starting the process with a written record. Managers who dislike asking their subordinates to keep diaries or fill in questionnaires, and who are faced with the need to start the interview from cold, could ask the subordinate for one or two critical incidents—examples of incidents that gave him problems, and of incidents he feels were handled successfully. (It is important to ask about both successes and failures here; although the 'success' question may not yield as much as the 'problem' question, the combination is less threatening.)

The aim of the interview itself should be the identification of areas of training need and the acceptance, on the part of the subordinate, that some or all of these training needs can be met using his daily experience as a vehicle. (There is a section later in this chapter on training managers in the requisite skills.) The two parties should have a short list—probably no more than three items—of things which they will do together or which the subordinate will do on his own, with success measures agreed between them. These measures are important, but managers should not believe that only those things whose performance can be measured to two decimal places are suitable activities; 'more than' and 'less than' also qualify as measures, and so does subjective judgement if the person who is making it can clearly state the basis on which his judgement is made—clearly enough for someone else to replicate his judgement. If the organisation has had an unsuccessful MbO programme care should be taken to emphasise the differences between the coaching programme— which covers only a part of the job, and is private to man and manager, and has no immediate pay-offs one way or the other— and the MbO programme, which covered all the job, was hierarchically organised from the top down, and may have been linked to the merit payment system.

At the setting-up meeting the two parties also agree when they will meet again to discuss progress.

C Activities

The developmental activities which are undertaken next include a wide range of possibilities. One common one is for the manager to start to take the subordinate to meetings from which he had previously been excluded, taking the time beforehand to discuss the object of the meeting, the balance of power, and his own tactics, and reviewing these things afterwards. As time goes on the subordinate may be asked to undertake more of the manager's preparation work for the meeting, or be encouraged to make his own contribution. Internal company meetings are the most often used, but the subordinate can also be taken on visits to customers and suppliers. He can also visit new people and places on his own—other parts of the firm, old customers prepared to do a favour, etc. Many a stores manager's performance has improved once he has gone to see where the parts he issues are actually used. Ranging more widely, subordinates can go to pick the brains of outside experts— lecturers, consultants, the firm's retired managers; or they can spend some time listening to what happens in an industrial tribunal.

Many activities involve the direct delegation of responsibility from the manager to the subordinate; thus the subordinate may chair the management meeting, with his manager in the crowd. He can prepare reports that his manager would normally prepare; act as a filter on fault reports that would normally have gone to his manager; prepare option reports on paper which his manager would normally have done in his head, and so on. The manager needs the skill to delegate well; he must not make petty alterations to the brief prepared for him, and he must not blame his subordinates in front of others while grabbing any credit for himself. As the coaching progresses, one of the most difficult things a manager has to do is to stand by and watch while the subordinate makes a mistake; but there are some things one only learns to do right by seeing how awful it looks when done wrong.

Other activities include more formal self-development techniques—reading books, taking correspondence courses, etc. One would hope that some of these things would happen anyway, but the coaching programme gives sanction to them: 'I needn't feel I'm wasting my time unproductively reading this book, my manager says I can and I must,' the subordinate says to himself. Again, this needs a change of heart by managers for whom being good is being busy.

D Review meeting

At the allotted time the two parties come together to review progress. It is important that a specific time be set aside for this—it should not be crammed in on the spur of the moment after a regular meeting has finished. The coaching manager's job is, most of the time, to keep quiet. He must encourage the subordinate to review for himself what he has learned. A good rule therefore is to start the interview with: 'Tell me how you think you got on,' and to ask lots of opening-up questions: 'Why did it happen like that?', 'Could that have been improved at all?', 'How was it different from the previous one?', 'How could you tell it was serious enough to call me?', and, most important of all, 'What would you do differently next time?' The manager must not say: 'Well if I were you, I would have done this . . .' because he is not there to show how clever he is, he is there to reflect the thoughts of the developing subordinate.

After the review comes the setting of some more activities and targets; maybe one or two new ones, and one or two of the previous ones renewed and made more challenging. It is not a good idea to change the activities each time—almost by definition some of the training needs take longer to work on.

Thus the cycle repeats itself. How ofter should the two meet? It should be more frequently in the early stages of the programme—maybe once a fortnight, or once a month. Later it can get less frequent, though an interval of more than four months is probably too long.

Most people, when they realise the demands that a coaching programme makes on the managers concerned, have one of two reactions. The first is: 'We cannot possibly spare the time,' and the other is: 'Where on earth in our organisation are we going to find managers with the skills necessary to perform such tasks? If they were all that good, we wouldn't need any training at all.' The answer to the first question has to be that coaching is a way of improving business performance and should be viewed in the same way as taking machines out of service in order to do preventive maintenance on them. To the second question there are a number of answers. One is that coaching helps the coach as well as the subordinate. Another is that you have to start somewhere—Houdini said that there is always one knot weaker than the rest, and that is where you start. In the extreme case where all the managers are utter duffers and couldn't teach anyone anything, there is the possibility of introducing an outside coach at senior management levels to start the ball rolling; but there is usually somewhere to make a start, and it is better politics for the trainer to select one division and do that well than to wait for the climate to be right everywhere.

E   The trainer's involvement

The trainer plays three possible roles in a coaching programme. He can make the initial suggestions, and persuade people to try coaching; he can train the managers who will act as coaches; and he can help in monitoring the coaching programme itself. We assume for simplicity's sake that a number of managers are likely to act as coaches; where only one manager is to be a coach the trainer may need to use external courses for coaching skills rather than run the course himself.

1   *Suggesting* the coaching programme must be done with tact, as with any staff inspired innovation. The trainer should realise that many managers will be coaches already, without having been labelled as such; claims for originality will not be well received by them. Nor should the trainer try to attract attention by selling the technique of coaching—all too easy when one has just seen a series of books and films about the topic. Many a useful tool has been rejected because the trainer has shouted: 'Hey! I've got this fantastic new technique!' when he should really wait until a problem comes along that he can apply it to. The best strategy therefore is to discover what operational problems could be helped by a coaching programme, and to suggest coaching as a possible cure. Of course, it is permissible to give the problems a little help in coming to the surface—an attitude survey sponsored by the training department could well reveal opportunities for coaching.

2   *Training* managers to act as coaches requires that three different training needs be met. Managers need the skills of listening and counselling well; they need some insight into the kinds of activities that can be set as part of a coaching programme; and they need some help with the strategy of coaching. These training needs fit nicely into a course of two or three days' duration—maybe shorter if your performace appraisal training already places a heavy emphasis on counselling skills.

(a) *Skills training* uses exercises such as the *listening exercise*, in which small groups of trainees are put together to discuss a controversial topic, under a time limit, with the objective of reaching a consensus. Afer twenty minutes or so they are separated and each person has to summarise on a sheet of paper the point of view of each person. Then everyone receives the summaries appertaining to themselves, which they score for (a) completeness and (b) accuracy. The trainer then reviews with them some of the lessons they learned. This is a good exercise when placed at the beginning and the end of each course, for practice and for evaluation. *Tape-stop* exercises (see Chaper 8) are also useful for developing questioning skills; make a tape of a coaching interview in which the interviewee is not very forthcoming, and arrange the stops so that the trainees must suggest questions that open up the issues. *Role plays* are also useful in this context, if advantage is taken of the learning opportunities that occur when one takes the other person's side; get the trainees role-playing subordinates who feel that their manager is not delegating enough, or not using their skills fully, or trying to feather-bed them. Managers who have had no interviewing training or experience previously will need reminding of the fundamental courtesies—no interruptions, for instance. They should also be told how coaching differs from performance appraisal interviewing—there is no rating or marking, no connection with the salary system, no need for senior managers to get involved.

(b) *Insights into activities* useful for developing subordinates is learned through exercises such as *brain-storming* as many possible activities as the group can think of to meet, for example, a need for better political skills, or a need to make a better précis. Managers can be asked to look back over their own history and give instances of tasks or activities which they themselves found useful in teaching them something—they should list the activities and what they learned from them as precisely as possible. They may work through old coaching records (which the trainer may invent if this is his first time, or steal from someone else) deciding what the best kind of activities would be for the people concerned. It is also useful to start a discussion about the measurement of success; pull an activity out of the hat and get the trainees to brain-storm as many possible related measures as they can think of. The arbitrariness of the procedure should help convince them that almost every worthwhile activity can be assigned success measures if one tries hard enough.

(c) *The strategy of coaching* is something the trainer can talk about in a general way, in the hope that some people will be warned off; it is difficult to practise strategy on a short training course, though, and some will have to be saved for later review meetings. Under the heading of strategy the trainer talks about the need to let people make mistakes rather than protect them, and the relevance of this consideration to the choice of activities. He talks about the Fat Aunt Ellen syndrome—the manager taking the credit for the trainee's learning, and crowing over him for having changed his mind. He talks about the fact that you can only coach and counsel the person being interviewed, so that neither party in the coaching interview tries to shift the blame onto someone who isn't there. These issues will be familiar in part to any practising manager, but it helps to have them put into the context of coaching. An example of a two-day course in coaching skills is shown in Figure 11.3.

3 *Supporting* the coaching programme is vital. The trainer has a number of jobs to do if the innovation is to survive its first six months. He must hold review meetings with coaches, at which they share their experiences and renew their commitment. He can help a great deal with simple things like paperwork—the design of a Preparation for Counselling form, or of a coaching interview record form. He can help design forms for the trainees to use for monitoring their own progress. He should be there to serve as a neutral third party if disputes arise between the coach and the subordinate—advertise this role discreetly or he could find himself coaching both parties simultaneously! He should also be concerned to consolidate the coaching programme into the management style of the company: coaching should be part of the training courses for new managers, coaching should be mentioned in the company newsletter, and coaching should be one of the dimensions on which managerial performance may be measured at appraisal time. Their responsibility to grow good subordinates must be openly acknowledged—and paid for—before managers can be relied upon to take it seriously.

The evaluation of the coaching programme must be planned from the start. A re-run of the Job Climate Questionnaire, or of the diary, gives a quantitative measure of the change in perception of the job; care should be taken not to attribute causality, as something else besides the coaching programme

Day One	
0900—0930	Introductions to each other, tutors, accommodation, etc.
0930—1015	In small groups participants review the training needs of their subordinates, producing a list of all the identified needs
1015—1045	Small groups report back in general session. Tutor then asks them which of these needs can be met by formal training courses, and stimulates discussion on how the rest of the needs can be met
1045—1100	Tutor gives short talk on the place of coaching in management training
1100—1115	Coffee
1115—1200	A tape recording of a coaching interview is played to the trainees in general session
1200—1230	In small groups they review the skills necessary to be a good coach
1230—1300	Small groups report back
1300—1400	Lunch
1400—1500	Listening exercise
1500—1515	Review exercise
1515—1530	Tea
1530—1615	In small groups go over a transcript of a coaching interview; first to classify each of the coach's contributions as helpful or unhelpful, secondly to say what the coach's strategy appeared to be
1615—1730	Tape-stop exercises using a coaching interview as vehicle
Evening session	Talk from a senior manager about the company's strategy for the next five years and how this will affect the new skills and knowledge managers will need to acquire

Day Two	
0900—1000	Tape-stop exercises again
1000—1030	Preparation of role-playing exercises
1030—1045	Coffee
1045—1215	Role-playing exercises; trainees form pairs, each pair doing two coaching interviews, swapping roles. Roles are chosen to give trainees practice as the subordinate, not the coach
1215—1245	Review
1245—1400	Lunch
1400—1500	Brain-storming exercises, in small groups, thinking of activities to meet given training needs
1500—1530	Groups report back
1530—1545	Tea
1545—1630	Discussion on the strategy of coaching
1630—1700	Individual task, preparing a plan of action to coach one subordinate
1700—1730	Group discussion of the next steps, and commitment from trainers to give necessary help

Fig. 11.3   Sample two-day course for managers in coaching techniques

may have caused the change; nor should much be read into small changes in the numbers. Nonetheless they are useful measures and would serve to start the next cycle of coaching, if required. More qualitative measures of change come from a re-run of the Preparation for Counselling form, or from another Critical Incident interview. More general attitude surveys could also be utilised. If all else fails, the performance appraisal records of those being coached could be studied, but the appraising manager is also the coach and has vested interest in saying that his people are improving. And of course there should be improvements in business performance—what, in Chapter 13, we have called *real life measures* of training.

Of course, the measures above are all applied to the subordinate—the one receiving the coaching. We expect also an improvement in the performance of the coach, and this can be measured in a number of ways. A before-and-after diary kept by the manager-coach should, if the coaching is successful, show changes such as:

> increased amount of work delegated to subordinates;
> less preparation time needed before meetings for which subordinate prepared the brief;
> fewer 'emergencies' referred to him which transpire not to be emergencies at all;
> more time spent interviewing subordinates;
> less time spent checking and correcting subordinates' work;
> more time spent initiating things, and less time in responding to things;
> less time dealing with complaints about the behaviour of subordinates,

and so on.

Changes in the manager's perceptions of his subordinates would be revealed if, at the same time as the subordinate fills in a JCQ or a Preparation for Appraisal form, the manager fills in one; a successful coach will have a greater insight into his subordinates after coaching than before. A very sophisticated form of before-and-after measurement applied to the coach is the Repertory Grid (see Chapter 5). Here the manager is interviewed using as elements the names of his subordinates—including both those who have been coached and those who have not, if both classes exist—together with his own name and any others that seem relevant. After coaching the manager should have more things to say about the people he has coached, on a wider range of topics, with more subtlety of judgement.

Coaching is not a complete alternative to training by formal methods, and the trainer will also help managers to decide when coaching must be supplemented by a course or other formal training activity. Thus slowly but surely the whole management style of the organisation becomes shifted towards planned personal development—everyone acting as resources according to his lights, with managers coaching and trainers acting as a central resource and as an interface between the coaching programme and the other training activities. If the coaching programme is installed from the top downwards there is a better chance of rapid success, because the middle managers who become coaches have themselves been coached and know what it is like. Although one sometimes hears it said that planning ahead in business is very difficult, if not impossible, there are some changes which can be foreseen if only people would look; the coaching programme is a splendid vehicle for getting people ready for these changes in plenty of time. For example, many organisations buried their heads in the sand when equal pay and opportunity for women was legislated; yet they had five years' notice, five years in which to think about the changes of attitude and work patterns which this legislation would inexorably bring to pass. Impossible to change attitudes overnight, when the legislation came in; one or two firms used the coaching programme, however structured, to get managers ready for the new demands that would be made on them, with the result that they were actually able to point to business improvements consequent on the installation of 'typists' lib.' or crèches or refurbished employee benefits schemes. Trainers with a little imagination and access to the seven-year plan can begin to interject into their coaches' review meetings suggestions as to new directions people should be taking, new skills that it would be useful for people to acquire.

The coaching programme thus is made responsive to organisational needs. We strongly suggest, however, that the trainer make sure that the information generated by the coaching programme is kept private to that programme, and to the manager and subordinate from whom it came. It would be awkward if someone from manpower planning wanted to use the information for his management audit; it would be catastrophic if ever the coaching records were quoted in an industrial tribunal, or as a basis on which to dismiss someone. The privacy of the records should be absolute, otherwise the risk to the learner is increased unacceptably.

F   Coaching by someone other than the immediate manager

Most of the time coaching happens between man and manager; only rarely should a third party be brought in. There are some firms where, at the annual performance appraisal, an 'uncle' figure is used by both parties to help clarify ideas and solve disagreements; in such cases, where it is already accepted that the manager may share his responsibility with another, coaching by the 'uncle' would be acceptable. Similarly there are some firms with a very strong personnel function, in which all developmental discussions take place with the personnel officer in the first instance; managers here manage commodities rather than people and it would be appropriate to use the personnel resource as a coach. Again, some graduate recruitment programmes recruiting direct into management training have an 'industrial tutor' system; here the new graduate is assigned to a manager normally, but also has regular meetings with a sympathetic senior manager whose task it is to bridge the gap between university and industry by means of informal chats and tutorials. In such firms a coaching programme would probably use both parties—the manager and the industrial tutor—though one would predominate.

This leaves us with two situations in which coaching is done by a third party—furthermore, by a third party from outside the firm. In the first instance the managing director of a firm appoints an outside consultant as his personal coach, or as coach himself and his immediate management team. The consultant follows the same pattern as the internal manager-coach; meetings followed by actions followed by review meetings. What the consultant contributes—if he is a good one—is almost impossible to describe on paper; he questions the directors, gets them to challenge their assumptions, gets them to consider alternative points of view. Because he has sanction to do it he can persuade them to play games, to try new ways of doing things, which an internal resource might have difficulty getting accepted—new techniques for increasing creativity, problem-solving techniques, and the like. This approach may seem familiar to readers who have experienced some organisation development consultants, and the two are not dissimilar in intent; in a coaching programme, however, the coach is more directive and places more emphasis on purely business results as opposed to concerns with human relationships.

In this case we have the unfair situation that a prophet is without honour in his own country; the consultant-coach is probably doing a job which could be resourced from inside (in many, but not all, firms), but where the credibility of the insider is by definition lower than the outsider's. The other case where outsiders are brought in to coach is when a genuine need exists for professional help unavailable in-house—when professionally qualified counsellors are required to help a person with a serious work problem.

Professional counselling services for managers have grown in recent years, in two main areas: redundancy counselling and personal financial counselling. A third area, counselling people with serious work problems whom the firm does not wish to make redundant, is also growing apace. We are not here concerned with redundancy counselling, but the other two areas are worth a mention.

Taking the last area first, a typical case is that of a manager who trained as a specialist, pursued a professional career path until promoted to first-line management, discovers he doesn't like management very much but thinks that he had become professionally obsolete by virtue of spending most of his time in management. Add to this a worry that his own specialism itself is becoming obsolete; a belief that he has been passed over for promotion because someone has a grudge against him; and a resurgence of his adolescent wish to become an artist and you have a potential problem, beyond the scope of most managers and personnel specialists to deal with. They called in a psychologist, who administered a series of psychological tests (of personality, motivation, and aptitude), asked for a self-report essay, and conducted a depth interview, after which he was able to make to both parties a series of recommendations about the possible career options for the man concerned, together with the training requirements and other considerations. On the basis of the joint decision—taken after reference to the psychological tests, etc.—the psychologist initiated a self-development programme with the man concerned, which he was able to hand over to the firm's personnel staff to continue. They were able to detect a problem and take action on it in plenty of time, and thus save themselves someone they had not wanted to lose.

Personal financial counselling hardly qualifies for inclusion in a book about management training, except that managerial salaries have suffered so much that many managers' performance is being impaired by financial worry. One or two organisations offer a service of total financial planning, which is something most managers do not normally think of getting; yet a long look at the total financial picture often produces major savings in outlay for people on middle and senior management salaries. It so happens that we have from time to time been involved in counselling a manager whose performance was giving serious concern, only to find that he didn't need a psychologist at all, just help with making ends meet; and we have sometimes been called to advise financial counsellors who discover that the problem is not solved when they have rearranged the finances. So the two must be mentioned together, especially for middle and senior managers who seem to have a serious performance problem necessitating counselling by an outsider; coaching alone may not help, and other practical assistance may solve the problem.

Our preference remains for coaching to remain in the hands of ordinary managers; rough and unprofessional though it may seem, it has enormous credibility when the managers believe in it and are supported by the training department. The outsider should be brought in only when political reasons dictate, or there is a need for specialist professional help.

G Summary

Where training needs cannot be met by formal courses because of their complexity and the length of time necessary, or because political and other reasons make alternative methods preferable, a coaching programme is a possible option. Coaching is undertaken (usually) by line managers, who in conjunction with their subordinates set developmental tasks and review progress together. The training department is not directly involved in the coaching programme, but provides support by selling the ideas, training the coaches, and helping to monitor progress. Very occasionally other people besides the line manager may be used as coaches.

H   Discussion questions

1   Look back over your career and think of the best manager you have ever worked for. Can you identify what he did to coach you, and how he did it?
2   Consultants who work by teaching people in organisations how to work the consultants' techniques often find themselves acting as coaches; in this case to people with whom they have no direct reporting relationship. What special problems, for the coaching relationship, are caused by the absence of line control? How would a good consultant overcome them?
3   'A Chinese emperor, on succeeding to the throne, was reviewing his new palace. One vista seemed to him incomplete; so he sent for the head gardener and asked that a row of cedar trees be planted in a certain line. The gardener asked whether the emperor realised that they would take five hundred years to grow. 'Then,' said the emperor, 'you had better start this afternoon; there isn't a moment to lose.'
The benefits of a coaching programme are more likely to show in the medium and long term than immediately. Are managers ever justified in putting off starting for these reasons?
4   Think of a subject about which you know very little (embroidery? Morris dancing? nursing? leading an orchestra?). If you had to coach someone who was practising this subject, how would you approach the first three stages? (If this question is discussed in groups, it need not be academic; choose pairs of people who have unfamiliar subjects to offer each other.)

I   Further reading

Readers contemplating a coaching programme will find two films about coaching, called 'I owe you' and 'Received with Interest' useful. They have been made by the Training Services Agency and the Air Transport and Travel Industry Training Board; the first deals with the philosophy of coaching, the second with its practical aspects. Language lovers will object to the glaringly incorrect use of the word 'disinterested'; otherwise they make a useful introduction.

Hawdon Hague's book *Executive Self-Development* (Macmillan, 1975) has several useful chapters on coaching and related techniques, including tips on the politics of getting acceptance from line managers.

12   Projects and assignments

A   Their place in the training plan

Just as not all training needs can be satisfied by formal courses, so there are some training needs for which coaching programmes are inappropriate. A long term development programme, for a manager thought to have potential to grow a good deal beyond his present job, needs more time and more specialised effort than is provided by training courses and coaching; so the notion of projects and assignments, in which a distinct part of the trainee's job is designed to stretch and develop him, arises. Many big organisations have small groups of people, identified as having top management potential, who undertake specially planned activities to develop this potential—the Chairman's group, the top management cadre, the 'A' list, etc. Other companies have project/assignment programmes not directly intended to train people for top management, but for other positions where the necessary skills take a long time to learn.

One of the main differences between projects/assignments and a coaching programme is the scale of the activities. Both are on-the-job training; both involve other people besides the trainer; both take longer to complete than most formal training courses. But a project or assignment takes up much more of the routine job than the tasks allocated in coaching; indeed, many involve leaving the routine job for a while and doing another one. There is thus more time and money involved, and a greater implied commitment on the firm's part towards the trainee. Because of the greater cost, projects and assignments tend to be used sparingly, to meet identified organisational manpower needs, rather than as a general rule; hence the top management cadres and the 'A' lists.

We can define projects and assignments as activities done as part of the routine job, or instead of the routine job, for a given length of time, with learning purposes planned in at the beginning, agreed by all parties, and reviewed during the activity and at the end. They can be set for one individual, or for a team of trainees working together; they can be woven into the regular job, or replace it for a while; they can take place in the normal work place, or in another of the firm's sites or offices, or outside the firm altogether.

The terminology used by different firms varies a great deal; all labels have at some time been assigned to all activities. In this chapter we refer to 'projects' as tasks done within one's own firm, and 'assignments' as tasks done outside one's own firm. We use the abbreviation P/A for the two together or undifferentiated.

B How are people nominated?

The trainer's first consideration when embarking on a P/A programme is the matter of how people get nominated. These programmes are usually intended for special people, to develop special talents; as the trainees are already thought to have some potential, the trainer's first job must be to question that judgement and make sure that it is correct. We have dealt at length with the topic of assessing management potential elsewhere, [1] so we can here summarise the main findings.

Judgements of potential are best made along a *number* of dimensions, by a *number* of judges, using a *number* of methods. The way many organisations assess potential—by asking the manager to fill in a little box at the end of the performance appraisal form—using a simple scale like: ready for promotion now/ready in one year/ready in three years/never ready, or:one year potential/three year potential/ultimate potential, etc.—is nonsense; the lack of regard in which these judgements are held is illustrated by the fact that very few firms bother to check their managers' predictions, and hardly any give their appraising managers training in filling out this part of the form. There are both systemic and psychological errors in this method: the manager's judgement is not usually questioned, there are no second opinions worth speaking of, and it is not possible for a manager to judge the potential of someone to hold a post senior to that presently held by the appraising manager.

Performance appraisal as an assessment of potential fails to meet the requirements of a good method because it uses one judge only, and usually only one scale; better assessments are made when the appraising manager must judge potential along a number of dimensions rather than the simple 'How far will he go in how long?' variety. Committees of assessors may be better, if the committee is managed so that the usual checks to decision-making by committee are removed. But any assessment method that relies upon track record alone is dangerous, especially if there is a large gap between the present job and the one for which potential is being assessed; also very few managers can recognise and make allowances for the poor track record of someone who has been put in the wrong job. In many cases therefore track record information should be supplemented by other information, gathered off-line; the results of psychological tests, for instance, or of a management assessment programme.

On a management assessment programme participants go through a series of exercises, singly and in groups, which have been designed to mimic the demands of the job(s) for which potential is being assessed, and to demonstrate the degree to which the participants possess the necessary skills for good performance in that job. As they go through the exercises they are observed by a group of trained observers, usually line managers one, two or three grades above them (but not in direct reporting relationship to them). The observers record each participant's performance on each exercise; then at the end of the programme they reach agreement about each participant's potential and the appropriate plans for his development, and conduct feedback and counselling interviews with each participant at which the development plans are discussed in detail. For assessment programmes designed to look for middle and senior management potential the development plans quite often include projects and assignments. The design of assessment programmes is covered in detail in *Tomorrow's Men Today*. [1]

Psychological tests similarly reveal developmental needs if well planned and interpreted. Deeply seated psychological traits cannot be changed except by unacceptably radical methods, but it is not unusual for tests to reveal a need to think more about subordinates, or to work more effectively in groups, or to evaluate arguments more powerfully, for example.

The point really is that if people are to be nominated for P/A activities then this should not be undertaken casually. We suggest that a manager's rating alone, on the basis of track record, should not be sufficient to put someone on the P/A programme or to keep him off; more than one manager, and maybe the trainer also, should be involved. They should look not only at the trainee's track record as revealed by his performance appraisal ratings, but at more detailed aspects of his track record—the reports he writes, the speed with which he solves problems, etc. And they should bolster the track record assessment by some form of off-line assessment—psychological tests, assessment programmes, interviews (as well as the previous two, not instead of), and so on. This will ensure a wider and more unbiased search than would otherwise have been the case.

A policy decision also needs taking at this point, about whether the P/A programme is going to be developmental in character, or is merely to be used to confirm the high flyers' position. In the latter case, people will be put onto the programme whom one knows will succeed; people will not be dropped from the programme unless they fail miserably; and participation in the programme will be seen as the promise of a job. If the P/A programme is really going to be developmental, then there will be people on it whose past performance was not necessarily outstanding; participation will not be seen as the promise of a job; and the philosophy will be one of training rather than of laying on of hands. Our preference is for the former, but you need a decision.

You also need a policy decision about whether to pay people for potential, if you are using the P/A programme to build a top management team; and we strongly advise against trying to spot future managing directors in your graduate entry.

We do not mean to give the impression that the P/A programme must have the atmosphere of an exclusive club. Such programmes happen to quite junior managers and on a fairly large scale in some firms. But their high cost and high visibility attracts attention, and induces some managers to think of them as hothouses for future directors, so it is as well to get the policy thought out with some care and to pay attention to how people get nominated.

Another way people are nominated, in some firms, is to put them up for assignment when there is a headcount freeze, or when there is a spare manager whom nobody knows what to do with. Occasionally this has led to pleasant surprises, as the ugly duckling turns into a beautiful swan (now marketable, and in someone else's pond, unfortunately); mostly it leads to a worse mess when the day of reckoning comes. We believe that P/A programmes should not be escalators leading automatically to the top; neither should they be railway sidings into which people are diverted because they're blocking the main line.

C   Who is involved?

The day-to-day running of coaching programmes is in the hands of line managers, quite deliberately. Managers who have subordinates on P/A programmes should have a hand in reviewing their progress and counselling them, but not unaided. The trainer takes a much more active part in setting up the P/A programme with each individual and helping him learn as he goes along. Other parties may also get involved—'uncle' figures, very senior managers, outside coaches and consultants, etc. A policy decision is needed about who has overall responsibility— the trainer or the manager—so that the trainee is in no doubt about whom to contact with problems.

One area here is fraught with danger unless responsibilities are clearly understood from the start. When the trainee leaves his normal job to undertake a full time project or assignment under the supervision of another manager, it is easy for that manager to regard the trainee as another pair of hands for doing the dirty work that no-one else will touch. Before handing over to a receiving manager the trainer must make sure that he has a plan of activity mapped out for the trainee, in accordance with the overall developmental plan, and that he is not merely treating the trainee as a free gift from an employment agency. The training plans which assign new graduates to work in a series of departments for three months at a time are very vulnerable to this kind of abuse.

D   What kind of project or assignment?

Ideally, the organisation has a job needing doing which fits the training needs of the trainee. In most cases a job has to be created, or an existing need modified, to allow the training needs to be met. Below are some examples of the activities that have been used as projects and assignments.

1   *Projects*, that is, activities undertaken within one's own firm on a full or part time basis. The following are examples:

(a) one manager was asked to design, conduct, analyse and report back on an attitude survey for all employees at one location. To do this he had to learn about survey design and methodology from an outside expert; negotiate with senior management and union representatives about the questions and the report-back strategy; organise a team of willing and unwilling helpers to process the survey forms: discover the implications of certain questions—how did his firm compare with others on morale, etc.? He learned a lot about the way expectations are raised by managerial action; about the design of surveys and questionnaires; and about the feelings of employees in a part of the firm he had never before had anything to do with.

(b) a manager was given the job of discovering how vulnerable a certain site was, in terms of security. He was given a sum of money to spend, and a covering title; no-one at the site knew his real purpose, except for a very senior manager who would vouch for him if he were found out. After a fortnight he presented a report showing the number of breaches of security he had been able to make: they included leaving suitcases at reception, leaving a car with a Northern Ireland registration number in the car park for a week, picking up interesting looking documents, getting information from secretaries by buying them drinks after hours. Then he was given the next task—to work with the people concerned on how the security should be improved.

(c) after a firm had spent a great deal of money training salesmen, with a particular emphasis on 'selling the benefits' to the client, a manager had the task of going through the previous two years' proposals and analysing them to see how many actually stressed the benefits (as opposed to merely rehearsing the features of the system). On discovering that only 15 per cent of the proposals met his criterion, he had to follow up the training programme with the trainer concerned and get him to make the necessary improvements, which they then monitored.

(d) a manager was given the job of recommending how a factory could cut down on its inventory without losing efficiency. This involved analysing the processes involved in manufacture, and conducting critical path analysis and other operational research programmes to see how savings could be made. This type of project, in various guises, is quite a common one; other examples are reorganising sales territories to cut down the amount of wasted travel time, reorganising the orders system, and working out more efficient ways of using the company's transport. All involve learning and using operational research techniques, as well as getting to know the workings of part of the firm that may be previously unknown. It is important that the project last long enough for the trainee to experience the teething troubles of his new system, and to make the appropriate recommendations for fine tuning.

(e) projects that involve planning for a major change are also frequently used. A project team working on the changeover from manual system to computer (or vice versa; it does happen) learns a lot about computers and about the jobs done. Decisions must be taken about how far the team's remit extends—should they be involved in the specification and purchase of the machine, or should they be involved after purchase but before installation planning? Should their involvement stop at designing the change-over in broad terms, or should they concern themselves with the re-training of staff? Again, it is important to make sure that wherever the project starts from, the trainees are involved long enough to get feedback on the results of their labours. Computers are only one example of a major change which provides a project team with learning opportunities: others are relocations (where? who? who not? how much? when?); the introduction of important pieces of legislation (Health and Safety at Work Act, Equal Opportunities Acts, Disclosure of Information Acts, etc.); the launch of a new product; the closing of a factory; the introduction of a new technology.

(f) a manager was allotted the task of producing real measures of effectiveness for middle managers. The firm were concerned that most of the ways middle managers' contributions were measured were second or third order: how much they spent, their performance appraisal rating, their salary growth relative to their peers. This manager was given the job of discovering what, if any, changes in the operation are made by the presence of middle managers in a given number of job categories. To do this he found himself interviewing managers and attending meetings; analysing the ways decisions were made, following particular decisions through the chain; looking at what happened when managers were ill or absent; interviewing subordinates to get their perceptions of the contributions their managers made, and so on. This was a more difficult task to manage as a project, because it was unlikely to have a definite ending and because success could be defined in so many ways; it proved useful development for a middle ranking specialist being moved across into management, because it taught him something substantive about management at the same time as allowing him to experience the ambiguities and uncertainties of middle management.

(g) on similar lines to the previous example, a team of managers had to produce a set of criteria against which the industrial relations climate of different parts of the firm could be measured. They had to begin with the macro measures familiar to most people—strikes, absenteeism, opinion surveys—and go on to refine these measures into something more sensitive to daily variation, more amenable to use by line managers and even foremen, and giving weight to positive measures, of good industrial relations, as well as indicators of when things were going wrong.

We could multiply examples of projects, but from the examples above several things emerge. Most projects involve investigation and recommendation; some involve implementation. In some there is emphasis on a set of technical skills to be learned—operations research, opinion surveying, data processing. All involve learning political skills and the skills required to get things implemented. Some projects have a definite conclusion, a point at which a line can be drawn and people say 'It's finished,' while others will never be completed to everyone's satisfaction. It is important that these considerations be identified at the start of the project; a serious mismatch between (say) the amount of ambiguity in the trainee's present job and his project could cause problems if he is put in and left to sink or swim. Later in this chapter we discuss the monitoring and control of projects and assignments.

2 *Assignments*, which are undertaken outside the firm, have an even wider range of coverage. Examples are:

(a) managers seconded to educational establishments or research institutes for a given length of time, usually not less than six months. Typically the manager would undertake a wide range of duties: some research of his own, or working with the establishment's regular staff on their research projects; teaching duties; and free time to be spent browsing in the library or on self-organised visits. There are a number of benefits possible here. The change in pace is useful for managers who have been rushed off their feet with no time to reflect. Having to prepare what one knows in order to teach it to other people is valuable for the new insights it creates; watching students tackling the new knowledge shows the kinds of misunderstandings people may experience, and how they link the knowledge into the rest of their course. If the research projects take the trainee into other companies this too is valuable; even a company one knows quite well as a customer or supplier looks very different when one tries to solve its problems. The contact with the rest of the teaching staff provides an opportunity to discuss new work in the management area, the research that they are doing, etc. The trainee may also learn new skills in the concentrated atmosphere of the establishment which he would not have had time to learn at home; many of the more esoteric skills required in a planning department, for example, have been developed by sending managers on assignment to research institutes.

(b) some managers have been seconded to work with management consultants on a similar basis—study and problem-solving, working alongside the consultant and being taught by him. This works well with those consultancies which have a research base and are confident enough of their approach to have it questioned by the manager-trainee; many of the benefits are the same as with an assignment to an educational establishment, except that consultancies tend to be a little more problem-oriented rather than technique-oriented. A manager who has worked all his life in small back rooms and who is to be moved towards a sharper part of the organisation is more likely to benefit from a spell in a consultant's than a spell in a research establishment.

(c) as part of a 'social responsibility' or 'good citizen' programme some managers working for large organisations have been assigned to work free for charities or for publicly funded agencies. One organisation alone has released managers to take part in urban renewal programmes, to help with the prison rehabilitation service, to help in marketing poorly used public services, and to teach school children about industry. This is used as training for the managers themselves, taking skills which would not be fully tested inside the firm and applying them outside. On a smaller scale other organisations allow full or part time assignments which meet social needs as well as developing their managers; a small group of firms in Sheffield co-operate in giving free job interview training to school-leavers, using developing managers to do the training; they kill a large number of birds with the one stone, for this scheme results in better liaison with the local schools, less acute induction crises for new hires, and a better public image.

(d) some firms exchange managers for a period of time, getting them to do each other's job. Professor Revans pioneered these planned exchanges (as far as we know) and they have been imitated by a number of firms since; among the more eye-catching exchanges lately has been that of a middle manager in a cider firm with a major in the British Army; here one of the purposes was to discover the extent to which leadership in the military resembles leadership in industry. Swaps have taken place at all levels, and between all sorts of organisations; insurance men have swapped with men making fertilisers, men selling toothpaste have swapped with men selling cars.

Because the assignment is spent outside the firm it throws into high relief some of the problems facing the trainer when setting up projects or assignments. Let us review these stages, using a full time external assignment as the example but bearing in mind that most of the comments apply equally to project and to part time activities.

D Setting up the assignment

1 *Diagnosis of training needs* is the first step. It has been emphasised before; at the risk of being repetitious we emphasise it again. It will not be possible to see if the money and effort were spent wisely if there is no diagnosis of training needs to refer back to. The needs should be written down in terms of things the trainee needs to do differently; and as the assignment needs his active co-operation he should be interviewed to discover his view of his training needs and to get his commitment to an agreed statement of training needs. This is doubly important because assignments are often encouraged by factors other than training needs—a problem arises, a vacancy occurs, someone asks for help—and the temptation is to say 'Splendid! We'll send so-and-so; been looking for an assignment for him'. With an agreed statement of training needs the opportunity can be looked at carefully, evaluated, and altered if necessary.

2 *Choice of assignment* is difficult, if only because one does not usually seem to have much choice. In the ideal situation, though, one asks questions such as:

what technical skills which he possesses already do we want him to practise further?
what technical skills which he does not already have do we want him to acquire?

what is his present job's time span of discretion, and what time span should the assignment have?

what is his present job's requirement for speed versus accuracy, and what requirement should the assignment have?

what is the level of ambiguity current in his present job, and what should there be in his assignment?

how much face-to-face contact does he have in his present job, and at what level; how much should there be in the assignment, and at what level?

how much political sensitivity does he require in his present job, and what should the assignment need?

consider his present subordinates— age, sex, type of job, number, method of working, etc. What should the assignment contain?

what is the reward system in his present job? what should it be in the assignment?

how much opportunity does he have to plan his own work at present? how much should the assignment give him?

One is not necessarily looking for a change along each of these dimensions, but if the questions are asked they may help in differentiating between assignments. They will help a great deal during the induction and counselling part of the project, where it is essential that the counsellor be aware of any major differences between the work demands of the assignment and those of the previous job. If there is a big difference it can be so overwhelming that the trainee cannot articulate it, and the counsellor must help.

3 *Agreeing responsibilities* between the trainer, the receiving manager, and the manager releasing the trainee covers a number of important topics. The actual activities the trainee will undertake must be specified, and a balance obtained between the ones done for the receiving manager and the ones done purely for learning purposes. Some performance measures on these tasks are also desirable. The manager releasing the trainee must promise not to entice him back before the assignment is completed (if the business will fail without him, then the return must be negotiated through the trainer, not direct). He must arrange for any review meetings the two of them are likely to have while the assignment continues, or any return visits the trainee is likely to make. Most important of all, *re-entry* must be committed to at this stage; far too many assignments finish poorly because the releasing manager forgets about the trainee

once he is out of the office, and has no place ready for him to return to; sometimes there is a place ready, but taking no account of the increase in skills and experience which the trainee now brings to the job. On a long assignment it may not be possible to negotiate a specific job for the trainee to return to; nonetheless the issue must be raised at this stage in the proceedings. The trainee should receive assurances that he is not being farmed out, and that a job will be ready when he returns. He should also know whom to contact with any query he might have about the management of the assignment—his old manager, his new manager, or the trainer. In most cases the trainer is the best person to contact, or someone nominated by him, because there is sometimes a need for an honest broker to go between the two managers and the trainee if job-related difficulties occur. At this stage too the trainee must be clear about such matters as where he fits into the performance appraisal system, how his merit pay (if any) will be calculated, what expenses he can claim and how.

4 *Induction* into the assignment is a separate exercise; it should not be assumed that because a manager has been working for thirty years he does not need induction into the new job. If there is a formal induction programme going on at the time of his joining, he should take part; if not he should have the same induction treatment as an ordinary employee would get. He will probably have an induction crisis, too, like other new employees; his receiving manager needs to give him lots of opportunities to ask silly questions and to find his way about, and the assignment counsellor must handle the first counselling meeting very carefully.

5 *The assignment counselling* programme takes a number of forms. People on assignment are there to learn, there for long term purposes of training; they can forget this easily in the press of the job to be done and the novelty. A series of regular meetings should be planned to review progress and give the trainee a chance to reflect on what he has learned. The trainer is probably best placed to conduct these meetings, which resemble the coaching interviews described in the previous chapter; that is beginning with an invitation from the trainer to 'tell me how you think you've been getting on,' and going through a widening and deepening discussion in which the trainee articulates what he has learned and what he has still to learn, finishing with the setting of a few more learning objectives for attainment between now

and the next interview, and commitments to action if they are needed. These interviews should be planned at regular intervals—the first one a fortnight to three weeks after the start of the assignment, and then monthly or bi-monthly. In addition the trainee should be able to ask for a counselling interview out of time if he feels it would be helpful. Preparation for Counselling forms, of the type quoted in the previous chapter, or other self-appraisal forms, make a useful start to the discussion.

There can be other counselling interviews besides the private one between trainee and trainer; if there are a group of people on assignment, separately or as a team, then formal or informal group meetings to discuss progress, hand on tips, tell funny stories, and get the news of what's been happening in the parent firm during their absence, are very useful. Where managers have swapped jobs the two may meet at regular intervals, with the trainer present, to discuss progress; the trainer should try to prevent any 'If I were you I wouldn't have got into that mess' comment from creeping in.

6   *Report-back* by the trainee to interested parties happens from time to time during the assignment; it helps to remind his colleagues that they have not lost him forever if they see him mentioned in the company newsletter or welcome him back to management meetings. If the manager who released the trainee has not been involved in the counselling process, he should receive reports also; and senior managers who may have taken a special interest in the trainee should be included. The purpose of report back is not only the information it contains, but also the way it reminds both parties that the assignment is only an assignment and there is a job to come back to.

7   *Winding-up* the assignment may take place because the job is done, or because people have run out of time. In either case the trainer should look ahead to the winding-up time, and have discussions with the receiving manager about the progress of the assignment, so as to time the departure well; it is very important that the trainee know how well his solutions worked, or sees the fruits of his labour in other ways. If this means altering the time of the finishing point slightly, then so be it. The actual winding-up consists of a long counselling interview, looking back over the whole assignment and reviewing what the trainee has learned; some action planning to incorporate the learning into the job he is returning to; and an arrangement to meet again in a few months' time. The receiving manager, now releasing his

charge to return to his old organisation, may want to give a farewell party; any suggestion that the road is now clear to the top should be avoided. Projects and assignments are for learning on, not promises of a job.

8   *Post-return* meetings, held for a while after the trainee has gone back to the old job, are useful in making sure that the learning really has been incorporated into the new routine, and that the assignment has not faded like the memory of a jolly holiday. These meetings also give the trainer a chance to check that the manager has fulfilled his commitment about keeping open a job that uses the newly developed manager; it cannot be over-emphasised that the usefulness of the assignment will be dissipated if the manager has no job to return to. We once saw such a person kept by his company as a professional course-goer for eight months after returning from assignment; they had no job for him, they kept holding out the promise of one, and in the meantime he was sent to every internal and external training course imaginable.

We suggest here that the trainer is the best person to manage the assignment—better than either of the managers involved, though they should not be left out. After a while, though, an assignment programme will have its veterans; people who have been on assignment, come back, perhaps been promoted, and can look back dispassionately at what happened. If the trainer can recruit some of these as helpers for the counselling and management of later trainees, he will almost certainly find their experience invaluable. Other third parties may also be involved—the director off whose budget the social responsibility programmes come, for example. He may also go for help to recently retired managers (if they are still sprightly) and to outside consultants who can operate under his broad guidance. Much depends upon the size of the firm and the number of people on projects or assignments.

The guide to action above assumes that the trainer is managing an assignment—the most difficult task. His job is roughly the same when managing projects, except that the politics may need different handling; there is a greater temptation for the trainee's own manager to give him back some of his routine work, with the excuse of urgency . . . he can always tackle his project tomorrow. The standards of performance may be distorted in a game of management politics unless the trainer has taken care to write them down beforehand. And while it is not possible to force a manager to accept someone temporarily onto his staff if he is implacably opposed, one should take with a pinch of salt such protests as 'only someone with intimate local knowledge can do this job', and 'you're trying to foist a baby from XYZ department on me'.

E Top management commitment

Many P/A programmes are set up to train future middle and senior managers. They ought therefore to be the concern of the top management in the firm. The trainer must make sure he has top management commitment to the P/A programme before going ahead. This means simple things, like having access to the strategic plan (there are many organisations where the personnel director does not have clearance for the five-year plan). It means having management's ear about business problems and opportunities, so that projects are selected with some relevance to future needs. Most of all, it means that if people working on a project come up with a useful-looking solution to a problem, the managing director ought to give it a try. In one organisation trainee managers are given current business problems to work on in project teams; the managing director himself introduces the problem to them, and states his commitment to putting the solution into practice if it looks like working; it is surely not a coincidence that this firm has turned in record performances at a time when its competitors have been going out of business.

F Summary

Long term development needs can be addressed by giving people projects to do or sending them on assignments. Because this is an expensive way of training people, extra care is needed in the selection of trainees. The line manager is involved during the training process, but much of the weight of management and counselling falls on the trainer. Particular care must be taken to see that problems of re-entry are dealt with, and top management's commitment to the programme is essential.

G   Discussion questions

1   Do you think that projects and assignments should be given only to those people identified (never mind how) as having high potential? or do you think that they should be more widely spread?

2   Fantasise for a while about job-swaps between: the managing director of a medium sized manufacturing company and a senior official in the recognised trade union; a sales manager in ethical drugs and a sales manager for nuclear power plants; yourself and the first name you point to in the internal telephone directory. What would the swappers learn from each other?

3   What would be the arguments for and against sending your best young (under 35) manager for a year to help organise rehabilitation programmes for prisoners? (Substitute another worthy cause if you're already established in prisoner care.)

4   You send a manager on a six-month assignment to a research institute. He is to have his own research project half-time, and to assist with another established project for the rest of the time. He tells you that this second project gives him access to sensitive data about the competition. What would you advise? (Don't get out of it by saying 'It depends what the data are'; choose different kinds of data and work out your answer for each kind.)

H   Reference

[1] A. STEWART and V. STEWART.   *Tomorrow's Men Today: The Identification and Development of Management Potential*, Institute of Personnel Management, 1976.

13   The evaluation of training

A   Relation to training needs analysis

Terms like 'evaluation' and 'validation' are argued over frequently by management trainers—what do they mean, and is it possible to evaluate or validate training anyway? Many people appear to have given up all hope of seeing whether their training efforts were worth while: 'You can never prove it was the training that caused the improvement,' they say. It's very rare in any part of business that one can point to simple cause and effect relationships, so why do so many trainers abandon the fight?

Partly because evaluation of training depends upon a good training needs analysis; the sort of analysis that tells you what people ought to be doing differently in order to perform better. Training needs analysis done by whipping round the training department asking people what subjects they like to teach is not likely to lead to training that can be evaluated. And it is certain that not all training activities *can* be evaluated; the trainer has to design the kind of training which it is possible to evaluate. As we shall see later, this leads to more efficient and economical training anyway.

Whether you call it evaluation or validation doesn't much matter. There are three questions that can be asked about training activities in order to gauge their success; these are:

(a) what are people doing differently as a result of the training?
(b) did they like the training or feel that it was useful?
(c) is the training paying for itself in terms of improved business performance?

The first and third are usually more important questions than the middle one.

B   What are people doing differently as a result?

Let us assume that the training activity we are evaluating is a

219

training course rather than a coaching programme or project. There are at least four stages during the course at which the trainer can evaluate it; after each exercise or group of exercises; at the end of the course; immediately on return to the job; and some time after return to the job. The reference books listed at the end of this chapter [1, 2, 3, 4] treat different aspects of these evaluation stages in detail; examples of evaluation at each of these stages follow.

1 *Evaluation at the end of an exercise.* The trainer has identified what it is he wants people to do better; suppose that he is running a course on the management of poor performers and wants to concentrate for the moment on the skill of treating the problem rather than accusing the person. As this is a skill, it must be learned by performance rather than by listening; so the trainer must devise an exercise that gives people lots of practice. For the exercise, he prepares a series of personal problem statements like this:

> Mary has been responsible for buying the department's supply of coffee and biscuits for over a year now. She collects money from everyone once a week, and the supplies are left in an annexe for everyone to help themselves. Recently she asked for more money to cover the increase in the price of coffee, quoting the amount by which a tin of Maxwell House has gone up. Following a series of complaints by other people in the department, your secretary has discovered that Mary is buying a coffee substitute at less than half the price she told you she was paying, and has apparently been pocketing the difference. You have asked Mary to come to your office to see you, without specifying what you want to talk to her about. She is outside now. What will you say to start the interview?

At the beginning of the exercise the trainees have pencil and paper in front of them. The trainer reads out the first statement, and asks the trainees each to write down what they would say. Then he gets them to read out their contributions, and to discuss the merits and demerits of each; he hopes to guide them towards discovering that it is better to confront the problem than the person, and better not to make assumptions about the nature of the problem. Probably he will make some headway in the discussion of the first problem; while they are still actively discussing it he interrupts to read them the second one:

George habitually returns from lunch twenty minutes late; he usually has a drink or two, but has never appeared drunk and incapable. His workmates are complaining that they are tired of having to cover up for him. You are in the office when George comes in at twenty past two and starts taking his overcoat off. What will you say to him?

and so on, gradually making the problems more difficult. After a while, a skilled discussion leader will lead them round to identifying for themselves five or six essentials in a good problem-analysis interview, and they can go back over their previous written replies and classify them to see how many of the

---

Quiz: psychological tests in industry

1   The 16PF test is a test of: intelligence
                                                      personality
     (please circle one)   clerical aptitude
                                                      managerial abilities

2   What do the following abbreviations stand for?
     EPI   MMPI   PAPI   AH5   MPI

3   All tests must be validated before they can be used. What is meant by
     each of the following terms?

     face validity   concurrent validity   predictive validity
     construct validity   conspect validity

4   Tick the objective tests in this list: Thematic Apperception Test
                                                      Differential Aptitudes Test
                                                      Strong Vocational Interest Blank
                                                      Rorschach Test
                                                      Blacky Test
                                                      Watson-Glaser Critical Thinking
                                                          Appraisal

5   For which of these tests are validation data nationally available?
     16PF   PAPI   Luscher Colour Test   EPI   Watson-Glaser

6   What is selector error? selectee error? How do these concepts relate to the
     predictive validity of the test? What other factors should be taken into
     account when assessing the need for a test in selection?

7   Write down the names of as many psychological tests as you can think of
     (not already named on this quiz).

Fig. 13.1   Pre-lecture quiz

essentials were contained in the early attempts. Thus they check progress. The pace may be speeded up later, with live interviews, real-life counselling exercises, etc., with people still monitoring the essential ingredients. At the end of the exercise the trainer is able easily to estimate the change in behaviour since the beginning.

Another example, from a different field entirely, of an exercise containing its own built-in evaluation is the self-assessment quiz given before and after a lecture or film. Assume that the trainees are about to be lectured to on psychological tests; before the lecture they are given a short quiz, shown in Figure 13.1. It will not take them long—the last item is to allow slow trainees to catch up with the rest. The quizzes are scored very briefly, by the trainer reading out the right answers but not entering into discussion. At the end of the lecture the quiz is re-administered. This gives a measure of increased knowledge, not only to the trainer but also to the trainees.

Evaluation can be built in thus to particular exercises, or to groups of exercises; a measure of change over a day, for example, might be more convenient. The basic principle remains the same: examine their performance before and after training on the relevant variables, wherever possible building this into the fabric of the training process itself.

2 *Evaluation at the end of a course.* This is similar in practice to evaluation at the end of an exercise, but spread over a longer period of time and covering (usually) a wider range of variables than any single exercise would. Some interactive skills courses begin with a simple behaviour analysis of the trainees, continue the analysis throughout the training, and compare the profiles before and after to see what the training has achieved. This must be done with care, as there is no 'right' profile which people should be striving for, and very few blanket judgements can be made about what is good behaviour and what is bad. Nevertheless, the before-and-after profile in Figure 13.2 gives an idea of how the change can be measured.

To get the results of which this table is an extract, the course began with a series of group discussion exercises designed to allow the participants to exhibit a wide range of behaviour. The results from the first three exercises are shown under the 'before' heading: the first three rows are self-explanatory; 'helicopter statements' is a measure of the number of times the trainee

Before training	After training
$\dfrac{\text{Caught proposals}}{\text{Escaped proposals}} = \dfrac{21}{54}$	$\dfrac{\text{Caught proposals}}{\text{Escaped proposals}} = \dfrac{16}{12}$
$\dfrac{\text{Stating difficulties}}{\text{Proposing solutions}} = \dfrac{12}{5}$	$\dfrac{\text{Stating difficulties}}{\text{Proposing solutions}} = \dfrac{6}{8}$
$\dfrac{\text{Bringing people in}}{\text{Shutting people out}} = \dfrac{2}{20}$	$\dfrac{\text{Bringing people in}}{\text{Shutting people out}} = \dfrac{12}{4}$
Helicopter statements$=0$	Helicopter statements$=5$
Listening score $= 2/5$ (accuracy) $\qquad\qquad = 2/5$ (completeness)	Listening score $= 4/5$ (accuracy) $\qquad\qquad = 3/5$ (completeness)
Self-analysis 23 mistakes out of 54	Self-analysis 12 mistakes out of 50
Suffixing score 20 mistakes out of 35	Suffixing score 8 mistakes out of 40
Group rating: helpful 6.5	Group rating: helpful 8.4
Trainer rating: flexible 3.0	Trainer rating: flexible 6.0

Fig. 13.2   Excerpt from before-and-after profile of training course member

looked at the company problem they were discussing from an overall viewpoint rather than his own narrow remit; the listening score derives from a listening exercise in which people had to summarise each other's points of view; the self-analysis scores derive from a prefacing game, and the suffixing scores from a suffixing game (see Chapter 8). The other two scores are a little less reliable as measures; the group members rated each other on a one to ten scale of helpfulness, and the trainer rated each person according to the perceived flexibility with which he could adapt his style to suit the needs of the occasion.

At the end of the course similar measures were taken in the last group of exercises (covering roughly the same amount of time, with the same number of people in each group). The changes are noticeable, and in the desired direction. The table does not show the other measures made, which are a little less right-or-wrong and much more sensitive to the needs of the company and the situation; the extract suffices to show the kinds of measure that are possible.

Similar before-and-after measures are possible with knowledge-based courses; a quiz at the beginning of the course, or Repertory Grid interviews, followed by testing at the end of the course.

It may seem as if we are advocating that the trainer spend all his time testing people and hardly any time training them. However, this viewpoint ignores two valuable uses to which the 'before' information can be put. The trainer can use this information to adapt his training to the needs of the people there; thus if it appears as a result of the quiz (Figure 13.1) that most of the audience know what validation means, but that none knows how to use the validity coefficient in calculating whether to use tests in selection, the lecturer skips lightly over his treatment of validity and spends more time on decision theory. And the second advantage is that the trainees may realise for themselves what they need to know, as a result of doing the quiz; or they can be told where they stand by means of feedback from a behaviour analysis or similar device; and this puts them in a much stronger position to manage their own learning and monitor their own performance. It has been shown many times [1, 2] that far from losing time by taking the before-and-after measure, the actual taking of such measures with feedback to the trainees greatly enhances the amount learned on the course.

3   *Evaluation immediately on return to the job.* This sort of evaluation is not normally in the control of the trainer. It asks the question: 'Given that he returned from the course on Monday, has he done any better this week?'; in other words, have the skills and knowledge acquired on the course been strongly enough embedded to be able to withstand the cold blasts of reality back at the job?

Here we have another messy experiment, from the purist's point of view; just as evaluating training on-course interferes (in the nicest possible way) with the training itself, so do most of the things that can be done to evaluate the course on return to the job interact with other considerations of getting the training to 'take'. Ideally, the returning trainee should give his manager a full account of what he has learned and how the knowledge could be applied by himself or by other people. This debriefing is assisted by work done towards the end of the course itself—action planning, forming good resolutions, syndicate or individual work on the problems the trainees brought. This kind of debriefing is possible when the training has been on using a particular technique—manpower planning, discounted cash flow, etc. There are other types of training where a too-intensive debriefing by the manager immediately on return would be the equivalent of digging carrots up to see how they are growing—courses designed to provoke thought (e.g. what if we stopped direct mail solicitation? put in cafeteria compensation systems? went over to team assembly?) and courses designed to give the trainee a fresh approach to dealing with people. There is a fine line to be drawn between making sure that the receiving manager debriefs his trainee with the thoroughness that denotes that training is being taken seriously, and crowing over him for having seen the light.

If evaluation on the course itself has been carried out properly this will cause no problem. All managers should carry out proper debriefing (by which we mean that he should not say: 'Well, you can forget all they taught you down there, because we'll carry on doing it my way'), but they should err on the side of caution when debriefing after an interpersonal skills course or a course designed to provoke consideration of radical changes in operation.

4 *Evaluation some time after return to the job.* Here any number of questions can be asked, by all sorts of people—trainer, manager, and trainee. Other people besides the trainee also act as sources of information.

The question : 'What is he doing differently?' should be asked, at a number of levels of analysis. If the course was to teach him a new technique, then is he operating that technique well and successfully? To return to our earlier example of psychological testing courses, we can ask: 'Does the trainee now use the right test in the right places for the right purposes, and has he stopped using the wrong ones?' If the course was to teach him to handle problem employees better, is he doing the right thing when he talks to employees with problems?

It will not always be easy to get direct answers to these questions, of course, but they should be asked; and they can very often be answered by the trainee himself, who is likely to be the best judge of his own performance. One should not ask: 'Do you think you are handling problems better as a result of the training?', but ask for a simple count of the number of problem interviews he has handled and how they rated on the criteria previously agreed on the training course. Provided all parties see the enquiry as genuine research, rather than a subtle form of empire building or performance appraisal, a surprising degree of honesty is often attained.

A second level at which to ask the question 'What is he doing differently?' is to repeat some of the training needs analysis techniques reviewed earlier. A manager's diary, before and after training, is often a good guide to the success of the training—is his day better controlled? does it have more of the desired activities and fewer of the undesired? does it now make proper allowance for the unexpected? has the balance altered amongst the subordinates with whom he spends his time, so that the middle-of-the-road men get more attention? is travelling time better managed? is there planning time built in before important meetings? is there thinking time built in? The categories into which the diary is broken down will, of course, reflect the training needs and the training offered.

A re-run of the content analysis technique may also be used to evaluate training; for example, one firm monitored the success of its appraisal training by scoring the completed appraisal forms on a number of simple dimensions, taking care that the person doing the scoring did not know if the appraising manager had received training or not. Histograms of the scores of trained and untrained managers showed clear differences—trained managers wrote clearer, more operational objectives, set more realistic standards of performance, and tried to write an account of what the employee actually said during the interview rather than stating that he agreed or disagreed. This simple operation allowed them to check the success of the training course in some detail. Other forms of content analysis suggest themselves—reports should be better written after a report writing course, sales proposals should stress the benefits after a selling course, project files reveal fewer false starts after a technical course.

Critical Incident technique may also be used to check the success of training; ideally, one would find that the type of critical incident had moved away from the area the training was directed to, into something completely different. The nature of the Critical Incident question makes sure that you always get a critical incident of some kind, of course. So if the original training needs diagnosis had uncovered lots of critical incidents relating to the managers' inability to persuade people to adopt courses of action which they had no power to enforce, thus leading the trainer to design a course in influencing skills, one would deduce that this training had been successful if on repeating the Critical Incident survey it now appeared that most of their problems had to do with an inability to budget during inflation. This new 'training need' must be taken on its own merits—what is it costing the firm not to have it met?—but as far as the first training need is concerned, the Critical Incident survey has shown it to have been satisfied.

Yet another way of asking the crucial question is by observing the behaviour of other people in various ways. The training of a shop manager may be assessed in part from the behaviour of his staff and his customers: are the staff well turned out? helpful? polite? do they give the right amount of information when requested? do they use the customers' names if they know them? do they make mistakes when recording the transaction? do they deal with complaints speedily and without upsetting other customers? And the customers: do they look as if they know where they're going, or do they look lost? Do they go to more than one person for the same piece of information? Do they show overt signs of stress? It can be argued, of course, that plenty of other factors influence these behaviours; nonetheless there have been studies comparing staff and public behaviour in the shops of trained and untrained managers, showing differences in favour of the trained ones. A manager's subordinates also provide a guide to the success of the training: how many grievances do they raise? how many leave? how have their diaries changed? how satisfied do they say they are with their manager's performance, in general and with regard to specific things like career management, performance appraisal, coaching?

Yet another way of evaluating the long term results of training is to look for associated changes in the business. Have there been fewer accidents as a result of the safety training? Have the salesmen responded more quickly to changes in the market? Have there been fewer unofficial stoppages? Have there been fewer customer complaints? Has there been less time spent in meetings? Has the wastage rate on new hires been cut down? Has the inventory been reduced? The sceptic will say, rightly, that it will never be possible to say that these changes are solely due to the training; and there are two answers to this objection.

The first is that in the muddy world of personnel research, it is often possible to find a control group, or pseudo-control, if you look hard enough. Compare managers who have been trained with managers who haven't. Compare this year's seasonal change with the last comparable year. Get your Industry Training Board to compare your figures with those of managers in comparable, untrained firms. Compare the post-course performance of managers on whom the training 'took' well with the performance of managers who did not seem to benefit. If you look hard enough, you'll find a control group; that's what the advertising men and the plant hire men and the fire prevention men and the heating and ventilation men have to do when they're selling their products, and they seem to manage all right.

The second answer is that even if you will never be able to claim that a particular performance improvement results from training, this should not absolve you from the necessity of trying; because if you don't try to find out how well you've done, you'll stop being a trainer and become either an entertainer or an administrator.

Management trainers can be divided into those who know evaluation is impossible, which is why they have never tried it, and those who treat evaluation as an integral part of training design. The real answer to anyone who objects that evaluating the training takes time away from the serious business of training is that any serious attempt to evaluate training is bound to lead to massive improvements in the training itself. Serious training evaluation is built upon the series of interlocking cycles— training needs analysis, evaluation of exercises, evaluation of the course, and evaluation immediately after the course and some time after, which together lead to training which is both flexible and controlled.

C Do they like it?

This is a question which is often confused with evaluation, leading to muddle and deception all round. Most people see it in the form of a slip of paper passed round at the end of the course, containing questions like:

> how useful was the content of the speakers' presentations?
> how well did they present their material?
> how useful were the exercises?
> how good were the visual aids?
> what was the quality of the food and accommodation?

In some training courses this form is actually labelled an Evaluation Form; and one of the commercially available Course Evaluation Services used to distribute these sheets at the end of courses subscribing to the service, after which the ratings given to each course were all added together to form a composite score, thus equating a 5 on *food and accommodation* with a 5 on *content*. They may still be doing it, but we haven't dared to ask a second time.

In the light of what we know about adult learning, it should be obvious that such a list of questions will be an imperfect guide to whether trainees will actually do anything differently as a result of the training. In the case where people come on a course because they need to know something, and where they and the trainer agree that this knowledge is lacking, then it is reasonable to expect that the trainee's statement of how much he has learned will correlate fairly well with what he does differently after the course. But there are plenty of circumstances where people's reactions to the training are not necessarily a good predictor of later behaviour change. Thus:

1   *Where prestige performers* send people away in a rosy glow of enthusiasm, having been entertained and soothed by a man with a Big Name. Sending someone to listen to a prestige performer may be good for his morale, and good for his understanding of the management problem, but it is unlikely to result in immediate improvements all round. This is fine as long as everyone knows what they're buying; but don't generalise from the warmth of the applause to subsequent improvements in performance.

2   *Where people have taken up positions* before the training which would make them look silly were they to admit that the training was useful. One of us was once administering a programme of counselling interview training for managers, the training having been deemed compulsory by senior managers. A potential trainee rang up to say that he didn't want to come on the course; after persuasion failed, the course was stated to be compulsory. He came; resentful, unco-operative, daring us to train him, he took up a position which made it impossible for him to admit that the training had in any way benefited him. (Of course, with hindsight, one can see that one should never have said it was compulsory, but should have trained every other manager in his branch so that he felt isolated and came of his own accord.) Wherever training is used as a possible punishment there is a danger of such positions being taken up; people feel compelled to show, before the course, that they don't need the training. There is a lesser danger where people are allocated so many training days as of right; then they may demand admission to the course not for any good it might do them, but because the book of rules says so.

3   *With some kinds of interpersonal skills training*: some courses dig fairly deep into people's beliefs and styles—listening

skills participation skills, delegation skills, negotiation skills, and so on. People come to the course not fully aware of and committed to their own training needs; during the course they learn to analyse their old ways of doing things, and to try new ways, often at some personal cost. Maybe the ideal outcome for the trainer is to send the trainees away having practised the skills of asking for the other's point of view, listening to it, summarising it, reflecting things back non-judgementally. He wants his trainees to go away thinking: 'Maybe there are two or three other strategies I ought to be trying; maybe I should be looking for the following extra things when monitoring my own success . . .' It's unreasonable to expect people who have learned some fairly fundamental new ways of dealing with people to be jumping up and down trumpeting what they've learned; better to expect a slightly thoughtful expression on the faces of trainees as they leave the course, rather than end-of-course euphoria. A number of studies has compared the later behaviour of participants on courses designed to make them feel jolly at the end with the behaviour of participants on courses designed to send them away thoughtful; the evidence is quite clear. The euphoria melts as they return to work, giving less overall transfer of training than with the second group.

4 *Where the group dynamics have been manipulated* so that people feel extra-happy at the end of the course and more likely to say nice things about the success of the training. We have outlined earlier in this book the various phenomena which the experienced manipulator can use on group courses, taking advantage of the fragmentation that happens about a third of the way into the course and the related cohesiveness that appears later, by setting exercises designed to make the group miserable on the Tuesday evening and bolstering them with success on the Thursday. Alternatively the trainees may be insulted, kept up late, made to make fools of themselves, made to break down; if they don't leave on the first day the chances are they will stick out until the bitter end, and say that the training was marvellous because that's the only way they can convince themselves their suffering was worth while.

5 *Where the trainees have little insight into their own behaviour.* This thorny problem affects some trainees more than others. Imagine a continuum of people's attitudes, with at one end the type of person who likes things to be governed by rules, prefers to have things in black and white, believes in strong

discipline and obedience to authority for its own sake; and at the other end the very *laissez-faire*, tolerant, individualistic sort of person. (Psychologists call these two types *high-F* and *low-F*; the F stood originally for Fascism, as this was very much on people's minds when the personality trait was first investigated, although having seen the fascism of the extreme left they tend nowadays to refer to the trait as 'authoritarianism!) Generally speaking, high-F people have a much narrower range of interpersonal insight available to them than low-F people; ask a low-F person to act as if he were high-F, and he will find it much easier and will do it more convincingly than a high-F person asked to take on the part of someone who is low-F. High-F people see other people as like themselves; low-F people see a wider spectrum. One consequence of this is that on an interpersonal skills course, for example, the low-F people are more likely to give an honest self-appraisal of how much they themselves have learned than are the high-F people; the high-F are less well equipped to see into themselves and see change.

This is, of course, the trainer's perpetual nightmare; it's always the more flexible trainees, the ones who are half-way there already, who seem to learn most; the blimps and the trotskyists, whom one would love to unbend just a little, stay rigid, even though the blimps may congratulate you on running a 'damn fine course' at the end. Part of the answer is in good design and group mixing; but one should not trust their reactions to the course as an indication of whether they will change.

An interesting example of the interaction between high-F attitudes and learning on courses comes from Rackham's research. [3] He examined trainees on a Coverdale course, on which the group members were expected to follow the Systematic Approach to Getting Things Done: identifying purposes, objectives, measures, assigning tasks, checking success, reviewing, etc. The Coverdale literature stated that following this approach taught one about teamwork. Yet a behaviour analysis of teams following the Coverdale approach showed quite clearly that the people most likely to make explicit references to the systematic approach were (a) more likely also to make wrong references, (b) less likely to show behaviour change in any other direction, e.g. supporting, building, proposing, disagreeing, than the other course members. Nonetheless they liked the course and thought it had done them some good. The Systematic Approach was pandering to the high-F members of the group, giving them a sequencing device to use during otherwise unstructured (hence uncomfortable) exercises. No wonder they liked it; and no wonder that by clinging to it they were able to protect themselves from venturing further into the waters of group discussion. The same warning applies to other occasions where tools of analysis—essentially systematic—are provided for a group to follow while the group is at the same time expected to analyse and experiment with its own processes; we have seen the Kepner-Tregoe approach modified by some trainers in the same way, and with similar results.

Beware, therefore, of asking the trainees to evaluate the course themselves by telling you, at the end of the course, how relevant and enjoyable it was. Where the training needs are straightforward, uncomplicated and openly acknowledged the trainee's evaluation may be a good predictor of later change in behaviour; but where attitudes and history make it difficult for people to have such insight, it should not be required of them.

It is legitimate to ask for 'reaction sheets' or 'comment sheets' at the end of a course, provided that they are not thought of as evaluations. Figure 13.3 shows one such reaction sheet. The feedback this provided is used to modify later courses in the series, if the comments are thought to be justified. They nearly always are, of course, but occasionally people have to be taught things which they may not want to hear, or at the end of the course are disappointed because the issues are not as simple as they would like them to be. We make no apology for including a session on validation in seminars on psychological tests, and are resigned to getting periodic disappointed comments from trainees who 'don't want to be bothered with this technical rubbish; give me a test that works'.

Reaction sheets are also necessary to get information about the 'hygiene factors' that can render training inefficient if they are not right: inadequate accommodation, indigestible food, unreadable slides, etc. Information here should be fed back to the people responsible as soon as possible, compliments as well as requests for change.

Internal trainers should also be wary of allowing their own performance to be appraised on reaction sheets, unless the appraisal acknowledges that they are reactions only, and not indicators of the trainer's success. It is difficult to do this, especially when there are few other forms of short term feedback as definite; but it is destructive of good performance in the end.

Predicting management potential, November 1977
Comments

1   Please let us have your comments on the workshop (content, speakers, opportunities for discussion, etc.)

2   *Workshop objectives:* How well do you think the workshop met its stated objectives?

	Very well	*Fairly well*	*Not very well*
1 To review current approaches to the assessment of management potential	....	....	....
2 To provide an opportunity to consider in detail, and have practical experience of, several methods for predicting management potential	....	....	....
3 To enable participants to assess the usefulness of existing methods for their own organisations	....	....	....

3   *Your own objectives:* If you had aims in attending the workshop in addition to those stated, what were they, and how well do you think they were met?

What use do you think you will be able to make of the contents of this workshop within your own organisation?

4   *Administrative arrangements:* was there anything about the administrative arrangements (room, timetable, accommodation, meals, etc.) which detracted from the success of the programme?

5   *Overall satisfaction:* Taking everything into consideration, how satisfied were you overall?

.... Very satisfied
.... Satisfied
.... Neither satisfied nor dissatisfied
.... Dissatisfied
.... Very dissatisfied

Name:...
Thank you.

Fig. 13.3   Reaction sheet for workshop in predicting management potential (condensed from one used at Brunel University, with permission)

D   Was it worth it?

This is often the most difficult of the evaluation questions to answer, for political and practical reasons; can one point to one's training activities and say how much money they have saved the company?

The first point to grasp is that this question cannot be answered to the last penny, because of the difficulties of following up all the trainees in detail and of attributing any performance improvement to the training; but this does not remove the need to make a good informed guess, just as the people in charge of advertising or employee benefits or machine maintenance have to do. The second point is much more important: financial evaluation has to be built in to the training programme from the start; it is not something that can be done well retrospectively. Without one or more attempts at training needs analysis, to show where the shoe is pinching most, one cannot tell how well one has remedied the situation. And the training needs analysis itself is a good place to start when counting the cost and benefits of training, because many of the analysis techniques quoted earlier lend themselves to having money values put on them.

In a Critical Incident survey, for example, be sure to ask what each critical incident cost—in time, reputation, and money. When discovered, for instance, that the majority of service engineers' critical incidents in one company were non-technical rather than technical in nature, the director responsible found the results interesting; he took action, however, when we were able to tell him that the only incidents which had cost money were the non-technical ones. Thus the Critical Incident survey for training needs analysis allows one to make a rough guess at the costliness of the training need; it is perfectly feasible to go to the trainees some time after the training with another Critical Incident survey, and see if there has been any change. If the nature of the critical incidents stays roughly the same, but the incidents cost less because they are managed better, or if the nature of the incidents has changed to something outside the scope of the training, then the training has probably done its job; it would be legitimate to ask the trainees what they are doing differently as a result of the training, after having conducted the Critical Incident questions; it is also a good idea to ask for example of successfully handled incidents at the same time, as (ideally) one would like to find that critical incidents had turned into successfully handled incidents.

This evaluation exercise will not give the answer to the last decimal point, but it is quick and cheap and surprisingly effective. If the training needs analysis originally was conducted using Content Analysis technique a notion of the cost of the training need could be gathered in similar fashion. For example, the analysis of reports-in-progress given in Chapter 4 allowed us to make some judgements about the costs of the various training needs; the most important of these were:

(a) the grammatical and syntactical errors needed correcting by someone in the publications department, who spent on average two hours per report correcting basic errors, mostly of grammar but also wrongly labelled diagrams. The time of the publications lady could be costed, though not the dissatisfaction with which she, a graduate in English, regarded the job of tidying up other people's spelling errors.

(b) the lack of editorial skill on the part of middle and senior managers meant that reports went through more stages than necessary, and took longer. The extra stages could be costed, in terms of the hours of the people involved; sometimes, too, the delays meant that material for a conference arrived too late to be printed with the rest of the conference papers, so that the home establishment had to run off their own Xerox copies—a surprisingly big expense.

It was not difficult to ask the publications specialist how long she had to spend correcting documents once the training courses had got under way, and to calculate how much time she was saving; and with a little persuasion it was possible to follow through the reports to the editing and conference stages, and see how much further time was being saved; we also made a judgement about the quality of the reports, because we did not want them to suffer in quality for the sake of speed.

Content analysis of other working files, for other types of training need, helps evaluate the training. For example, many industries would like managers to act as their own personnel/industrial relations specialist, only calling in help from the personnel department in real emergencies. One way of estimating the size and cost of this training need is to examine the working files of the personnel department, together perhaps with asking one or two personnel officers to keep diaries. Here, one would look for:

(a) how many times did experienced managers ask for help from personnel on trivial matters, things that they should have handled themselves? How much of personnel's time was this taking up? Is it possible to identify other important personnel functions that suffered as a result?

(b) how many times did experienced managers not call in help from the personnel department in an area where, on reflection, it was obvious that specialist assistance was needed? What were the associated costs? (e.g. costs of strikes, go-slows, unfair dismissal cases, etc.).

After training the managers, one would expect to find changes in the desired directions indicated in the personnel department's working files; changes to which it would be possible to attach some notional costs. Indeed, as this is not a training need that can be addressed quickly, it is possible to follow through the earlier trainees before the later managers are trained; thus one can improve the training further and get additional ideas on where to look for cost savings.

One's first steps in evaluating the costs and benefits of training are best directed towards simple measures like: how much time is this training saving? Many beginners start by trying to put everything into the equation: time, customer relations, materials, the costs of industrial tribunals, etc. Then they finish with an equation so unwieldy that it is impossible to manage, let alone defend to a sceptic; so they stop. It is good discipline to limit oneself to just one or two simple measures, in the knowledge that one is not asking all the questions, but asking one or two thoroughly. For example:

(a) follow up an *interviewing course* for selection officers by asking how much time the line manager interviewers (who do the second interviews, after the selection officers have acted as a first filter) spend interviewing candidates whom they then turn down.

(b) follow up an *appraisal interviewing* course by asking how much time managers now spend on preparation for appraisal, and how much time their managers or the personnel department spend in grievance-handling as a result of unsatisfactory appraisal interviews.

(c) follow up a course on *decision-making* by asking for how long items are discussed in committee, and how many times referred back.

This over-simple approach to putting money costs and benefits on training will by no means cover everything, but by following it the trainer will get a good introduction to the methods to use and the other questions he should ask later when his skill has improved. It's not a bad rule of thumb, however, that if a training course doesn't appear to be saving anyone any time, then it is unlikely to be making savings in any other direction; this is not a universal rule, but it helps to save unnecessary effort.

Having mastered the time-saving approach to training evaluation, the trainer should then look for more sophisticated measures that can be expressed in money terms; number of sales made, number of industrial tribunals attended, travelling expenses reduced, number of negotiations concluded without industrial action, and the like. Again, the starting point must be the training needs analysis and the costs of the needs it reveals. In this more sophisticated analysis of cost savings, the trainer should probably look for general trends over groups of trainees rather than trying to follow individual people through. It is easy to argue about individual cases, violently for or against the training; much more difficult to quarrel with a general trend, even if it is less spectacular. The trainer should probably reconcile himself to the fact that if a manager says: 'I came off your course and the following Wednesday I saw a bloke about to do a repair, and I thought to say "Hey, get that pipe stressed before you put it in", and if he hadn't then we'd have had another Flixborough on our hands', there is probably no way of putting money costs on the value of that particular piece of training.

When managers are trained through projects, assignments, and coaching programmes it is often possible to enlist the aid of the line manager responsible for them, in evaluating the training. One should not look for cost savings in the early days; in fact, if training includes the freedom to make mistakes, the beginnings of a project or coaching programme may be costly. Towards the end, though, it is appropriate to discuss how much the new skills the trainee has acquired will save him and the company, and to encourage him and the supervising manager to do a cost-benefit analysis of the proceedings. Often the answers arrived at this way are more detailed, and more imaginative, than the training department could derive; they have more credibility, too, as they come from the managers themselves.

Putting money measures on the benefits of training will never be an exact science. To some degree we have made an artificial split between the different types of evaluation: what are they doing differently, did they like it, and is it saving money. It is difficult to answer one without going some way towards answering the rest, especially if the answers refer back to the training needs analysis. Sometimes, too, a training programme will be run when it is known to produce no tangible money savings, because people believe it is the right thing to do; some firms run training courses for managers about to be made redundant, many more run pre-retirement training, and the money benefits of these are probably negligible. If some attempt has been made at evaluating all training in money terms, then the decision to run some courses out of goodwill becomes an informed one, rather than one which people are forced into.

E Summary

Evaluation of training consists of finding the answers to a group of questions: what are the trainees doing differently? what do they think of the training? and does the difference in performance cover the cost of the training? Trainee reactions to the training should not be taken as firm evaluations, though reactions are important in avoiding discomfort. The question of what people do differently is addressed at a number of points in the training cycle—after each exercise, at the end of the course, on re-entry to the job, and some weeks or months after the training. Little of this is possible without a good training needs diagnosis.

F Discussion questions

1 Here are some common managerial training needs. For which ones would trainee reaction, taken at the end of the course, be a good predictor of behaviour change back on the job? For which ones would trainee reaction not be a good predictor?

appraisal interview skills	safety consciousness
security	inducing creativity in others
project management	budgeting
finance for production	exporting into Europe
managers	managing specialist staff

participative management
selection interviewing
problem analysis
communications
clear thinking

negotiating skills
decision-making
influencing skills
sales management

2   Is it reasonable to expect every trainee to show some improvement after the training course? Under what conditions (course content, numbers, participant mix, nomination strategy, etc.) should the trainer be satisfied with less than 100 per cent strike rate? How much less?

3   In one organisation it was traditional for managers in the Research and Development department to be given a course on Creative Thinking one year after appointment. A new trainer performed a training needs analysis and came to the conclusion that creative thinking was working perfectly well without the need for a special course. The Personnel Director and the Head of R & D together said that they were not prepared to see the course stopped. What should the trainer do? How should he evaluate his course?

4   The following five descriptions of training programmes are taken from the large engineering organisation where they had been run. Suppose that you were responsible for advising the company on the evaluation of the training courses, what would your priorities be? Are there any of the courses which would probably have a higher or lower priority for you than others in terms of training improvement? Put the five programmes into rank order, starting with the one which you believe has the highest priority for pay-off from validation.

Programme A is a general management course for eight senior managers. This was a one-off programme run about six months ago, consisting of material provided by London Business School and run by them, lasting five days.

Programme B is an induction course for new employees. Run twice a month with an average of fifteen course members lasting two days, and mostly resourced by speakers from various departments in the company rather than by the training department.

Programme C is a course which has been requested in conjunction with a new performance appraisal system. Senior management has asked for a course which will give the 270 managers who use the system:

(a) a knowledge of the paperwork and procedures which they must handle, and

(b) some skill in handling face-to-face appraisals. Management is prepared to budget on the basis of a three-day programme to be run during the next budget year.

Programme D is a safety training programme for supervisors. The target population is 112 of whom 70 have already been through. A very popular course, well supported by management, with objectives to do with knowledge gain in areas such as the Factories Acts and attitude change.

Programme E is an action-centred leadership programme run for the company by the Industrial Society, with mixed knowledge, attitude, and skill objectives, at a supervisory level. Currently ten per year are run with an average of twelve people per programme. The course lasts three days and costs £500 in consultancy fees.

(This question is based on an exercise designed by Neil Rackham, and quoted here with his permission.)

G Further reading

[1] P. B. WARR, M. BIRD and N. RACKHAM. *The Evaluation of Management Training*, Gower Press, 1970.

[2] N. RACKHAM, P. HONEY and M. COLBERT. *Developing Interactive Skills*, Wellens Publishing, 1971.

[3] N. RACKHAM and T. MORGAN. *Behaviour Analysis in Training*, McGraw-Hill, 1977.

These three are landmarks in the field of training evaluation. The first two are particularly good for showing the kind of improvement made to the content of the training itself when evaluation is built in from the first; the second two show evaluation in action when the subject of the training is interactive skills. All three are clearly set out and a model for action.

[4] A. C. HAMBLIN. *Evaluation and Control of Training*, McGraw-Hill, 1974.

An in-depth work, clearly written, covering the whole field of training in industry. Particularly good when considering—and forcing the reader to consider—the organisational and cost consequences of training.

[5] G. S. ODIORNE. *Training by Objectives*, Macmillan, 1970. Another detailed treatment, considering training from the systems point of view, which though it might appear gimmicky at first, in fact reinforces the idea that training evaluation is rooted in training needs diagnosis.

[6] R. I. DRAKE and P. J. SMITH. *Behavioural Science in Industry*, McGraw-Hill, 1973. Simplified but partial account of behavioural science in industry, with very clear exposition. Chapter 7 gives a strategy for understanding and coping with organisational problems, with built-in measures of success; good reading because of its clear approach and because it provides ideas for evaluation of training activities other than courses.

14 What next?

We believe that the personnel function in organisations is at a crossroads. At the time of writing, more and more people are grumbling about the weight of legislation pressing down on the manager, and about the effect this has on the personnel department; the choice appears to be between a retreat into a new kind of legal department, where personnel is exclusively concerned with keeping out of trouble, or branching out into new areas which involve taking the initiative, doing research, getting out into the field and persuading managers to see new ways of doing things. Personnel as the pay-and-rations department will disappear, we feel sure, to be replaced in many instances by personnel departments which make a positive and unique contribution to the management strength of the company. It is this kind of department which, we hope, will use some of the ideas in this book. Perhaps we can conclude by speculating about some of the new challenges that the future is likely to bring for the management trainer.

A New products

Management training is notoriously prone to fads and fashions; one week we tear each other apart on a Blake's Grid course, then we learn to be adults by using Transactional Analysis, then in a couple of months we decide that all the airy-fairy human relations stuff is rubbish and what we want is nice rational Kepner-Tregoe training. We are fortunate in the UK, in that most of these fads originate in the USA, where people tend to make more spectacular mistakes with them, from which we could learn a lot if we chose to listen.

It would be foolish, and possibly libellous, to name the next serious of fads we ourselves see looming on the horizon. May we instead refer the reader back to Chapter 9, on the choice of external training courses; and offer also the following list of questions which should sort the men from the boys as far as most fads go:

1   What, exactly, is the training supposed to do?
2   Does it have a specified behavioural end-point?
3   Can that end-point be safely revealed to potential trainees?
4   Is the training intended to affect the whole of the trainee, or just his performance at work?
5   Does the training assume that people are sick or maladjusted?
6   If the training offers the trainee an analytical framework for looking at other people, is their use of the framework validated during the course?
7   Where was the training designed and evaluated? If in a different country, how has it been adapted?
8   Are the skills needed to run the training transferable to other people?
9   Must a licence fee be paid, and what do you get for it?
10 How do you know it does the job?
11 How do you know it's worth the money?

Most of these questions are common sense, but we emphasise them because they will be particularly useful for testing the next likely batch of training fads. There are courses offering sensitivity training in all its awful variants, or an instant solution to all the problems you didn't know you had, or (would you believe?) fast Zen. Test them. Ask what people are supposed to do differently at the end of the course, and if you get an answer like 'It depends on what you bring to the course', or 'Take what you get', be cautious. Any training that starts from the assumption that people are mentally sick should not be used; any training that tries to change the whole man, rather than the bit he sells to the employer, should be viewed with caution.

There is an increasing number of courses that train people in analysing other people's behaviour—using transactional analysis, variants on behaviour analysis, body movement analysis, etc. If the givers of the training take it seriously, then during the training itself they will include checks to see that each trainee observes consistently with himself, and that he sees roughly the same thing as the people around him. If these checks are missing—if it is assumed that people can use the analytical framework correctly as soon as it is presented to them—then the course is not worth the money. When the analysis is based on extra-weird characteristics, e.g. body movements, handwriting, the shape of the head, etc., ask for a full explanation of the link between the surface characteristic and the deeper characteristics they are supposed to imply.

And, distrust the science that dies with the scientist. If the salesman says 'This is the only course in the world that will improve your management performance', or 'These are the only two people capable of operating this procedure', be wary. In the early days, the designer of a new system will probably operate it better than anyone else, and may not want to let it out of his hands until he has checked everything; but after the development stage we believe it is better to share your secrets than to hug them to yourself. People will copy, anyway; much better to be open about as much as possible, because then people will believe statements like 'This bit really ought to be left to a qualified psychologist', or 'You shouldn't use this procedure until you've been through stages x, y, and z'.

Fads from foreign countries need translation. We sympathise with the training manager who was forced to accept dozens of training films from an Australian subsidiary; most of the message was lost because the audience were falling about with laughter because the films reminded them of Barry Humphries, and the rest of the message failed because the visual clues in the films meant nothing to the UK audience. If a training package comes with a licence that says it can't be altered in any way, bounce it back; nothing loses credibility in the eyes of the trainees faster than films and case studies which are ever so slightly wrong.

B New problems

We think that trainers will be faced with new jobs, new training assignments, in the coming years. Some of them are:

1 *Women moving into management.* Much has been written about the problems and opportunities faced by women who are moving into management, either because they have elected for a full time career or because they wish to return to productive and interesting work after having raised children. Social attitudes are changing so rapidly, and women's apparent skills also, that it is difficult to make statements about the average woman's training needs. However, the following are some of the things the trainer might think about:

(a) *Induction training* is especially important for women, who are more likely to be unfamiliar with the organisational world. Women returning to work after having children are in special need, because they may feel that they have forgotten everything and are irretrievably out-of-date. Here, induction training should consist not only of showing them around the building and the organisation chart, but of instilling into them confidence; housewives with children have to exert a number of useful management skills, did they but realise it, and there is more transfer of training than they might at first believe.

(b) *Early failure* is often more daunting to women than it is to men. We were once asked the question: 'Why won't women go into management?', and on pinning the questioner down discovered that what he was worried about was a pre-management training course that his firm ran, based on performing two or three short talks to a camera in front of the rest of the trainees, with a trainer who made a habit of being severely critical of the first talk. Our questioner said that women were making all sorts of excuses to avoid going on the course, and therefore losing their chances of promotion. We explained that women have a greater tendency than men to be cast down by early failure, and suggested to him that he re-structure the course so as to give successes in the first task rather than failures, and to have the trainer 'give feedback' about successful things rather than make negative criticism. He came back later with news that delighted us—everyone's end-of-course performance, male or female, had improved, but that of the female trainees had improved more. This is an important point for the design of all sorts of training, as we have stressed elsewhere; but to throw women trainees into a 'sink-or-swim' game is especially wasteful of potential.

(c) *Help them structure their own feedback* on performance, because the chances are that if they have been away from organisational life for any length of time, they will need help in convincing themselves that they are doing a good job. The trainer can help by giving extra-rich feedback on training courses, paying special attention to ensuring that it is reasonably objective, and by stressing the need for feedback on performance when planning performance appraisal courses, etc.

(d) *Stop thinking about 'women's careers'* when giving training in career counselling, planning projects and assignments, etc. It's illegal and may get you into trouble. And, as a courtesy, if you do have a 'statutory' woman on a training course, don't flap round for the first half-hour telling her that; one gets awfully tired of hearing speeches larded with phrases about 'in these days of women's liberation', and so on. On a point of etiquette, the correct way to address a group of men and one woman is 'Good morning, Miss Jones, gentlemen', *or* 'Good morning, madam, gentlemen', but *not* 'Good morning, lady and gentlemen'.

2 *Mid-career change.* Because of redundancy, or manpower planning difficulties, or sheer restlessness, many people in their forties and fifties find themselves changing careers and/or employers. The trainer can help to ease the transition in a number of ways:

(a) *Handling redundancy* is a traumatic experience which can be made worse by pussyfooting round it. If a lot of managers are going to have to make people redundant, have them in for training first; brief them on the legal background, on the other employment opportunities in the areas concerned, on the help people can expect from the DHSS. More importantly, train them to face up to the unpleasantness they will cause, so that they don't tell the bloke he's redundant when they're both half way to Manchester on a crowded train; train them to prepare for the interview, to select the time as well as possible, to withstand the hostility they are bound to experience. This is an area where role play exercises are useful; the manager will do a better counselling job if he has role played people in the position of being made redundant.

People who are being made redundant can also be helped by the training department. At the very least, they should be offered training in applying for jobs and attending selection interviews; it is easy to forget how daunting it must be to find oneself on the job market again after twenty years. An off-the-cuff briefing from a selection officer, telling about his experiences, the things he looks for in a job applicant, the etiquette of selection interviewing, is very valuable; while a formal presentation of these matters is necessary, it's just as important to have drinks round the bar afterwards as the selection expert tells some 'inside stories'.

Skilled trainers could help with face-to-face counselling of the redundant managers, with or without help from psychological tests; it is a good idea to get the redundant man to write a short autobiography, which will almost certainly remind him of the difficulties he has already overcome and the successes he has had; a good counsellor will then use this material to build further on his identified strengths. Some of the techniques available for training needs analysis may also be helpful, turned on their heads and used as aids in career counselling.

Some firms who have had to make managers redundant have turned the problem into a benefit; instead of making the oldest or the youngest go, they have identified some managers in the middle whose entrepreneurial spirit is stifled by the size of the organisation. These managers are offered money, training, and support to set up business on their own. By moving out they create more room for manoeuvre in the manpower planning system; and in a number of cases the parent company finds that its financial support is being repaid handsomely, as the newly released entrepreneurs zoom into success.

Very little of the redundancy training will take, however, if the managers are worried about money. It is surprising what a difference good financial counselling makes; if you are going to spend money helping managers re-train, spend a little more to help them make their redundancy money go further.

(b) *Handling mid-career change* without redundancy is also an area where the trainer can help. Much will depend on the number of people changing, their reasons for doing so, and the amount of notice the trainer has to give him time to prepare. Where a number of managers are involved in mid-career change it is worth running an assessment centre or similar device (e.g. a series of psychological tests) both to let people show what they are capable of to the observers, and to allow them to rediscover this for themselves. If there is plenty of notice of the need for change, a good match between the people and the new jobs is possible, because the assessment programme generates enough developmental information for people to train in areas identified as deficient. Trainers may also help by offering training to the line managers whose subordinates are affected by the need for change; training in career counselling, in delegation and team management, etc.

Mid-career change presents some painful short term problems; but your short term problems today were someone's long term problems a few years ago, and many trainers could provide a useful service by offering to new employees a training programme which gave them experience of life in other departments, so that they did not get stuck in one career path without seeing other options. For example, in one firm new graduates—

about a year after hiring, so that the early leavers have gone—are given a programme in which a series of modules is run; each module consists of (a) a presentation about a particular division from a senior manager therein, (b) group work on a problem which that division is presently experiencing, watched by the manager, (c) a discussion with the manager about the proposed solutions, (d) opportunities for self-assessment and peer-assessment of the trainees' performance in the exercise. At the end of the series each participant has a dossier containing the notes he made about the divisions and the exercises, and the notes his peers made about his performance. At any time later he can take that file to a manager from personnel department, or to one of the managers who visited the course, and ask for career counselling based on the file. There is no promise of a job transfer, but people's options have been opened at a time when normally they would have started to close off; thus the problem of the specialist in his mid-thirties who suddenly thinks he has nowhere to go may be alleviated somewhat.

3 *Matrix management*, or project management, is likely to spread. In this system, there is no fixed hierarchy; people are assigned to tasks, and to projects within those tasks, on the basis of competence. This gives senior managers a chance to retain their technical expertise, and encourages mutual respect based on proficiency rather than seniority. Matrix management has often been used for teams of specialists—R & D men, management consultants, serving soldiers, etc.—and interest is spreading for a number of reasons. There are many contributions a trainer can make in a matrix managed firm. For example, as there are no stable, fixed man-manager relationships, procedures which in a hierarchical organisation depend on such a relationship (e.g. appraisal, coaching, training nominations) must be modified to fit. Personnel departments may legitimately take on more of line management's responsibilities here. A particular problem with matrix management is that when a manager is choosing a team, he will pick the people best qualified for the job; thus specialists get more and more specialised, unless preventive action is taken. The trainer could find himself helping to negotiate job assignments that assist people's long term career development and broadening, based on identified training needs. Matrix management is reviewed thoroughly in Knight. [1]

4 *International movement of managers* is certain to increase

as the United Kingdom becomes more firmly a part of Furope. At a fairly basic level this presents problems for the trainer, who is likely to find himself asked for language courses or to discover that most of the foreigners on his course have arrived with lists of things to get from Marks and Spencer so that no matter what you have on the programme, they're going shopping on Wednesday afternoon. Sometimes, though, the training problems are enormous and involve ventures into the unknown; many firms find they have great difficulty recruiting or developing managers to go to the Arab countries, or to black Africa, no matter how much money is offered. In many firms there is a list circulating of the various things to do on board the aircraft or on the tarmac which will ensure a speedy return by Customs and Immigration.

This is a serious problem, of economic importance at a time when most profitable ventures, for some companies, involve overseas work in countries which managers find uncongenial. It is best if the problem comes to the personnel department as a selection problem, not as a training problem; it is easier to select out those people who will not survive than try to change them. It is worth spending a good deal of time in selection, using some fairly probing psychological tests (this is one of the rare cases in industry where we would use the full, clinical version of the 16-PF personality test). For long assignments, whether accompanied or separated, we would also interview and test the spouse. Many firms find, when recruiting from outside to fill such jobs, that ex-servicemen settle down best, as they and their families are already used to the experience.

Training people to go abroad to potentially uncongenial countries requires expert help, if the firm has not gone there before. One or two establishments exist to fill this training need; at Farnham Castle, in Surrey, for example, intensive briefing courses lasting several days are given, covering all aspects of business and personal life; wives of men sent abroad are also included. There is so much material to cover in one of these briefings, some of it about areas a trainer would not normally touch—servants, schooling, health, sexual customs, bribery, tipping, etc.—that an outsider is almost by definition equipped to handle the subject better. Where managers have been abroad and returned successfully, they may be used on internal training courses as speakers and resources; but the session round the bar is just as important here as the formal presentation, and if spouses can join for their own sessions then they should be asked.

Major reappraisals of management practice are sometimes forced when the company seeks work abroad; for example, trade unions are illegal in Saudi Arabia, so that a British firm employing a British work-force out there may not recognise the unions with whom it has an amicable relationship back home. Equal opportunity legislation fades into the background in countries where women have no separate identity. Petty theft is a different kind of problem when the thief can have his hand chopped off. It's not the sort of problem the average trainer should try to tackle alone; our advice is to get professional help before the problem becomes expensive.

What else is new? What sort of management training would we like to see? Managers in the UK are often spoken of as depressed, defeated, defeatist; we would like to see training in assertiveness, training to build up the need to achieve, training to enhance the enjoyment of business. Robert Townsend's question 'If you're not in business for fun or profit, what the hell are you doing here?' is as valid today as when it was first uttered; yet the thing which often gets missed out of books like this is the fun, the enjoyment, the sense of achievement and of having done something creative. Doing a training needs analysis is fascinating work; watching the pictures, the patterns, the differences and similarities emerge as one analyses the data is, for us, as exciting the fiftieth time as it was the first. Teaching a group of people, watching them take the technique and do things with it one hadn't thought of, watching the light dawn as someone changes his mind, puts things together, masters himself—these are intensely rewarding experiences. Helping a manager to coach his subordinates, and thereby enabling a whole team to grow and do better, is a unique professional contribution from the trainer. With this book we wish you proficiency, we wish you mastery—but above all, we wish you enjoyment.

C   References and further reading

[1] K. KNIGHT. *Matrix Management: A Cross-Functional Approach to Organisation*, Gower Press, 1977.
[2] M. FOGARTY. *Forty to Sixty*, Centre for Studies in Social Policy, 1975.
An interesting and committed book about the way middle-aged

people are disregarded and the contributions they could make.
[3] S. BEER. *Platform for Change*, Wiley, 1975.
Iconoclastic and imaginative book about the changes that may
affect people and organisations, and some of the things they
might care to do about them.

Bibliography

Alberts, C., *The Good Provider: H. J. Heinz and his 57 Varieties,*
Arthur Barker, 1973.
Argenti, M., *Corporate Collapse,* McGraw-Hill, 1976.
Bacie Case Studies, British Association for Commercial and
Industrial Education, 1970.
Bannister, D., and Fransella, F., *Inquiring Man: The Psychology
of Personal Constructs,* Penguin, 1971.
Beer, S., *Platform for Change,* Wiley, 1975.
Berger, M. L., and Berger, P. J., *Group Training Techniques,*
Gower Press, 1972.
Berne, E., *Games People Play,* Penguin, 1971.
Bligh, D. A., *What's the Use of Lectures?* Penguin Education,
1972.
Blumberg, A., and Golembiewski, R. T., *Learning and Change
in Groups,* Penguin Modern Psychology, 1976.
Cooper, C. L., and Bowles, D., *Hurt or Helped? A Study of the
personal impact on managers of experiential, small group
training programmes,* Training Information Paper 10,
Training Services Agency, 1977.
Cooper, C. L., and Mangham, I., *T-Groups: A Survey of
Research,* Wiley, 1971.
Dixon, N. F., *On the Psychology of Military Incompetence,*
Jonathan Cape, 1976.
Drake, R. J., and Smith, P., *Behavioural Science in Industry,*
McGraw-Hill, 1973.
Dunnette, M., *Handbook of Industrial and Organisational
Psychology,* Rand McNally, 1976.
Farnsworth, T., *On the Way Up,* McGraw-Hill, 1976.
Fineman, S., 'A Modification of the Ghiselli Self-Description
Inventory for the measurement of the need to achieve amongst
managers', *International Review of Applied Psychology,*
vol. 25, no. 1, 1973.
Fineman, S., 'The Work Preference Questionnaire: a measure of
managerial need for achievement', *Journal of Occupational
Psychology,* vol. 48, 1975.

252

BIBLIOGRAPHY 253

Fineman, S., 'The influence of perceived job climate on the relationship between managerial achievement, motivation, and performance', *Journal of Occupational Psychology*, vol. 48, 1975.

Fogarty, M., *Forty to Sixty*, Centre for Studies in Social Policy, 1975.

Guion, R. M., *Personnel Testing*, McGraw-Hill, 1965.

Hague, H., *Executive Self-Development*, Macmillan, 1975.

Hamblin, A. C., *Evaluation and Control of Training*, McGraw-Hill, 1974.

Handy, C. B., *Understanding Organisations*, Penguin, 1976.

Houlton, Bob, *The Activist's Handbook*, Arrow Trade Union Studies, 1976.

Howe, M., *Adult Learning*, Wiley, 1977.

Jaques, E., *Time-Span Handbook*, Heinemann Educational, 1964.

Kay, H., Dodd, B., and Sime, M., *Programmed Instruction*, Penguin, 1968.

Kelly, G., *The Psychology of Personal Constructs*, Norton, 1955.

Kinnersley, P., *The Hazards of Work, and How to Avoid Them*, Pluto Press, 1973.

Knight, K., *Matrix Management: A Cross-functional Approach to Organisation*, Gower Press, 1977.

McLeish, J., Matheson, W., and Park, J., *The Psychology of the Learning Group*, Hutchinson University Library, 1973.

McLennan, R., *Cases in Organisational Behaviour*, Allen & Unwin, 1975.

Mant, A., *The Rise and Fall of the British Manager*, Macmillan, 1977.

Miller, K. M., *Psychological Testing in Personnel Assessment*, Gower Press, 1975.

Odiorne, G. S., *Training by Objectives*, Macmillan, 1970.

Peters, G., 'The Crash of Trident Papa-India', in Bignell, V., Peters, G., and Pym, C., *Catastrophic Failures*, Open University Press, 1976.

Rackham, N., 'Controlled Pace Negotiation as a technique for developing negotiating skills', *Industrial and Commercial Training*, vol. 4, no. 6, 1972, pp. 166-275.

Rackham, N., Honey, P., and Colbert, M., *Developing Interactive Skills*, Wellens Publishing, 1971.

Rackham, N., and Morgan, T., *Behaviour Analysis in Training*, McGraw-Hill, 1977.

Rogers, J., *Adult Learning*, Penguin, 1971.

Stewart, A., and Stewart, V., *Tomorrow's Men Today: The Identification and Development of Management Potential*, Institute of Personnel Management, 1976.

Stewart, R., *Managers and their Jobs*, Macmillan, 1967.

Stewart, R., *Contrasts in Management*, McGraw-Hill, 1976.

Stewart, V., and Stewart, A., *Practical Performance Appraisal*, Gower Press, 1978.

Thomas, L., and Harri-Augstein, S., 'Learning to Learn: The Personal Construction and Exchange of Meaning', in Howe, M. (ed.), *Adult Learning*, Wiley, 1977.

Townsend, R., *Up the Organisation*, Coronet Books, 1971.

Warr, P. B., Bird, M., and Rackham, N., *The Evaluation of Management Training*, Gower Press, 1970.

Index